Corporate Social Responsibility and Local Community in Asia

The idea of corporations exercising corporate social responsibility has spread from the West and is now firmly embedded in Asian countries and in Asian corporations. The latest trend in corporate social responsibility, evident also in Asia, is for corporations to apply corporate social responsibility to local communities and to those at the bottom of the social hierarchy. This book explores corporations' social responsibility engagement with local communities in a range of Asian countries. It provides examples of corporate social responsibility in a wide range of industrial sectors, focuses extensively on 'social enterprises' and on governments' and corporations' schemes to encourage them, considers how relations with employees and with local workforces fit into the pattern of corporate social responsibility, and discusses the question as to how far corporations engage with local communities as a way of developing new markets for their products.

Kyoko Fukukawa is a Senior Lecturer in Marketing at Bradford University School of Management, UK.

Routledge International Business in Asia Series
Series editor: Hafiz Mirza
Bradford University School of Management

The primary aim of this series is to publish original, high-quality, research-level work, by both new and established scholars in the West and East, on all aspects of international business in Asia. Works of synthesis, reference books and edited collections will also be considered. Submissions from prospective authors are welcomed, and should in the first instance be sent to the series editor: Professor Hafiz Mirza, Bradford University School of Management, Emm Lane, Bradford BD9 4JL. Email: h.r.mirza@bradford.ac.uk

Corporate Social Responsibility and Local Community in Asia

Edited by Kyoko Fukukawa

Routledge
Taylor & Francis Group

LONDON AND NEW YORK

First published 2014
by Routledge

2 Park Square, Milton Park, Abingdon, Oxfordshire OX14 4RN
711 Third Avenue, New York, NY 10017

Routledge is an imprint of the Taylor & Francis Group, an informa business

First issued in paperback 2018

British Library Cataloguing in Publication Data
A catalogue record for this book is available from the British Library

Library of Congress Cataloging in Publication Data
Corporate social responsibility and local community in Asia/edited by
Kyoko Fukukawa.
  pages cm. – (Routledge international business in asia series; 7)
  Includes bibliographical references and index.
  1. Social responsibility of business – Asia.
  2. Community development – Asia. I. Fukukawa, Kyoko.
  HD60.5.A78C667 2014
  658.4′08095 – dc23   2013039415

ISBN: 978-0-415-62765-8 (hbk)
ISBN: 978-1-138-37705-9 (pbk)

Typeset in Times New Roman
by Florence Production Ltd, Stoodleigh, Devon, UK

Contents

vi *Contents*

Illustrations

Figures

Tables

Boxes

Notes on contributors

Sharad Agarwal is a PhD candidate at the Indian Institute of Management Ranchi, India. He had completed a BTech and MBA before joining the doctoral programme at IIM, Ranchi. He has previously worked at the Indian Institute of Management, Indore, as an Academic Associate.

Stefan Altmann is a research assistant and PhD candidate at Humboldt University of Berlin. His research is focused on competitive dynamics, particularly multi-point competition. He graduated from Technical University Dresden, Germany. His current research concentrates on competitive structures in the oligopolistic US film industry, developing tools to identify and predict which films actually do compete for the same audiences. He is also developing a method to apply multi-point competition logic to the dynamic temporal markets of film release dates.

Fara Azmat is a Senior Lecturer in the School of Management and Marketing at Deakin University, Melbourne, Australia. Her areas of research interest are: corporate social responsibility in developing countries, international governance, particularly governance of emerging economies, women's entrepreneurship, poverty and sustainable development. She has published her work in highly ranked peer-reviewed journals such as *Journal of Business Ethics*, *Australian Journal of Management*, *European Management Journal*, *International Journal of Public Administration*, *Contemporary South Asia*, *Thunderbird International Business Review*, *Social Responsibility Journal* and *International Review of Administrative Sciences*. She has also presented at numerous international conferences and is a reviewer of a number of journals.

Olga Bobrova is Associate Professor at St Petersburg State Economic University, Russia. She has had experience of comparative studies of corporate social responsibility in Finland and Russia (2004) and in Japan and Russia (2011). Olga has also studied NGOs' activity in St Petersburg in the context of Russian civil society development and business involvement. Her current key research focus is stakeholder management of innovative firms.

Eric Chen graduated from Loyola Marymount University, Los Angeles, with an MBA in Marketing and Entrepreneurship. He currently conducts market research and concept testing for the pharmaceutical and medical device industry. He is passionate about how technology can improve lives.

Nelarine Cornelius is Full Professor of Human Resource Management and Organisational Studies and Associate Dean Research at the School of Management, University of Bradford. She is currently Visiting Professor at the University of Paris (Nanterre, La Défence) and Distinguished Visiting Professor at the University of Lagos. She has conducted research and consultancy in the areas of diversity and inequality, social enterprise and social entrepreneurship, and business ethics. Nelarine's work has appeared in international journals that include *Human Resource Management Journal, International Journal of Human Resource Management, Journal of Business Ethics, British Journal of Management, Organization, Information and Management, Information Systems Journal, Critical Perspectives on Accounting* and *Urban Studies*. She is a founder member of the Voice and Ethnicity Research Network (VERN) and a member of the scientific committee of Paris Research in Norms, Management and Law (PRIMAL). She is co-editor of *Personnel Review*.

Kyoko Fukukawa specializes in research on CSR and ethical decision making in consumption and business practices. She edited a book titled *Corporate Social Responsibility in Asia* (2010, Routledge). She was a Japanese Studies Fellow of the Japan Foundation in 2006, during which time she conducted research on multinational companies to examine the communication and practice of CSR in Japan. She is currently serving as an editorial board member of the *Asian Journal of Business Ethics*. She also co-edited a special issue of the *Journal of Business Ethics* on Corporate Identity, Ethics and CSR (2007). Before coming to the UK, Kyoko worked in the construction industry in her home city, Tokyo.

Edmund R. Gray is a Professor of Management at Loyola Marymount University, Los Angeles. He specializes in social and environmental issues in business.

Janti Gunawan is a Lecturer at Institut Teknologi Sepuluh Nopember (ITS) in Surabaya, Indonesia. She is a member of the Laboratory for Industrial Management and Systems Development, as well as the Research Center for Regional and Community Development at ITS. Her research interests are entrepreneurship, industrial clusters and CSR, with a specific focus on small to medium-size enterprises and local economic development. She has extensive research and consultancy experience with the Indonesian government, Indonesia Central Bank and a number of international non-government organizations operating in Indonesia.

Maria Elena B. Herrera, who holds a PhD in Organization Development from the Southeast Asia Interdisciplinary Development Institute, is Professor at the Asian Institute of Management. She is a fellow of the Actuarial Society of the Philippines and is Research Director of the AIM Ramon V. del Rosario Sr Center for Corporate Social Responsibility. Her fields of consulting and research are corporate strategy, corporate finance, enterprise risk management, governance in family firms, health policy and finance, CSR and organization performance measurement and management. She has worked in the insurance and consumer goods industries and is currently President of Solutions Incorporated, an employee benefits and actuarial consulting firm.

Ashique Ali Jhatial is Senior Lecturer in International Human Resource Management at Sindh University, Pakistan. He was previously a post-doctoral research fellow at the School of Management, University of Bradford. In addition to publications in academic journals in Pakistan, his work has appeared recently in the journal, *Business History*. Ashique's research is in the areas of international human resource management, business history and colonial and postcolonial influences on the evolution of management practices.

Christoph Lattemann is Professor for Business Administration and Information Management at Jacobs University Bremen, Germany, and a Visiting Scholar at Harvard University. He has taught courses in top MBA programmes such as those at the Copenhagen Business School, Hasso Plattner Institute for Software Engineering, Educatis University in Switzerland and Universita Cattolica de Sacro Cuore. Having published more than 130 publications in reputable journals, books and conference proceedings, his latest articles are about corporate governance, CSR and information management. He is a member of various review boards and professional associations.

Nancy Lieu has an Asian Humanities Bachelor of Arts degree from UCLA, where she studied East Asian history, languages and cultures. She also has an MBA with a focus on entrepreneurship from Loyola Marymount University, Los Angeles. She is a licensed US accountant and currently resides in Seattle, Washington. She is passionate about educational quality worldwide.

Satoshi Mizobata is director and professor of the Kyoto Institute of Economic Research at Kyoto University, Japan. He was awarded his doctorate in Economics at Kyoto University in 1997. His research areas are comparative studies in economic systems, corporate governance and business organization, and the Russian and East European economies and Japan, focusing on the enterprise and market structure. Recently, he has focused on researching CSR in Russia and Japan, and corporate society in emerging economies. He is editor of the *Journal of Comparative Economic Studies*. He is an executive director of the Japan Association for Comparative Business Management and has an executive position in the European Association for Comparative

Economics. His recent publications are: *Melting Boundaries* (2008), *Two Asias* (2012) and articles for journals such as *Society and Economy*.

Francisco L. Roman, who holds a DBA in International Business, minor in Agribusiness, from Harvard Business School, is Professor at the Asian Institute of Management and is currently the Executive Director of the AIM Ramon V. del Rosario Sr Center for Corporate Social Responsibility and the Associate Dean for Research and Publications. His area of research and consulting covers Southeast Asia, with additional work in China and India, Korea and Bhutan. His expertise includes governance in family firms, corporate social responsibility, competitiveness and cluster development, agribusiness and small and medium-size enterprise development.

Anna-Maria Schneider is a postdoctoral researcher at Humboldt University Berlin. She has specialized in corporate social responsibility in China. Her current research is mainly focused on the realization of CSR processes in emerging countries, especially in China and at Chinese supplier firms. This field of research contains in particular the implementation of CSR measures along the supply chain of multinational enterprises (MNEs) and the underlying incentive and enforcement mechanisms. Furthermore, she examines the impact of particular phenomena in China, such as labour shortage and relocation of production facilities, on working conditions and the realization of CSR.

Ramendra Singh is Assistant Professor (Marketing) at the Indian Institute of Management Calcutta, India. He holds a PhD from IIM Ahmedabad, an MBA from XLRI Jamshedpur and a BTech from IIT-BHU. He is also a 2008 AMA-Sheth Doctoral Consortium fellow. His research has been published in reputed international journals, including *Industrial Marketing Management*, *Journal of Personal Selling & Sales Management*, *Journal of Business and Industrial Marketing* and *Marketing Intelligence & Planning*. Ramendra has previously worked for six years in sales and marketing in several multinational companies.

Eddy Soedjono is a Senior Lecturer at Institut Teknologi Sepuluh Nopember (ITS) in Surabaya, Indonesia. His research interest involves the environment and sanitation. He has been engaged with various community programmes in the areas of health, sanitation and energy.

Patnaree Srisuphaolarn is a Lecturer at the Department of International Business, Logistics and Transport, Thammasat Business School of Thammasat University, Thailand, where she teaches cross-cultural management, comparative business systems, and doing business in Asia. She is invited guest lecturer at the Vienna University of Economics and Business, Austria, and Hitotsubashi University, Japan, on marketing for emerging countries and social innovation in Thailand. Her research interests include the development of corporate social responsibility in Thailand and the internationalization of healthcare services from Thailand to Japan. She writes for local and international academic journals, including the *Journal of Social Responsibility*, *Chulalongkorn Business Review* and the *Journal of Business Administration*. Recently, she serves as Deputy Director of the Institute of East Asian Studies at Thammasat University to promote the joint seminar and research collaboration regarding East Asia.

Britney Teeple graduated from Loyola Marymount University, Los Angeles, with an MBA in international business and finance. Her research interest includes the relationship between the environment and business, especially energy efficient development and real estate. She has worked in the corporate governance and the intelligence and securities industries with expertise in marketing and trend analysis. She currently resides in the Washington, DC, area of the United States.

Anthein Thomas has an MBA in entrepreneurship and finance from Loyola Marymount University, Los Angeles, and a Master of Science in civil engineering from Syracuse University, New York. He works in watershed management to improve water quality, conservation and flood control capabilities.

Lantip Trisunarno is a Lecturer at Institut Teknologi Sepuluh Nopember (ITS) in Surabaya, Indonesia. He is the coordinator for the university's entrepreneurship programme.

Agnes Tuti Rumiati is a Senior Lecturer at Institut Teknologi Sepuluh Nopember (ITS) in Surabaya, Indonesia. She lectures in the Statistics Department and is a researcher in the Research Center for Regional and Community Development at ITS. Her research interest and experience is in the field of CSR (social mapping, planning and evaluation). She also has extensive research and consultancy experience with private firms in the oil/gas and cement industries, central and local government in Indonesia and international organizations.

Sam Vahedi graduated from Loyola Marymount University, Los Angeles, with JD/MBA. His practice is focused primarily in the areas of business litigation, business transactions and business consulting.

James Wallace is Senior Lecturer in Quantitative Methods and Director of PhD Training and Development at the School of Management, University of Bradford, UK. A Fellow of The Royal Statistical Society, James has undertaken research in the main areas of information and management, social enterprise and social regeneration, and business and society, applying his statistical expertise to the exploration of these fields. He is Visiting Research Fellow for the research centre, Paris Research in Norms, Management and

Law (PRIMAL), an international network of scholars coordinated by the University of Paris. He is currently involved in two PRIMAL projects on mentoring, including a national project conducted in collaboration with the research unit of the CFDT union in France. James's work includes articles in *Business History*, *European Journal of Marketing*, *Journal of Business Ethics*, *International Journal of Public Sector Management* and *Information and Management*. James heads the Research Methods section for PRIMAL.

Introduction

The multiplicities of CSR

Kyoko Fukukawa

This book is a sequel to *Corporate Social Responsibility in Asia* (2010), and retains the underlying aim to offer alternative perspectives to the existing dominant discourse of corporate social responsibility (CSR). Having previously examined the goals of CSR and their perceived 'import' into Asia, this volume, *Corporate Social Responsibility and Local Community in Asia*, looks further to ask what is at the root of all discourses, disciplines and implementation of CSR across the Asian region. When I first researched the perceptions of CSR in Japan (Fukukawa and Moon, 2004), I came to understand a number of subtle and alternative viewpoints about how CSR practices can be situated *between* both internal and globalized markets, and this prompted me to pursue editing my first book on CSR in Asia. While I was always aware I could not capture the area of research in its totality, I was struck with how readings of CSR varied across Asian countries; and subsequently how tall a task it was to present a fully representative view, particularly with regard to understanding the beginning of the supply chain. It has taken a second book, then, to focus attention on CSR in Asia in terms of issues of progress and local community engagement. This book aims to offer more insights from a wider set of Asian countries, which in part is to appreciate the variance of practices in these countries.

Having noted in the previous volume the importance of human connectivity as an emerging theme, this book turns to look more directly at the notion of connectivity. More specifically, it is framed around the concept of local community, with particular emphasis upon the 'bottom of the pyramid' (BOP). A key tenet of the book is that in order to complete the circuit of CSR, to gain a more complex and nuanced understanding of CSR, we need to bring into focus a consideration of the poorest socio-economic groups. The BOP has been identified as a site of opportunity for corporations to tap into new markets, with varying degrees of responsibility to local communities. There is an obvious tension between employees being part of the global supply chain and yet typically having no real choices and opportunities to prosper within a local economy. In terms of CSR, businesses operating at the base of the economic pyramid are all too frequently labelled as 'laggards'. Yet, arguably, we are all lagging behind when someone, somewhere in the overall chain is lagging behind. CSR cannot be the preserve of the rich. In line with the previous volume, which sought to deconstruct dichotomies of 'East' and 'West' and 'buyers' and 'sellers/suppliers', this sequel aims to challenge the categories of 'rich' and 'poor'. Ultimately, we need to look ahead to understand what businesses can do to operate at *all* levels in the global trading 'village'. The chapters examine a range of issues, including philanthropy, social entrepreneurship, employee relations and community engagement. In so doing, the contributions brought together here enable us to ask afresh what is meant by CSR across all stratifications, whether of a country, region, community and/or organization; and probe further into how corporations can properly locate responsibilities in local community and global operations.

Of multitudes and multiplicities

Adam Smith's notion of the 'invisible hand' of the market remains a highly evocative metaphor, underpinning the belief of many – arguably a majority – that the free market system maximizes the benefits for *both* individuals and society. Smith's economic theory valorized the profit motive of the individual, arguing that competition leads to improvements and efficiencies in the marketplace. The effect of this is not solely individual gains; indeed, Smith argues that while the individual operates for self-interest motives, it has the effect of promoting the interests of society as a whole. Smith, then, saw no need for public intervention, and in fact actively argued against such activities:

> By pursuing his own interest, [the individual] frequently promotes that of the society more effectually than when he really intends to promote it. I have never known much good done by those who affected to trade for the public good. It is an affectation, indeed, not very common among merchants, and very few words need be employed in dissuading them from it.
>
> (Smith, 1976: 456)

Smith's account has continued to dominate debates about the economy well beyond his time of writing in the late 1700s. The Nobel Prize-winning economist Milton Friedman accentuates Smith's view, arguing forcefully that the only social responsibility of any business is to increase its profits. Conversely, John Maynard Keynes's writings of the 1930s, during the period of the Great Depression, reacts against Smith's account. Keynesian economists argue that inefficiencies of the private sector do in fact accrue; as such, at the macro-economic level there is the need to stabilize the economic cycle through active intervention by the public sector.

We might consider the concept of CSR to lie somewhere *between* Smith's and Keynes's theories. CSR is undoubtedly of the private sector, yet has its eye on the public sector, or at least, to echo Smith's words, is the affectation to 'trade for the public good'. And while CSR can be said originally to have developed as a managerial response to anti-corporate activism, operating more as a strategy for corporate reputation, today its moral agenda has gained traction. Recent events regarding the global downturn (and the related banking crisis of 2008) have renewed the challenge to classical economics and capitalism more generally. In a recent primer on Smith's *The Wealth of Nations*, McCreadie 'cannot help but wonder what Mr Smith would make of the excesses of capitalism we've witnessed in the twenty-first century'. McCreadie's hunch is that:

> [Adam Smith] might wish that he had added a little more emphasis on the importance of a strong moral and ethical compass, if the benefits of a free economy are to be reaped without making room for the exploitation and evil that has been such an unfortunate by-product.
>
> (McCreadie, 2009: 2)

Of course, Smith does pay specific and critical attention to the moral thinking of his time; notably with the publication of *The Theory of Moral Sentiments* (1759). One's conscience, he argues, arises through social relationships; with our ability to form moral judgements occurring despite a natural inclination towards self-interest. It is reasonable to read Smith's theory of sympathy – whereby observing others allows us to be aware of our own morality – as being in conflict with the ideas presented in *The Wealth of Nations*, which focuses on self-interest. Yet, at a more philosophical level, the two accounts need not seem so opposed, as becomes apparent with Smith's well-known dictum:

> It is not from the benevolence of the butcher, the brewer, or the baker, that we expect our dinner, but from their regard to their own interest. We address ourselves, not to their humanity but to their self-love, and never talk to them of our own necessities but of their advantages.
>
> (Smith, 1976: 26–7)

Of course, Adam Smith could never have imagined the complexities of today's global and networked economy. The idea that we might 'address ourselves' to those we trade with is now substantially more difficult to comprehend. Who are we 'facing' when we make everyday purchases on the high street, for example, and what would it mean for us to talk of their advantages? We can grasp at some answers to these questions, though perhaps all too sadly we tend to speak less of advantages than of deceptions and inequalities. The manuscript for this book was being prepared just at the time Western media broke the news of the tragic collapse of the Rana Plaza factory in Bangladesh, killing over 1,100 workers (BBC News Asia, 23 May 2013). The factory supplied garments to many high-street outlets in the United Kingdom and elsewhere. Primark, a high-street chain store selling low-end fashionable clothing to UK consumers at very low prices, was one of the named companies receiving wares from the factory – in fact one whole floor of the building was dedicated to supplying the chain.

The news of the building's collapse led to protests outside Primark's flagship store on London's Oxford Street. A few days later the company announced a package of aid for those working at the Bangladesh factory. And further to this, several Western retailers signed a pact to improve working conditions in Bangladesh (though with some notable exceptions – including Walmart and Gap – who refrained from signing up to collective action, favouring their own, independent approach to tackling issues).

The numbers killed and badly injured at the Rana Plaza factory (many lost limbs in order to be pulled from the wreckage of the building) is a deeply felt tragedy. Yet, what makes this industrial accident even worse is just how poorly the people working in the factory, and others like it, are represented. The collapse of the factory was a particularly dramatic example of failure in health and safety, yet what was revealed (to those outside the country) is that many smaller-scale instances are occurring on a regular basis both in Bangladesh and in other countries to where fashion production is outsourced. Of course, in the main these instances go unreported – certainly in the Western media. Three weeks later, for example, the headline 'Cambodia shoe factory collapse kills workers' appeared in *The Guardian* (16 May 2013), which arguably only received attention due to the prior event in Bangladesh. The Rana Plaza factory has become the most recent emblem of the globalized supply chains and corporate relationships that this book seeks to examine. The rubble of the factory is the dark symptom and symbol of the *unfettered* hand of capitalism that lies at the bottom of the global economic pyramid. What it revealed, sadly again, to the wider global community, is an army of workers dispossessed, a multitude that is mute and in this case most likely back looking for work among the plethora of textile factories. The problem is not simply the inability of the workers to uphold their rights, but the inability for us to share in this responsibility. Just as Ostrom (1990) has written of the governance of natural resources requiring the common pooling of resources, we too need to understand labour as a common experience.

The gestures of support offered by Primark and others in the wake of the collapse of the factory in Bangladesh – while undoubtedly genuine and generous – can be said to come about only because of such an event. And there is a history to such aid. Since the 1990s, corporations have poured billions of dollars into building CSR teams and conducting social audits, prompted initially when the sweatshops supplying Nike and Kathie Lee Gifford came to the world's attention. However, rather than wait to respond *after the event*, we need to find ways to better elucidate the complexities of globalization and to make better judgements about our sense of social responsibility and connectedness. In overcoming the duplicitous nature of a global economy that can show genuine concern for the poor, and yet continue to serve the rich, the difficulties faced are perhaps less to do with a multitude than with our own multiplicities of behaviour.

Despite the scale of casualties and fatalities at the Rana Plaza factory, and the widespread reporting of the event, the government leaders attending the

G8 Summit of 2013 had another pressing matter to attend to, to attempt to fix the international tax system, which currently allows multinational corporations (MNCs) to legally avoid vast sums of tax. Profits are being collected up from the dusty floors of factories and the clean interfaces of online shopping sites, siphoned off through complex corporate accounting structures. If it is hard to fathom the true nature of such business practices, we might at least ask what it is about profit that is so motivating. If you are a factory manager, you feel obliged to increase the efficiency and productivity of the factory floor, leading you perhaps even to control your workers' time allowed in using the toilet. If you are an accountant, with the best of your professional knowledge, you will try to identify how to make things financially advantageous for a company. These are individual nodes in a complex network, within which it is all too easy *not* to know the impact of one's decisions and actions. During classes at my university I ask students if it is acceptable to make a decision based on profit while undermining environmental and social impacts. The answer will typically come back along the lines: 'We have to. It should be permissible as a manager, however as a person I won't do it.' Arguably, it is through the deterritorializing experience of the global economy that we have adopted a multiplicity of responses as a means to cope. CSR itself has enabled different perspectives to be upheld simultaneously. Specifically, it pertains to both moral and legal perspectives. In espousing the virtues of transparency and auditing, CSR is a system to help ensure companies uphold legal responsibilities. Equally, CSR gives voice to a variety of moral issues, to which companies are seen to pay attention. A dilemma arises, however, if we confuse these two perspectives, to think by observing legalities companies are forwarding a moral agenda. There is a definite relationship, but not necessarily a direct correlation.

Shakespeare's *The Merchant of Venice* offers a neat allegory of the balance between moral and legal business practices. Bassanio, a Venetian noble suffering hard times, seeks aid from his friend Antonio, a wealthy merchant of Venice. Antonio is short of cash, but agrees to guarantee a loan from the moneylender Shylock. The moneylender stipulates the dramatic condition: if Antonio is unable to repay the load, Shylock may take a pound of his flesh. As we might expect, the play culminates with the forfeiting of the loan and a scene in which Shylock prepares to claim his 'pound of flesh', having refused Bassanio's offer to repay double the amount of the loan. The climax of the play revolves around a legality rather than morality. A court grants Shylock his right to a 'pound of flesh'. Antonio prepares for the incision of a knife, but is saved by a deft legal appeal in which it is pointed out the contract only allows Shylock to remove the *flesh*, not the blood of Antonio. Since he can only remove the flesh by spilling the blood, the 'repayment' of the loan is forfeited. In today's complex global environment, while the removal of the 'flesh' may well be legal, we need to remind ourselves of the coursing of the blood that allows transactions to flow in the first place. In reading the chapters of this book, I hope readers might feel and want to connect (and indeed see ways to connect) with others in the globalized marketplace.

Being aware of what we *do* (and not just what we say) impacts upon all those in connection with us.

Overview of contributions

The take-up of CSR practices has become more prevalent in Asian countries, right across the region. While companies would not want to be hindered by implementing procedures with cost implications, the need for legitimacy for pursuing social and environmental objectives has come squarely into focus, and can be understood even to lead to economic benefit. The chapters of this book cover a wide range of geographic and cultural contexts, and in doing so present varying accounts and critiques of CSR and CSR-related practices. In the opening chapter, which considers the context of China, Schneider, Lattemann and Altmann examine the impact of international companies relocating production facilities to lower-wage regions. The chapter analyses the impact of relocation on working conditions and portrays the impact on the local community. It goes on to elucidate three critical levels, governmental, industrial and the firm, and proposes the extent to which each may influence the nature of working conditions through three scenarios specifying working conditions. The chapter captures a tension between the opportunities and ethics of foreign direct investment (FDI). While FDI can be seen to bring brighter prospects to an area, factory workers are often worse off (as we see with the recent incident in Bangladesh). A key question we can extrapolate from this chapter is where the balance lies between the benefits from low-cost production to a region, and mere exploitation.

The second chapter is the product of collaboration between six researchers – Teeple, Lieu, Thomas, Vahedi, Chen and Gray – and is based on a series of projects on Singapore, India and Hong Kong. Each country can be seen to have identified social or environmental needs and subsequently to have used entrepreneurial principles to innovate solutions to address these needs. The authors note that funding, talent recruitment and retention are the most common barriers for progress across all regions. The study further identifies four common practices to tackle these challenges: (1) the use of performance indicators and metrics, (2) strategic partnerships, (3) networking and (4) relevant technology implementation.

The context of India is further analysed in Chapter 3, with Singh and Agarwal's study of CSR practices among the top 200 Indian corporations. Importantly, the companies in their sample are those listed on the Bombay Stock Exchange (so excluding foreign multinationals such as Coca-Cola and IBM etc.). As such, they offer an account of India's indigenous corporate landscape, giving insight into national, social and cultural distinctions. The authors provide some important elucidation of perceptions towards CSR in the Indian context, and examine corporate processes of engaging with local communities, which can be seen to bring change to the lives of many disadvantaged members of the community.

A similarly broad consideration of business sectors is made by Jhatial, Cornelius and Wallace, in Chapter 6, which looks at the context of Pakistan. Their study evaluates the corporate engagement of commercial and non-commercial organizations with the local community. They draw results from an analysis of online disclosure of CSR policies and impact statements of high-profile MNCs and private and government-owned companies. They also conducted interviews with senior executives across business sectors and non-governmental organizations (NGOs) to further understand how CSR activities impact on local communities. The authors comment on the effectiveness of government regulations in Pakistan to set minimum standards of CSR disclosure, and provide insight into the distinctive aspects of CSR activity in Pakistan, as informed by local cultural norms and values.

Chapter 4, by Mizobata, Bobrova and Fukukawa, focuses on corporate engagements with local communities in Japan, particularly after the devastating Great East Earthquake in 2011. Following the earthquake, further pressure was placed upon companies in relation to CSR activities. Companies became closely involved in the remedial operations rebuilding towns and villages and even tasks to bring whole communities back to normality. Yet, the authors note how the overreliance of the communities on local government prevented corporations from establishing or developing closer ties with these communities. Thus, the relationship between corporations and communities can be said to remain relatively static while the importance of NGOs/NPOs (non-profit organizations) has been reconsidered to bridge among all stakeholders.

The previous book on CSR in Asia featured a chapter focusing on the ready-made garment sector in Bangladesh, which gave an account of the exploitation of labour. The chapter remains highly pertinent for its critical analysis of the situation, not least given the high-profile example of the Rana Plaza factory, noted above, and the ensuing debates over 'ethical' shopping and fashion. The chapter in this book by Azmat, Chapter 5, presents another critical issue for the context of Bangladesh: the environment, and in particular waste management. Azmat offers a more positive picture of Bangladesh, exploring the potential for social entrepreneurs to work with communities to respond to persistent social problems. In presenting a case study of Waste Concern – an initiative of social entrepreneurs in Bangladesh – the chapter brings together the discourses on the BOP and social entrepreneurship. Azmat shows how social entrepreneurs have the potential to reduce poverty and make a difference to the local community.

Chapter 7, by Gunawan, Rumiati, Trisunarno and Soedjono, offers an account of two types of organizational implementation of CSR in the context of Indonesia. On the one hand there is the multinational enterprise of the private sector, and on the other state-owned enterprises (SOEs). The authors describe how the practice of CSR by multinational enterprises (MNEs) is driven by international values, standards and norms, while implementation by SOEs is driven by domestic, or national, values, standards and regulations. The authors draw upon institutional theory to explain how companies conduct CSR in order to obtain legitimacy. The case studies demonstrate perspectives on legitimacy, which are different from one business to another. Yet, nonetheless, the beneficiaries of CSR activities are similar. The chapter also considers the importance of the role of intermediaries such as university and marketing partners, which help in bridging between organizations and communities in Indonesia. The authors note how intermediaries are positively associated with CSR implementation because of their ability to meet social values. One of the SOE cases shows that CSR implementation is driven explicitly by external pressure and the adoption of a bottom-up approach.

The cases presented in Chapter 8 by Srisuphaolarn illustrate proactive community engagement of corporations in Thailand. As 'change-makers', to use Srisuphaolarn's term, corporations help support capacity-building and capability development. The relationship between corporations and community is detailed as being collegial, based upon co-production rather than the handing out of donations. The chapter brings attention to affective components, such as trust and perceived autonomy (relating to issues of confidence), as key features of successful knowledge exchange among those involved. Srisuphaolarn argues how CSR programmes enable companies to fill institutional voids and correct government failures in redistributing economic benefits to citizens. It is not insignificant, of course, that corporations are privileged in terms of resources and knowledge. The idea, however, is that once community members learn how to manage resources, they can go on to seek resolutions for themselves to subsequent challenges. Thus, this chapter clearly examines processes for balancing economic, social and environmental variables to create tangible sustainability.

In the final chapter, Herrera and Roman present an innovative modelling of CSR strategy development, which they discuss in relation to a range of Asian countries. The authors argue that a strategic approach to CSR needs to align external and internal business realities, in particular taking account of the macro-environment, stakeholder concerns and a company's ecological 'footprint' in developing a community engagement strategy. In order to create shared values for the company and its stakeholders, community engagement is described as being key in creating sustainable partnerships. Based on investigations of CSR practices in Cambodia, China, India, Indonesia, Laos, Malaysia, Philippines, Singapore, Thailand and Vietnam, the chapter presents a set of factors, which the authors draw together for a tool or framework, which they call the Influences (Hexagon) Framework. The chapter shows positively that progress can occur in supply-side CSR engagement with the BOP, where corporations combine internally generated initiatives with information about and inputs from affected community stakeholders.

Putting the social back into CSR

There are inevitably many challenges when researching CSR management and practices. Access to internal data is guarded and sensitive, and there is no fixed consensus over criteria for evaluating practices. In order to overcome such methodological issues, early studies approached CSR in terms of transparency, so typically studying levels of (self-)reporting. While this offered a first window on how corporations engage with CSR practices, the findings were presented with caution, since what a corporation communicates can be different from what actually manifests. Inevitably, firms quickly learnt to talk the talk on CSR (often referred to as 'green-wash' and 'window dressing'), but were not necessarily ready to walk the talk.

Paul Klein, the president of Impakt (an organization that helps corporations and civil groups become 'social purpose leaders'), is critical of the *concept* of CSR that grew out of crisis management from the 1970s in response to anti-corporate activism. Following this period we arrived at the widely accepted view that CSR contributes positively to both business and social change. Yet, Klein argues 'the degree to which [CSR] delivers measurable business value and meaningful social change isn't clear'; and goes on to suggest this is perhaps because 'the original intent of CSR had nothing to do with what many practitioners now call "shared value"' (Klein, 2013). Klein's criticisms are not levelled at socially orientated activities that a firm may engage in, but rather at a 'CSR industry' that he sees as divorced from business interests:

> Business has . . . a vitally important role as an agent of social change but this has little to do with corporate social responsibility. Executives aren't lying awake at night worrying about their company's charitable donations, partnerships with non-profit organisations, employee volunteer programs, and corporate social responsibility reports. These initiatives aren't wrong but they need to be embedded in the fundamental priority of business.
>
> (Klein, 2013)

For Klein, this fundamental priority is the generating of profit. He makes explicit reference to Friedman's much quoted statement:

> There is one and only one social responsibility of business – to use its resources and engage in activities designed to increase its profits so long as it stays within the rules of the game, which is to say, engages in open and free competition without deception or fraud.
>
> (Friedman, 1970)

The argument that follows is that corporations have largely only altered behaviour due to what Klein describes as 'more robust rules of the game'. There is something convincing about Klein's pragmatic point of view, yet we need not stick solely to a mantra of profit to draw out the more interesting suggestion that business play a key role as agents of social change.

We have come to value the fact that corporations at least talk of a commitment to pursue responsibilities beyond that of profit; and we might suggest the scope of the debate has moved on even further. While we look to companies to 'walk the talk', we are also witnessing the emergence of new company ethics, leading firms to 'walk the walk'. In other words, rather than match up ethical concerns to existing practices as a means to measure and temper the activities of the company, there is a growing appetite among both producers and consumers to take ethical principles as a starting point and work outwards in building new socially orientated businesses. The development of such businesses and organizations has an important effect beyond their own operations, including upon those firms that are not pursuing similar goals, but that nonetheless now find themselves necessarily operating within a newly evolving and credible social-orientated discourse.

It was a noticeable fact in the time following the publication of my first edited volume on CSR in Asia that there had been shift in the terms being used. The term *sustainability*, for example, has generated a lot of interest in recent years, being suggestive of greater emphasis upon environmental issues following the effects of a number of natural disasters. The recent conference and book, *The Necessary Transition* (2013), which took place at Griffith University in Brisbane, Australia, in 2012, brought together leading international researchers and practitioners to debate key *necessary* transitions required for societies across the globe to attain sustainable enterprise economies. These transitions included, for example, moving from high- to low-carbon economies, from inequality to egalitarianism, from human rights abuses to social justice, and from corruption to cohesion and integrity (McIntosh, 2013). Similarly, the term *social entrepreneurship*, seeking legitimacy for business practices *as* environmental and social initiatives, has gained greater traction as a key concept. A recent special issue on the topic appears in the *Journal of Business Ethics*, which points out that research is at an embryonic stage and suggests four key areas to be addressed: (1) the characteristics of individual social entrepreneurs, (2) their sphere of operation and the social needs and constituencies targeted, (3) the process and resources used and (4) the mission of the social entrepreneur/enterprise (Pless, 2012: 111).

Thus, since publishing the first volume, I have had my doubts for the efficacy of the term CSR. As the chapters of this book bring to the fore, when turning attention to the local community, corporations are frequently working alongside all manner of organizations from non-profits to government-sponsored agencies. An obvious question, then, is why we need to refer to *corporate* social responsibility, rather than a more broadly defined constellation of social responsibility. Stakeholder theory, for example, has been an important guiding discourse in understanding and developing the concept of CSR. However, rather than simply acknowledging various different stakeholders, we should recognize that multiple persons are in each of us. CSR is, and always was, multifaceted in its scope and manifestations. All things are interrelated, and as such all things are socially defined. Al Gore's line is that 'if there is no Earth, no us'. We read this to mean that, if the Earth is undermined, so too is humanity. Yet, equally, it is through our social communication that we give definition to what we mean by the Earth. Similarly, then, as we continue to approach the study of CSR, we need to remember a more fundamental social definition of business and responsibilities. This book, hopefully, offers the reader a wide range of examples, from different cultural contexts within Asia, that remind us of the 'social' in corporate social responsibility, helping to extend and enrich our critical understanding of global business-society.

Acknowledgements

I would like to thank the contributors to this book for all the effort they have put in and also for the conversations we had during the process of developing the manuscript. Continuing on from the previous book on CSR in Asia (Fukukawa, 2010), I am very lucky to have worked with contributors, as included here, from a wide range of geographical areas. Each of the contributions is unique and I believe many aspects presented here have not been discussed elsewhere (and most likely will not be discussed and/or analysed in academic or professional journal papers). The chapters in this book are not only the presentation of intellectual research, but will also be of value as teaching materials to provide critical accounts of ethical issues in international business and CSR management. As an editor, I have thoroughly enjoyed the exchanges I have had with the contributors (and their texts), sensing the intellectual challenges and tensions as a formative and informative process for all involved. With the support of a copy editor and writer, the best effort has been made to make these texts accessible to the reader. Establishing connectedness and bringing to light the relevance of local practices within the global market/business lies at the heart of this book. Each chapter reveals that such a process is not at all straightforward, but is nonetheless always important.

References

Friedman, M. (1970) 'The social responsibility of business is to increase its profits', *The New York Times Magazine*, 13 September.

Fukukawa, K. (ed.) (2010) *Corporate Social Responsibility in Asia*, London: Routledge.

Fukukawa, K. and Moon, J. (2004) 'A Japanese model of corporate social responsibility? A study of website reporting', *Journal of Corporate Citizenship*, 14: 45–59.

Klein, P. (2013) 'CSR built around crisis management won't deliver enough value', *The Guardian Professional*, 24 June 2013. Available online at www.theguardian. com/sustainable-business/csr-crisis-managment-shared-value (accessed 10 December 2013).

McCreadie, K. (2009) *Adam Smith's 'The Wealth of Nations': A modern-day interpretation of an economic classic*, Oxford: Infinite Ideas.

McIntosh, M. (2013) *The Necessary Transition: The journey towards the sustainable enterprise*, Sheffield: Greenleaf Publishing.

Ostrom, E. (1990) *Governing The Commons: The evolution of institutions for collective action*, Cambridge: Cambridge University Press.

Pless, N.M. (2012) 'Social entrepreneurship in theory and practice – an introduction', *Journal of Business Ethics*, 111: 317–20.

Smith, A. (1759) *The Theory of Moral Sentiments*, ed. D.D. Raphael and A.L. Macfie (1982) *The Glasgow Edition of the Works and Correspondence of Adam Smith*, vol. 1, Indianapolis, IN: Liberty Fund.

Smith, A. (1976) *The Glasgow Edition of the Works and Correspondence of Adam Smith*, vol. 2a, ed. R.H. Cambell and A.S. Skinner, Oxford: Clarendon Press.

1 Impact of relocation on working conditions in Chinese supplier firms

Does a downgrade have to be expected?

Anna-Maria Schneider, Christoph Lattemann, and Stefan Altmann

Following economic reforms and opening to the world in 1978, China has been industrializing rapidly. In the last three and a half decades, China has been a preferred target for outsourcing by international companies because of its cheap labor force and low-wage manufacturing of consumer goods (Fang *et al.* 2010). As China's economic reforms supported especially the development of the coastal regions with special economic zones, coastal provinces were prioritized destinations for outsourcing (Wen 2004).

Appropriate treatment of workers is protected by law, labor unions, and non-governmental organizations (NGOs) in Western market-based societies (Krueger 2008). While China is well known for its low-cost manufacturing, foreign investors and customers have remained skeptical about working practices and conditions in China (Lübcke *et al.* 2007). In the past 15 years, there have been efforts by buyer firms, especially Western multinational enterprises (MNEs), to improve working conditions in Chinese supplier firms in order to maintain their own reputation in their Western markets. Western buyer firms, mostly in the business-to-consumer sector, have imposed codes of conduct on their Chinese suppliers that are often based on general social standards (Seuring and Müller 2008), such as SA8000 or International Labour Organization (ILO) Conventions. Codes of conduct define principles related to working conditions and human rights. Aspects such as health and safety conditions, forced labor, child labor, freedom of association, discrimination, disciplinary practices, working hours, and wages are covered by codes of conduct (Ciliberti *et al.* 2009). During the past two decades, small but continuous improvements concerning working conditions in Chinese supplier firms have been observed (Schneider and Schwerk 2010).

In recent years, producing and sourcing in the coastal regions of China has become increasingly expensive due to growing input factor costs (Fang *et al.*

2010). The labor shortage in the southeastern provinces has promoted the competition for unskilled workers and has been leading to higher production costs in the labor-intensive manufacturing sector. Rising prices for energy and raw materials negatively impact production costs (Huang *et al.* 2011). The rising costs of production induce manufacturers to look for cheaper production locations in other regions of China (*The Economist* 2010).

Relocation from developed coastal regions of China has already started in several industries (Huang *et al.* 2011). The labor force in industrialized central and western regions of China is much bigger than in China's coastal regions. By relocating to these regions, businesses can benefit from a greater labor supply, lower wages, and lower production costs, for example through lower electricity costs and tax reductions (Jing 2010). The relocation trend will affect both the environment and the social pattern in the local communities of the new destinations. On the one hand, relocation of factories may cause increasing environmental pollution in the new locations with negative effects for the local community. On the other hand, employment rates and wage levels may increase at the new destinations, potentially causing a raise in living standards (e.g., through increased purchasing power and education). Migrant workers profit from this trend as they now can take jobs in their home regions and do not have to find jobs far away.

Relocation from China's coastal regions to the Chinese hinterland is a very recent phenomenon. Academic research on this topic is still scarce. Literature predominantly focuses on economic aspects and reflects the incentives to relocate, that is, mainly cost aspects (e.g., Chen *et al.* 2009; Kumar *et al.* 2009; Platts and Song 2010) and new markets (e.g., Bo and Chen 2009; AmCham Shanghai and Booz & Co. 2010). However, relocation is not only based on purely economic reasons such as cost reductions. Instead, strategic decision making for relocation also has to take environmental and social issues into account, as relocating Chinese companies are integrated in international networks. Aspects such as proper management of hazardous waste and working conditions are of crucial importance for long-term relations because they signal reliability to buyers and help to build up trust. Moreover, market pressure may force companies to comply with prescribed codes of conduct.

Particular impacts of relocation on social aspects such as working conditions have mostly been neglected in research. Most China-related research covers working conditions as only one small part of a broader corporate social responsibility (CSR) concept (e.g., Wong 2009). Human resource-related issues in China are, in general, not sufficiently reflected in academic literature (Cooke and He 2010). This chapter considers these issues further. After years of efforts by Western MNEs to improve working conditions in their supplier firms in China, the impact of factory relocations to the Chinese hinterland or other low-cost areas on working conditions and the determining factors of these relocations need to be analyzed. Will there be a worsening of working conditions in the relocated factories? Is it likely that supplier firms will instead maintain or improve already established working conditions in their relocated plants?

This chapter presents theoretical considerations on alterations of working conditions due to the relocation of companies' manufacturing plants. First, companies' motives to relocate their manufacturing within China are briefly described. Second, current working conditions in Chinese firms are discussed. Three different scenarios (stable, better, and worse working conditions) are then derived and impact factors are analyzed on the basis of a literature review. Subsequently, variables on government-, industry-, and firm-levels are summarized in an explanatory framework, which serves to explain probable developments of CSR and working conditions in relocated production facilities. Derived propositions on impact factors provide a basis for further research.

Motives for relocation

Research on international production essentially focuses on the question whether MNEs establish production plants in foreign markets (Fisch and Zschoche 2012). Different motives and types of foreign direct investment (FDI) are distinguished in traditional management theories (e.g., Lewis 1954; Dunning 1994, 1997) to explain why companies engage in greenfield FDI, strategic alliances, or mergers and acquisitions (Lattemann *et al.* 2012).

Lewis's (1954) model explains why companies in labor-intensive industries tend to relocate their manufacturing plants in particular to developing countries. It assumes that in the early stages of an economy's development there is an unlimited supply of labor. This unlimited labor force will keep labor prices (i.e., wages) down and support the economic development of the country (Tignor 2004). Increasing labor costs due to a shortage of labor lead to higher production costs (Lewis 1954). Therefore, companies from labor-intensive industries start to move their plants to developing or underdeveloped countries, or to regions with a high surplus of labor. We assume that the discussed motives and Lewis's model can explain the relocation of factories in the given Chinese context.

So far, however, economic-driven relocation decisions widely neglect social and environmental (CSR) aspects. At the same time, existing international business theory has failed to integrate CSR into its explanatory models. It can be observed that during the past two decades, Western MNEs have started to impose codes of conduct on their emerging market partners, in particular in China (e.g., Wong 2009; Cooke and He 2010), in order to improve working, environmental, and other social conditions in and around partnering factories and to activate responsible behavior in supplier firms. Hence, MNEs' CSR and local working conditions are certainly not among the main criteria for relocation or internationalization, but they constitute constraining factors as proper CSR practices influence the MNEs' reputation and risk. A recent study (AmCham Shanghai and Booz & Co. 2010) shows that labor cost savings, material cost savings, access to quality labor, utility cost savings, access to the Asian market, and global competitive strategies are the main reasons for

FDI in China. Hence, intended cost savings and strategic business expansions are presumably also the main reasons for relocating away from China (e.g., Chan *et al.* 1995; Wen 2004). This is in line with Dunning's (1994, 1997) well-known classification of resource-, efficiency-, strategic asset-, and market-seeking motives for FDI.

Labor shortages can be noted in labor-intensive manufacturing clusters. Around 90 percent of the labor-intensive clusters, producing goods such as clothing and textiles, footwear, toys, and bicycles, are located in 15 provinces in the eastern and coastal regions of China (Wang and Mei 2009). In 2004, early indications of an imminent labor shortage were observed (Inagaki 2006) and, in 2005, the labor shortage became apparent in the industrial centers of the coastal regions (Zhang and Figliozzi 2010). This situation has been reflected in sharp increases of wage levels of more than 200 percent in five years (e.g., Barboza 2006; Schneider 2012)—from 2004 to 2009, the wage level rose by about 120 percent in Guangdong and Shandong and by more than 200 percent in Jiangsu and Zhejiang.

Not only labor costs, but also the general costs of manufacturing, are lower in the inland provinces than in eastern and southern China (Jing 2010). For instance, in Chongqing the costs of labor, water, electricity, and natural gas are almost 30 percent lower than in the coastal provinces (Ying 2010). Furthermore, in the coastal regions, manufacturing plants frequently also have to cope with unexpected power cuts leading to sub-standard products and a reduction of productivity (Wang and Pei 2010).

The relocation of export-oriented factories to China's inland provinces requires a sufficiently developed infrastructure and logistics systems with a high transportation load capacity in place in order to remain capable of export (Zhang and Figliozzi 2010). Local governments have realized that good infrastructure constitutes a major incentive for companies to relocate and invest in the Chinese hinterland. For example, Chongqing has started to invest in the expansion of its airport and established a direct cargo service to the Belgian city of Liège and hence to the European market (Ying 2010). The railway route is being expanded as well (Ying 2010). As a result, transportation and infrastructure issues are slowly becoming less of a limiting factor for many manufacturers in some of the Chinese inland provinces.

At the same time, many natural resources vital for industrial production are actually mined in China's hinterland, which explains why Chongqing has China's largest aluminum processing plant as well as China's largest acetic acid plant (Bo and Chen 2009). Another motive for relocation, therefore, is the proximity to natural resources and the availability of building land, which has become scarce in the coastal regions but is relatively abundant in the hinterland (Wang and Pei 2010). In order to stimulate the relocation of manufacturing operations from coastal to western provinces, tax incentives such as duty-free zones have been set up and the development of industry clusters similar to those in Chongqing is supported by the government (Jing 2010). In principle, manufacturers from Chinese coastal regions can choose

Figure 1.1 Location choices for Chinese manufacturers.

either to keep producing in the coastal regions or to partially or completely relocate to the Chinese hinterland. Figure 1.1 depicts the options for manufacturers' location choices and their respective benefits (motives) and challenges.

Working conditions in Chinese manufacturing firms

Occupational distributions and working conditions differ among Chinese labor groups, namely migrant workers and local residents (Wong *et al.* 2007). Working conditions include employee-related aspects such as working time, extent of overtime, wage level and overtime payment, (the existence of) working contracts, the physical environment, housing opportunities, health and safety issues, and treatment by supervisors and management. The definition of "appropriate" working conditions differs between nations (Wong 2009) because of the institutional and cultural frameworks that affect ethical perceptions (Matten and Moon 2008).

Mostly, migrant workers are employed in the production plants of the coastal regions (Messinis and Cheng 2009). Such workers migrate from rural to urban areas in order to find jobs. This is mainly caused by the income disparity between regions (Shi 2008). Migrants typically come from western and central provinces, which are rich in labor force, and move to southern and eastern provinces where export-oriented, labor-intensive industries are located (Chan 2008). Migrants accept physically demanding jobs that local urban workers disesteem (e.g., Wong *et al.* 2007; Démurger *et al.* 2009). The *hukou* system, a household registration system, aims at impeding migration between rural and urban areas. Institutional barriers lead to discrimination of migrant workers who have been living a marginalized life excluded from urban welfare systems (e.g., Wong *et al.* 2007; Démurger *et al.* 2009).

Migrant workers are often exploited at manufacturing facilities. They often work much longer than their local urban colleagues (Schneider and Schwerk 2010) and longer than the law allows, and perform excessive overtime

(Démurger *et al.* 2009). Workers face high-pace shifts of up to 15 hours or more on six, often seven, days a week. They receive lower wages than urban citizens or do not get the compulsory minimum wage (Wong 2009). A large number of migrant workers have to cope with delays in wage payments, a common strategy used by manufacturers to reduce employee turnover and to tie workers to their respective manufacturing plants (Wong *et al.* 2007).

Due to the *hukou* system, migrants are excluded from urban housing markets and are therefore living on the factory premises. Cramped accommodations and a lack of private space are the norm. Usually, between eight and 20 workers share a room. Washrooms and bathrooms are shared by roommates, floor mates, or even all the housing unit's occupants (Pun and Smith 2007). Human rights abuses have been apparent (Wong 2009; National Labour Committee 2010) and the level of occupational safety is often low (Wong 2009). Furthermore, there is no possibility to build labor unions or to bargain collectively with factory management (Wong 2009). Migrant workers are often less aware of their rights and less protected by local governments (Démurger *et al.* 2009). The costs of living have significantly increased in the coastal regions while wages have not risen to the same extent (Schneider and Altmann 2010). However, the continued scarcity of labor in the coastal regions has strengthened the power of workers and workers' communities. Increasing awareness of labor rights has made workers more likely to strike for their rights and for improvements of their working and living conditions, as happened at the Honda factories in Foshan in 2010 (Bradscher and Barboza 2010). Nowadays, migrant workers choose more frequently to stay closer to their home towns. Lower wages and poorer working conditions in the factories in the Chinese hinterland are compensated by lower living costs than in the coastal regions and greater proximity to the respective home provinces (Tsang 2010).

Poor labor standards in Chinese supplier firms constitute a reputational risk for MNEs' brands. Codes of conduct have become the MNEs' most frequently used instrument to manage and monitor their suppliers' ethical and socially responsible practices (Waddock *et al.* 2002; Egels-Zandén 2007; Schneider and Schwerk 2010). Consequently, codes of conduct are often part of MNEs' CSR strategies. For example, Mattel has imposed global principles, which include social and environmental requirements and which have to be adopted by their supplier firms (Wong 2009). Chinese companies are frequently integrated into extensive global supplier networks and seek to maintain or improve their position in the network. In order to build long-term relationships with buyers or to become a strategic supplier, a firm has to be reliable and must guarantee stable conditions in terms of product quality and social as well as environmental requirements (Andersen and Skjøett-Larsen 2009). In recent years, global players and international buyers have set much value on social and environmental standards, including appropriate working conditions, because investors, NGOs, and the media have demanded such standards (e.g., Yu 2008; Andersen and Skøjett-Larsen 2009). The implementation of codes of conduct is a medium- or long-term process that takes time to be completely implemented and realized (Schneider and Schwerk 2010). Since the 1990s small steps toward improved working conditions in Chinese manufacturers have been observable, mostly driven by MNEs' imposed codes of conduct (Cooke and He 2010).

Scenarios on working conditions

Research shows that CSR could become a source of sustainable competitive advantages (McWilliams *et al.* 2006), but adherence to international CSR standards and to industry-specific codes of conduct implies costs for both buyer and supplier firms. At the same time, worldwide cost pressure leads to relocation and to a rethinking of strategic investment decisions. Thus, an area of conflict between opposing forces of change becomes apparent. It implies the question as to how working conditions will change due to the relocation of factories to the Chinese hinterland or to other low-cost countries. Questions can be raised as to whether renewed efforts and investments for appropriate working conditions can be expected because supplier firms use the opportunity to step back from costly previous achievements. In which case, we need to consider if working conditions remain stable, or if indeed it is possible for improvements to be in working conditions. Predictive scenario analysis (Börjeson *et al.* 2006) can be used to forecast developments in working conditions in relocated Chinese manufacturing plants. For an MNE it is important to understand the factors that drive the development of working conditions. The respective probabilities of stable, improving, and worsening working conditions lead to action implications for MNEs that want to protect their reputations and ensure appropriate working conditions in their supplier firms. The following scenarios can be drawn up:

(S1) Stable working conditions: Compliance with international social and environmental standards is an increasingly important precondition for being selected as a supplier for international corporate networks. Even when relocating, the buyers still require certain global standards and codes of conduct. Companies have to meet these requirements or face their potential exclusion from the supplier network (Schneider and Schwerk 2010). Companies that have to comply with labor standards imposed by buyers have already gained experience with the implementation and realization of social standards. It can be assumed that the transfer of these labor and CSR standards to new factories in inland China or in lower-cost countries may not generate inadequately high costs due to the previously gained experiences and accumulated know-how. Hence, the first scenario (S1) is based on the assumption that being a partner in international supplier networks, which respect social standards, is of pivotal importance for Chinese manufacturers. Relocation will not change working conditions.

(S2) Better working conditions: The position as a pioneer in business networks might predestine suppliers to distinguish themselves from their competitors—especially if the network relies on social compliance and ethical

worker treatment or if end customers prefer products made under fair working conditions (Kirby *et al.* 2008). If a company can gain competitive advantages due to ethical working conditions and appropriate CSR practices, it probably will use the relocation to implement better working conditions and higher CSR standards for all local stakeholders at the new production plants. Such a step enables relocated firms to integrate good working conditions into the planning process from the outset. This strategy is focused on long-term benefits. Hence, the second scenario (S2) is based on the assumption that Chinese supplier firms use CSR to create sustainable competitive advantages. They will improve social standards or pioneer high working standards and ethical worker treatment.

(S3) Worsening working conditions: The third scenario is based on the assumption that Chinese manufacturers primarily aim at reducing costs. As a consequence, these companies will relocate their factories to regions with a perceived unlimited labor supply to benefit from lower wages. In a manifestation of the classic buyer's labor market concept (as compared to the seller's labor market emerging in the coastal regions), workers might be willing to accept worse working conditions as local jobs remain scarce and alternative jobs in, for example, agriculture yield even lower incomes. Moreover, if buyers do not request social standards and only price, quality, and delivery time are crucial for network partners, supplier firms will have no incentive to improve working conditions or to treat workers fairly (Zadek 2004). Under these assumptions, the third scenario (S3) describes a situation where relocation or expansion strategies to the Chinese hinterland or to low-cost countries go hand in hand with a considerable decline in working conditions.

The three described scenarios are simplifications of the reality in order to identify clear and distinctive scenarios, to create a framework to derive clearly stated propositions, and to be able to determine factors and their impacts.

Factors influencing working conditions in relocated factories

Forecasting is a well-known method in scenario analysis (Börjeson *et al.* 2006). Factors that influence the occurrence of scenarios can be grouped into the national phenomena (e.g., government regulation), the economic environment (e.g., in industries and on markets), and the organizational structure of a company (Börjeson *et al.* 2006). We will use this classification to cluster factors, derived from a literature review, into three levels: the government level, the industry level, and the firm level.

Government-level factors: Supported by the Chinese central government or by local governments, Chinese firms are incentivized to relocate or expand to regions in China's hinterland. The local administrations of inland provinces pursue duty-free policies in order to attract large companies. For instance, the Chongqing Xiyong Comprehensive Bonded Zone is the largest duty-free zone in inland China (Jing 2010).

A country-wide minimum wage does not exist in China. Regions and cities impose their own minimum wages (Kumar *et al.* 2009). Such policies may in particular attract low-cost manufacturers that focus on a reduction of overall production costs. However, these policies are not accompanied by rules for better working conditions. In general, there is a lack of local government support to foster CSR and the improvement of working conditions. Further, due to weak law enforcement in China (Lam 2009), there is little motivation for manufacturers to improve working conditions. Therefore, we derive the following proposition:

> *P1: Without an accompanying setting of social standards and enforcement mechanisms by the (local) government, working conditions will get worse (S3) after relocating production when operating in a low-cost segment.*

If other motives for the relocation are predominant, such as seeking new markets, strategic competitive moves, or affiliation to an industry cluster in order to share knowledge, technologies, or the supplier networks, cost reductions might be of minor importance for the relocation decision.

Industry-level factors: Premium goods usually generate higher profit margins than low-priced goods. The latter are characterized by small profit margins and quick returns. For businesses in this market segment, controlling costs is of crucial importance to stay profitable. Fang *et al.* (2010) show that companies that seek the cheapest production conditions are likely to leave China's coastal regions and relocate their factories to the inland provinces or other low-cost regions. As CSR goes along with higher production costs (Cooke and He 2010), we propose:

> *P2: Relocation of low-cost product manufacturing leads to a worsening of the working conditions (S3).*

Park-Poaps and Rees (2010) identify three conditions that promote inadequate working conditions in supplier firms: (1) labor-intensive and limited-automation production, (2) competitive pressure to lower production costs, and (3) multiple layers of subcontracting firms and complex production networks. This shows that the industry itself has an impact on the level of the working conditions. Hence, we derive the following proposition:

> *P3: The greater the labor intensity in the industry, the more likely a worsening of the working conditions (S3) is after a company's relocation.*

Firm-level factors: External pressure from international stakeholders encourages the introduction of codes of conduct (Park-Poaps and Rees 2010). Chinese firms that have Western buyers or produce for Western markets more frequently consider an active stakeholder management than locally acting Chinese firms (Huang and Gardner 2007). Buyers' attitudes toward social standards is an influencing factor for the improvement of working conditions (Kolk *et al.* 2010). Western buyers have started to require social and environmental standards as criteria for supplier selection (e.g., Egels-Zandén 2007; Seuring and Müller 2008; Lam 2009). Compliance has been of increasing importance for Chinese supplier firms in order to survive in global competition (Lin 2010) and to become or remain strategic partners in global production chains (Schneider and Schwerk 2010). Assuming that the client structure of a Chinese manufacturing firm remains constant after relocation, we propose:

> *P4: The more important the business relation to a Western buyer firm for a Chinese supplier, the more likely the working conditions will remain stable (S1) or improve (S2) in the newly relocated factories.*

Western buyers cannot be said to do business in an intrinsically more moral way or behave more ethically than domestic buyer firms (Lam 2009). MNEs with a global network just have a broader and more diverse customer base than locally acting Chinese firms. Therefore, they are faced with higher public expectations (Krueger 2008). A broader customer base, especially in the retail sector, increases the likelihood that CSR practices are taken as a relevant selling factor (Krueger 2008).

Many companies present glossy brochures in order to prove their CSR-related activities, such as the implementation of social and environmental standards along their supply chain. However, often there is a gap between the actual working conditions in supplier firms or subsidiaries and the standards that are publicly expressed and advertised (Andersen and Skøjett-Larsen 2009). At the same time, most domestic and some international buyer firms do not require social standards at all or tolerate deviations from international social standards (Lam 2009). The domestic market in China is price-sensitive and highly competitive. Often, there is not much pressure on companies with poor labor standards (Lam 2009). If a buyer firm tolerates deviations from its officially requested social standard, a deterioration of working conditions in case of relocation becomes more likely. Therefore, we derive the following proposition:

> *P5: The more a buyer firm (or the network) tolerates the supplier's non-compliance with codes of conduct, the more likely a worsening of the working conditions (S3) is.*

A top-down approach to CSR is typically taken within supply chains. The buyer firms set the standards and the suppliers comply with the codes of conduct in place. There is no incentive for suppliers to establish their own, stricter codes of conduct as the supplier firm's production processes are ultimately shaped by the lowest common CSR denominator in the supply chain.

According to Tsui (2009) company size plays an important role in predicting the probability of compliance with social standards. Cooke and He (2010) also find that financial performance and company size have a strong influence on the realized CSR practices. Relocation is linked with sunk costs. Small and medium-sized firms naturally have more substantial budget constraints than larger companies. Only firms with a solid capital base may be able to relocate (Huang *et al.* 2011). Smaller firms frequently do not pay proper attention to good working conditions due to a lack of resources (Ciliberti *et al.* 2009). If smaller firms decide to relocate, they usually will be mainly concerned about their financial situation and liquidity while they will be paying little attention to working practices. Thus, non-compliance with CSR practices is more likely to occur after relocation. Conversely, bigger firms have a greater number of employees, giving demands for improvements a greater weight. Therefore, we propose:

> *P6: The greater the number of employees of a Chinese company, the more likely the working conditions will remain stable (S1) or improve (S2) in the newly relocated factories.*

The Chinese government has been a main driver for CSR in China (Lam 2009) since becoming aware of the potential long-term benefits of CSR programs including social standards. It introduced a campaign to support domestic firms' CSR (Schneider and Schwerk 2010) and imposed a code of ethics (Fu and Deshpande 2012). State-owned companies are tightly monitored and controlled by government representatives (their shareholders) to ensure adoption of these rules and regulations, which is not the case for privately owned companies (Cooke and He 2010; Fu and Deshpande 2012). Moreover, state-owned companies had already been accustomed to meeting social obligations before market liberalization started, and having been transformed into international or global players, they still remain familiar with taking over social responsibilities (Moon and Shen 2010). It can be concluded that the ownership structure influences working conditions. Therefore, we propose:

> *P7: The greater the Chinese state's ownership share in a firm, the more likely the working conditions will remain stable (S1) or improve (S2) in the newly relocated factories.*

Positive consequences of compliance with social standards and appropriate working conditions in production plants become visible only in the medium or long term, while costs are incurred immediately (Schneider and Schwerk 2010). Research shows that CSR practices correlate positively with job satisfaction and lead to a higher commitment of workers to their employers, while improvements in working conditions lead to higher productivity and better organizational performance over time (Brammer *et al.* 2007; Cooke and He 2010). However, short-term thinking and the setting of goals accordingly (e.g., focused on quarterly results) are prevalent among manufacturers in China, determining management processes and putting managers under pressure to succeed quickly and cheaply (Lam 2009).

A firm's focus on short-term profitability leads to a relentless search for cost savings and is thus a main driver for the deterioration of cost-incurring decent working conditions. Consequently, short-term orientated companies are presumably more likely to shy away from the costs resulting from maintaining or even improving working conditions in the course of their move to the hinterland.

Meanwhile, firms subscribing to a long-term perspective may recognize value in motivating workers through good working conditions. Hence, medium- or long-term orientated companies are more likely to transfer their achieved standards of working conditions to their new production facilities in the Chinese hinterland.

> *P8: Long-term orientated companies will keep working conditions stable (S1) or even improve (S2) them after relocation. The relocation of short-term orientated companies will cause worse working conditions in the new factories.*

Figure 1.2 provides an overview of our propositions concerning the identified factors and the proposed negative or positive impacts on the working conditions in the relocated firms. Based on these propositions future research can provide empirical evidence.

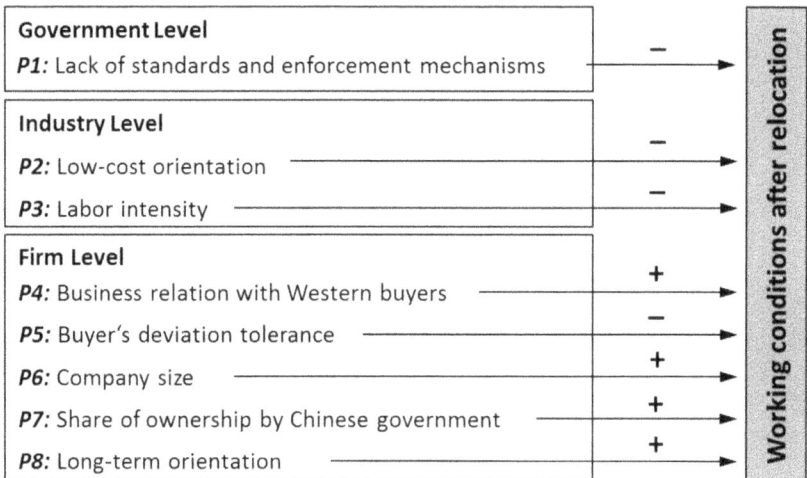

Figure 1.2 Exploratory framework of impact factors on working conditions.

Conclusion

China's coastal regions have recently started to experience labor shortages and increasing production costs. As a consequence, Chinese manufacturers have been starting to relocate their factories to China's hinterland or to other low-cost countries. Since the early 1990s networks of Western firms have invested in CSR, including the improvement of working conditions in China. As a consequence, working conditions and other CSR activities in networks of Western firms have been considerably improved. This chapter analyzed the consequences of the relocation of firms for established CSR standards as well as working conditions and practices by examining potentially influential impact factors that were identified based on a literature review. Three scenarios that differ in their outcomes were presented: stable, improving, and worsening working conditions. Eight propositions about factors' impacts were derived. These propositions constitute the basis for future research. Especially, further empirical research should analyze which factors do indeed lead to improved working conditions, and which to stable ones.

The integration and implementation of social standards and appropriate working conditions in companies necessitate a medium- to long-term strategy. In the short term, implementation costs dominate. Many Chinese firms are short-term orientated and consequently skeptical about long-term, positive effects of providing good working conditions and CSR standards. Such companies relocate due to cost pressures. Under these circumstances, the low bargaining power of labor unions, a lack of CSR requirements, and an insufficient enforcement of labor laws in Chinese provinces lead to worse working conditions.

However, in the medium to long run, three factors prevent working conditions from falling too far behind the average level established in the coastal regions: (1) government intervention (central and local), (2) pressure from network partners, and (3) the rising bargaining power of workers. First, the Chinese government's promotion of CSR and social standards is much greater than in the past. For instance, this is visible in the introduction of various recent labor laws, even though enforcement continues to differ from region to region (Moon and Shen 2010). Furthermore, the provinces may influence wage levels by setting appropriate minimum wages. Second, empirical data from China's coastal provinces show that both wages and social standards start to rise when labor demand outpaces labor supply (Kumar *et al.* 2009). In the medium to long term, the share of exports from the central and western regions will rise and Western firms will thus have to be present in these regions. They will increase pressure on their Chinese suppliers to comply with international labor and CSR standards to protect their reputation (Andersen and Skjøett-Larsen 2009). Third, in the medium to long term, labor demand will outpace labor supply in the Chinese hinterland, too, while workers are becoming more aware of their rights and no longer hesitate to engage in collective actions such as strikes or bargaining with plant management in order to improve their working and living conditions (Chan and Ngai 2009).

In the medium to long run, relocation will increase employment and wages in the new areas with many effects for the local community, both positive (e.g., higher living standards, former migrant workers can work in their home towns) and negative (e.g., increasing pollution). The lack of empirical studies in this new field provides great potential for future research, which particularly needs to deal with the empirical validation of the developed framework and the derived relations. Hence, with this work, we encourage further studies in the field of CSR and relocation in China on the basis of our proposed research framework.

References

American Chamber of Commerce in Shanghai (AmCham Shanghai) and Booz & Co. (2010) *China Manufacturing Competitiveness Study 2009–2010*, March 2010, Shanghai.

Andersen, M. and Skjøett-Larsen, T. (2009) "Corporate social responsibility in global supply chains," *Supply Chain Management: An International Journal*, 14(2): 75–86.

Barboza, D. (2006) "Labor shortage in China may lead to trade shift," *New York Times*, April 3, 2006. Available online at www.nytimes.com/2006/04/03/business/03labor. html?pagewanted=all&_r=0 (accessed February 29, 2011).

Bo, Z. and Chen, G. (2009) "Bo Xilai and the Chongqing Model," East Asian Institute (EAI) Background Brief No. 465, July 17, 2009.

Börjeson, L., Höjera, M., Dreborg, K.-H., Ekvall, T., and Finnveden, G. (2006) "Scenario types and techniques: towards a user's guide," *Futures*, 38: 723–39.

Bradscher, K. and Barboza, D. (2010) "Strike in China highlights gap in workers' pay," *New York Times*, May 28, 2010. Available online at www.nytimes.com/2010/05/29/ business/global/29honda.html?pagewanted=all (accessed May 30, 2011).

Brammer, S.J., Millington, A., and Rayton, B. (2007) "The contribution of corporate social responsibility to organizational commitment," *The International Journal of Human Resource Management*, 18(10): 1701–19.

Chan, C.K.C. and Ngai, P. (2009) "The making of a new working class? A study of collective actions of migrant workers in South China," *The China Quarterly*, 198: 287–302.

Chan, K.W. (2008) "Internal labour migration in China: trends, geographical distribution and policies," United Nations Expert Group Meeting on Population Distribution, Urbanization, Internal Migration and Development, UN/POP/EGM-URB/2008/05, January 3, 2008.

Chan, S.H., Gau, G.W., and Wang, K. (1995) "Stock market reaction to capital investment decisions: evidence from business relocations," *Journal of Financial and Quantitative Analysis*, 30(1): 81–100.

Chen, V.W., Wu, H.X., and van Ark, B. (2009) "More costly or more productive? Measuring changes in competitiveness in manufacturing across regions in China," *Review of Income and Wealth*, 55(Special Issue 1): 514–37.

Ciliberti, F., de Groot, G., de Haan, J., and Pontrandolfo, P. (2009) "Codes to coordinate supply chains: SMEs' experiences with SA8000," *Supply Chain Management: An International Journal*, 14(2): 117–27.

Cooke, F.L. and He, Q. (2010) "Corporate social responsibility and HRM in China: a study of textile and apparel enterprises," *Asia Pacific Business Review*, 16(3): 355–76.

Démurger, S., Gurgand, M., Li, S., and Yue, X. (2009) "Migrants as second-class workers in urban China? A decomposition analysis," *Journal of Comparative Economics*, 37(4): 610–28.

Dunning, J.H. (1994) "Re-evaluating the benefits of foreign direct investment," *Transnational Corporations*, 3(1): 23–51.

Dunning, J.H. (1997) *Alliance Capitalism and Global Business*, London and New York: Routledge.

Economist, The (2010) "Is China's labour-market at a turning-point?," June 10, 2010: 86.

Egels-Zandén, N. (2007) "Suppliers' compliance with MNCs codes of conduct: behind the scenes at Chinese toy suppliers," *Journal of Business Ethics*, 75(1): 45–62.

Fang, T., Gunterberg, C., and Larsson, E. (2010) "Sourcing in an increasingly expensive China: four Swedish cases," *Journal of Business Ethics*, 97(1): 119–38.

Fisch, J.H. and Zschoche, M. (2012) "The role of operational flexibility in the expansion of international production networks," *Strategic Management Journal*, 33(13): 1540–56.

Fu, W. and Deshpande, S.P. (2012) "Factors impacting ethical behavior in a Chinese state-owned steel company," *Journal of Business Ethics*, 105(2): 231–7.

Huang, X. and Gardner, S. (2007) "A stakeholder view of strategic management in Chinese firms," *International Journal of Business Studies*, 15(1): 1–13.

Huang, Z., Lu, J., Sun, H., Hu, J., and Song, Y. (2011) "Sticky factors in the industrial relocation of a cluster: a case study of Zhili children's garments cluster in China," *The Social Science Journal*, 48(3): 560–5.

Inagaki, H. (2006) *South China's Labor Shortage: Will the current worker shortage escalate?*, Tokyo: Mizuho Research Institute.

Jing, M. (2010) "High-tech companies go west," *China Daily*, May 11, 2010. Available online at www.chinadaily.com.cn/business/2010-11/06/content_11511214.htm (accessed April 30, 2011).

Kirby, W.C., McFarlan, FW., and Manty, T.Y. (2008) "Esquel Group: integrating business strategy and corporate social responsibility," Harvard Business School Case 307-076, December 17, 2008.

Kolk, A., Hong, P., and van Dolen, W. (2010) "Corporate social responsibility in China: an analysis of domestic and foreign retailers' sustainability dimensions," *Business Strategy and the Environment*, 19(5): 289–303.

Krueger, D. (2008) "The ethics of global supply chains in China: convergences of East and West," *Journal of Business Ethics*, 79(1): 113–20.

Kumar, S., Medina, J., and Nelson, M.T. (2009) "Is the offshore outsourcing landscape for US manufacturers migrating away from China?," *Supply Chain Management: An International Journal*, 14(5): 342–8.

Lam, M. (2009) "Beyond credibility of doing business in China: strategies for improving corporate citizenship of foreign multinational enterprises in China," *Journal of Business Ethics*, 87(1): 137–46.

Lattemann, C., Alon, I., Fetscherin, M., Chang, J., and McIntyre, J. (2012) "The globalization of Chinese enterprises," *Thunderbird International Business Review*, 54(4): 145–54.

Lewis, W.A. (1954) "Economic development with unlimited supplies of labour," *The Manchester School*, 22(2): 139–91.

Lin, L.-W. (2010) "Corporate social responsibility in China: window dressing or structural change?," *Berkeley Journal of International Law*, 28(1): 64–100.

Lübcke, E., Ruth, K., and Yim, I.-S. (2007) "Corporate social responsibility 'Made in China'," ITB working paper No. 60, Bremen, Germany: University Bremen.

McWilliams, A., Siegel, D., and Wright, P.M. (2006) "Corporate social responsibility: strategic implications," *Journal of Management Studies*, 43(1): 1–18.

Matten, D. and Moon, J. (2008) "'Implicit' and 'explicit' CSR: a conceptual framework for a comparative understanding of corporate social responsibility," *Academy of Management Review*, 33(2): 404–24.

Messinis, G. and Cheng, E. (2009) "Earnings, education and training in China: the migrant worker experience," working paper No. 42, Centre for Strategic Economic Studies, Victoria University, Melbourne, Australia.

Moon, J. and Shen, X. (2010) "CSR in China research: salience, focus and nature," *Journal of Business Ethics*, 94(4): 613–29.

National Labour Committee (2010) "China's youth meet Microsoft: KYE factory in China produces for Microsoft and other U.S. companies', National Labour Committee Report, April 10, 2010.

Park-Poaps, H. and Rees, K. (2010) "Stakeholder Forces of Socially Responsible Supply Chain Management Orientation", *Journal of Business Ethics*, 92(2): 305–22.

Platts, K.W. and Song, N. (2010) "Overseas sourcing decisions: the total cost of sourcing from China," *Supply Chain Management: An International Journal*, 15(4): 320–31.

Pun, N. and Smith, C. (2007) "Putting transnational labour process in its place: the dormitory labour regime in post-socialist China," *Work, Employment and Society*, 21(1): 27–45.

Schneider, A.-M. (2012) "The movement of factories to the Chinese hinterland or to low-cost countries: renewed struggles or appropriate working conditions ahead?," paper presented at the ICCSR 8th Annual Symposium—Corporate Social Responsibility in China, Nottingham University, Ningbo Campus, July 11, 2011.

Schneider, A.-M. and Altmann, S. (2010) "Competition for unskilled workers in southeast China: an analysis of drivers and response options," paper presented at the 4th China Goes Global Conference, Harvard University, Cambridge, October 8, 2010.

Schneider, A.-M. and Schwerk, A. (2010) "Corporate social responsibility in Chinese supplier frms," *Zeitschrift für Betriebswirtschaft*, Special Issue 1: 39–59.

Seuring, S. and Müller, M. (2008) "From a literature review to a conceptional framework for sustainable supply chain management," *Journal of Cleaner Production*, 16(15): 1699–710.

Shi, L. (2008) "Rural migrant workers in China: scenario, challenges and public policy," working paper No. 89, Geneva: International Labour Office, Policy Integration and Statistics Department.

Tignor, R. (2004) "Unlimited supplies of labor," *The Manchester School*, 72(6): 691–711.

Tsang, D. (2010) "Labour shortage in delta worsens after holiday: workers' no-show alarms factories," *South China Morning Post*, February 26, 2010.

Tsui, A.P.Y. (2009) "Labor dispute resolution in the Shenzhen Special Economic Zone," *China Information*, 23: 257–84.

Waddock, S.A., Bodwell, C.B., and Graves, S. (2002) "Responsibility: the new business imperative," *Academy of Management Executive*, 16(2): 132–48.

Wang, D. and Pei, H. (2010) "Transfer of Shenzhen's hi-tech industries: an empirical study," *Chinese Management Studies*, 4(4): 401–18.

Wang, J. and Mei, L. (2009) "Dynamics of labour-intensive clusters in China: relying on low labour costs or cultivating innovation?," Discussion Paper Series No. 195, Geneva: International Institute for Labour Studies.

Wen, M. (2004) "Relocation and agglomeration of Chinese industry," *Journal of Development Economics*, 73(1): 329–47.

Wong, D.F.K., Li, C.Y., and Song, H.X. (2007) "Rural migrant workers in urban China: living a marginalized life," *International Journal of Social Welfare*, 16: 32–40.

Wong, L. (2009) "Corporate social responsibility in China: between the market and the search for a sustainable growth development," *Asian Business & Management*, 8(2): 129–48.

Ying, W. (2010) "Chongqing emerging as fresh IT center in China," *China Daily*, June 11, 2010. Available online at www.chinadaily.com.cn/cndy/2010-11/06/content_11510320.htm (accessed May 26, 2011).

Yu, X. (2008) "Impacts of corporate code of conduct on labor standards: a case study of Reebok's athletic footwear supplier factory in China," *Journal of Business Ethics*, 81(3): 513–29.

Zadek, S. (2004) "The path to corporate responsibility," *Harvard Business Review*, 82(12): 125–32.

Zhang, Z. and Figliozzi, M.A. (2010) "A survey of China's logistics industry and the impacts of transport delays on importers and exporters," *Transport Reviews*, 30(2): 179–94.

2 Social entrepreneurship in Singapore, India, and Hong Kong

Britney Teeple, Nancy Lieu,
Anthein Thomas, Sam Vahedi,
Eric Chen, and Edmund R. Gray

Social entrepreneurship is a significant worldwide movement that has emerged over the past two decades. It represents the merging of corporate social responsibility (CSR) with entrepreneurial zeal and ingenuity. Social entrepreneurship bears a wide variety of definitions. Academician J. Gregory Dees (2001), for instance, views social entrepreneurship as a combination of the passion for a deeply felt social mission and a business-like mode of operation. Popular author David Bornstein (2005) describes it as an innovative and transformative force for solving social problems. Based on our research, we view social entrepreneurship as the application of entrepreneurial principles to facilitate social change. Social entrepreneurs utilize traditional business techniques, and employ available resources and innovation to tackle social and environmental challenges. Social enterprises are the vessels through which these entrepreneurs pursue their social ventures. While the traditional business entrepreneur typically measures performance in terms of profit and financial return, a social entrepreneur also considers positive returns to society. Social enterprises can be either for-profit or not-for-profit as long as they share the common principle of pursuing business-led solutions to achieve social and/or environmental objectives (Choi and Gray, 2010: 12).

The impact of social entrepreneurship has increased significantly in recent years due to several prominent factors. First, although there have always been social and environmental needs, they appear to be more numerous and perilous now than in the past. Need gaps are human needs that are either addressed inadequately or not at all by markets, governments, or traditional nonprofit institutions. Many of these unfulfilled needs are significant for human wellbeing, such as education and vocational training, and some are essential for human survival, such as clean water, sanitation, and the availability of food. Second, while recent trends, including growing populations in certain parts of the world, increasing economic inequality, food and water shortages, and an ever-mounting burden on our physical resources and ecosystems are accentuating dire needs gaps, the potential has increased for business acumen to be applied in solving the problems resulting from these gaps. With the advent of the internet, and accelerating communication and information retrieval, there is an increasing awareness of these needs gaps.

As people have become more aware of the problems and struggles around the globe, the idea of social entrepreneurship as a change agent for alleviating these problems has grown in recognition, and resources for social entrepreneurial organizations have become more widely available. Social entrepreneurship has also increasingly become an academically accepted discipline, as indicated by a 2008 study that identified 250 professors from 35 countries teaching or researching social entrepreneurship (Brock *et al.*, 2008). At the 2009 Global Social Ventures Competition for MBA students held at the University of California at Berkeley, there were over 200 entries, compared to the typical 20 to 50 entries at new venture competitions. All indications suggest that interest in social entrepreneurship is continuing to grow among both faculty and students.

The purpose of this chapter is to report an exploratory study that compares and analyzes social entrepreneurships in Singapore, Hong Kong, and two major cities in India—Delhi (including New Delhi) in the north and Bangalore in south, explores and analyzes common barriers they face in pursuing their missions, and discusses potential solutions. After conducting extensive secondary research, our team interviewed representatives from social enterprises in each location—25 altogether. Our hope is that the research will highlight social entrepreneurship in Asia and provide helpful insights and guidance for a new generation of social entrepreneurs.

Environment for social entrepreneurship in Singapore, India, and Hong Kong

Each of the three target regions faces its own set of unique social and environmental problems. Governments, because of their position of authority, are often the agents in the best position to address their jurisdictions' social issues, and therefore play a significant role in shaping their regions' current social environments. Despite the participation of governments, as well as profit-making entities and traditional charities in resolving these issues, many needs remain unfulfilled. Such gaps are the domain where social entrepreneurs thrive. This section briefly examines the social environment and the role of the government in the three countries with an eye toward the challenges and opportunities for social entrepreneurship.

Singapore

The Singaporean government is intricately involved in managing the nation's economy, infrastructure, and society. It provides many services for its citizens—a safe environment, with a 0.6 percent crime rate (Department of Statistics Singapore, 2012); subsidies for homeownership leading to the highest percentage of homeownership worldwide (Department of Statistics Singapore, 2012); an efficient infrastructure (Lim, 2007); and a favorable corporate tax rate (IRAS, 2012), to name a few. It also, however, imposes many restrictions on its citizens that limit their freedom in some areas, such as levying fines on chewing gum and littering and corporal punishment for vandalism (Gannon and Pillai, 2010). The government's high degree of control and oversight contributes to a city-state that faces far fewer serious social problems than India or Hong Kong.

In relative terms, the control of the Singaporean government, coupled with the country's small size, allows for social and economic needs to be dealt with swiftly and effectively. The country boasts a highly developed and successful economy with a relatively high per capita GDP and an unemployment rate of a mere 2 percent (Central Intelligence Agency, 2012a). Singapore, however, is not entirely devoid of social and environmental concerns. Its principal issues emanate from its diminutive geographical size and a population that is rapidly aging. The government and society in general are grappling with how to care for the aging population and assist those who are mentally ill and disabled. These issues are exacerbated by the nation's low birth rate (Saad, 2011). Singapore has one of the lowest birth rates worldwide, ranking among the bottom ten countries and, thus, the dilemma of a shrinking and an aging workforce (Central Intelligence Agency, 2012a).

Another major challenge for the country stems from its limited landscape. Singapore lacks natural resources and is heavily dependent upon other nations for its resource needs (Morrison and Conway, 2006). For instance, it imports roughly 40 percent, the largest percentage of its water supply, from its neighbor, Malaysia (Morris, 2007). It also imports all of the natural gas it consumes (Central Intelligence Agency, 2012a). Thus, the country is far from being self-reliant in regard to natural resources.

The Singaporean government's definition of social entrepreneurship is limited to organizations that help disadvantaged Singapore citizens, such as ex-offenders; older, less educated citizens; and those who are disabled or recovering from psychiatric illnesses (Government of Singapore, 2011a). This is a far narrower perspective on social entrepreneurship compared to the predominant views in other regions. Because of this perspective, many Singaporean social enterprises focus on the needs of disadvantaged and at-risk groups that are not already addressed by governmental programs. Enterprises whose missions address environmental issues or other concerns outside of the needs of disadvantaged citizens do exist, but are far fewer in number. Consequently, any Singapore enterprise with a mission outside of the prescribed definition will find it difficult to be officially recognized as a social enterprise and will be ineligible for government funding, and, therefore, must look elsewhere for money.

India

The Government of India, also known as the Union Government or Central Government, is a federal form of government that acts as the governing authority over 28 states and seven union territories. Roughly three million people are employed at the federal level and another seven million work at the state level, creating a large and convoluted network of government officials (*The Economist*, 2008). A high level of bureaucracy among the different levels of authority creates a governmental structure known for its inefficiency and corruption. Most development spending never reaches the intended recipients. A recent example of this is the shortage of food for India's poor despite increases in the food budget every year. India's budget to feed its poor was over $13 billion in 2011 alone, yet decade-long food heists by politicians and government officials continued to leave many without rations. India's Central Bureau of Investigation cited that within the Sitapur district of India's Uttar Pradesh state in 2005, 2006, and 2007, "100 percent of the food meant for the poor was stolen" (Srivastava and MacAskill, 2012). In addition, government officials stole approximately $14.5 billion of the state's food over the last decade, yet no one has been prosecuted (Srivastava and MacAskill, 2012). These fairly typical examples illustrate why India's government has been ineffective in ameliorating the country's social problems.

Compared to Singapore and Hong Kong, India faces many far larger-scaled social issues. India has the second largest (soon to be the largest) population in the world with over 1.2 billion people (Central Intelligence Agency, 2012b). This massive population is at the root of India's many social challenges, including poverty, sanitation, food and water shortages, healthcare, and education. Although the country is rapidly developing economically—from 2007 to 2011, the economic growth rate was 8.2 percent—poverty declined by only 0.8 percent (Agazzi, 2012). Consequently, there is rational fear that rapid population growth is offsetting many of the potential benefits of economic growth. Nearly 51 percent of India's population defecates in public, severely affecting sanitation (Agazzi, 2012). Close to a million Indian children die annually due to malnutrition. Between 2010 and 2011, India spent 11.6 billion dollars on education, which is merely 1.2 percent of what the United States spends (Forbes India, 2012). These far-reaching problems are daunting and seemingly overwhelming. The stark imbalance between the wealthy and poor is further cause for concern in India. Of the 1.2 billion people, the middle class is estimated to be anywhere from 60 to 250 million, while 2.5 percent, or about 30 million, make up the upper class (Hardgrave and Kochanek, 2008). The rest live in poverty, many in abject circumstances (*Deutsche Bank Research*, 2010). Estimates indicate that at least 40 percent of all Indians in rural areas and at least 25 percent in urban areas live below the internationally accepted poverty line (World Bank, 2011).

Because the government and traditional markets have failed to adequately address the critical needs in India, there is a strong demand for other agents, especially social enterprises, to provide solutions. While there are no official statistics as to how many social enterprises exist in India, research suggests that the numbers are on the rise (Segran, 2008; Seth and Kumar, 2011). Social entrepreneurship in India was originally viewed as simply an extension of corporate social responsibility and philanthropy, but the idea of financially sustainable organizations established to create change is beginning to grow in recognition and make progress toward becoming mainstream. In particular, social enterprises in both the healthcare and the natural resources and energy industries are estimated to have the largest growth (Segran, 2008; Seth and Kumar, 2011). Social entrepreneurship has recently become more popular among India's youth who are slowly showing increasing interest in the field. However, entrepreneurship, let alone social entrepreneurship, is still a new field in the traditional Indian education system. Entrepreneurship courses are rare and found only in select business management programs (Seth and Kumar, 2011).

In addition to the dearth of education in the field, Indian entrepreneurs are disadvantaged by the absence of government involvement and funding. Although the government openly recognizes the value social enterprises provide for society, it provides no resources, funding, or tax breaks to social business ventures (Seth and Kumar, 2011). Consequently, social entrepreneurs must fend for themselves. Additionally, with the second largest population worldwide and the seventh largest land mass, India is a heterogeneous nation. Consequently, the majority of social entrepreneurships are unable to apply a one-size-fits-all approach, and thus their impact remains limited in scale and regionalized (Segran, 2008; Singh and Pollock, 2011).

Hong Kong

Much like Singapore, Hong Kong is small in size but high in population density. Unlike Singapore, which is an independent nation, Hong Kong is a special administrative region of the People's Republic of China. Its government takes a minimalist position toward involvement in the economy and society, allowing market forces to be the primary driver. Hong Kong is a trading state and, like Singapore, is highly dependent on the international economy and global markets. Hong Kong's solid financial sector, lack of public debt, relatively corruption-free government, strong legal system, and deeply embedded relations with Mainland China have all helped it withstand the recent global economic downturn and adjust effectively (Central Intelligence Agency, 2012c).

However, despite surviving the difficult economic conditions in the past decade, Hong Kong is now facing several issues that affect the country's social development. Hong Kong must determine how to cope with an increasing wealth gap, controversial education reform, and population concerns. According to Hong Kong's Census and Statistics Department, the city's wealth gap has surpassed the wealth gaps in countries and major cities known for their inequality, including Singapore, the United Kingdom, and Australia, as well as New York and Washington, DC in the United States (Chen, 2012). Property prices have soared since 1997 and overall inflation is on the rise, allowing the wealth gap to widen further as a small circle of tycoons continue to prosper while the middle class struggles to make ends meet (Chen, 2012).

The state of education in Hong Kong has also been a source of concern. In 2012, thousands took to the streets to protest the introduction of Mainland China's national educational model into the Hong Kong school curriculum (*The New York Times*, 2012). Concern about the education system is believed to be one of several reasons why Hong Kong's fertility rate is now at an all time low of 0.966 children per woman (Hong Kong Industrialist, 2007). Moreover, rising educational costs coupled with rising inflation is drastically increasing the cost of raising a child, and consequently many couples are waiting into their late thirties or forgoing parenthood altogether (*Hong Kong Industrialist*, 2007).

Even with the low birth rate, Hong Kong's population is at an all time high. This is primarily due to an aging population that is living longer because of modern-day medicine and improvements in sanitation. An aging population presents two major predicaments: shrinkage in the workforce and added pressure on welfare and health services. This in turn creates a higher tax burden on the younger population, which can affect their productivity (*Hong Kong Industrialist*, 2007).

Despite its current challenges, Hong Kong suffers from far fewer sweeping social problems than India. However, for those issues that the region does have, its government is far less engaged than is the Singaporean government in Singapore's societal problems. Hong Kong's government does provide some support to social enterprises through startup funds and seed grants. It also recognizes a variety of organizations with social or environmental causes as social enterprises, although, like Singapore, not all social enterprises are eligible for funding. To qualify for government funding in Hong Kong, social enterprises must focus on poverty prevention, employment for the disabled, or the increased self-reliance of the underprivileged (Government of Hong Kong, 2012).

Social organizations in Hong Kong typically cannot expect to receive much in the way of charitable donations or volunteer work from the local community. Chinese culture strongly emphasizes taking care of one's own proximal community, particularly the immediate and extended family. In general, each family member reaches out to those in need in the family and does not feel responsible for people or causes beyond the family (Gannon and Pillai, 2010). As a result, the Hong Kong public tends to view charitable giving and social work as issues beyond individual responsibility and more within the realm of religion and government.

Despite this cultural outlook, the idea of social entrepreneurship as a viable change agent is beginning to spread in Hong Kong, especially in academic circles (Ho, 2010). Social entrepreneurship practitioners and universities are encouraging students to find and create solutions for communitywide issues through social innovation. The Center for Entrepreneurship of the Chinese University of Hong Kong, for example, hosts the Chinese University Social Enterprise Challenge. This competition promotes students' "entrepreneurial spirit through the achievement of both economic and social objectives, as well as enhancing public understanding on social enterprise" (Ho, 2010).

Common barriers and efforts to overcome them

After researching each region in depth, to include basic country statistics, top concerns facing the region, as well as the history and current state of social entrepreneurship in each location, we conducted interviews at social enterprises in Singapore, Delhi, Bangalore, and Hong Kong. Most interviewees were founders or top executives of their respective organizations. Over the span of ten months, we conducted interviews with more than 25 social enterprises. The interview questions focused on the barriers associated with the organizations' startup, operations, and growth phases and what, if anything, each organization has done to overcome its problems.

Through these interviews, we learned that social entrepreneurs adapt their unique ventures to the social needs of their respective countries. A social entrepreneur in Singapore may seek to empower the disadvantaged by offering employment opportunities within the enterprise's internal operations; a social enterprise in India may seek to provide a reliable light source to rural villages that have no electrical infrastructure; and a venture in Hong Kong may recycle old vinyl banners into fashionable bags to help reduce city debris and waste products. Irrespective of the specific mission, we discovered that, in establishing and running their ventures, the social entrepreneurs from all three regions faced many similar challenges and barriers. Here, we identify and examine the three most common barriers—funding, talent recruitment and retention, and social resistance—and the strategies employed to overcoming them.

Funding

Barriers related to funding and financial operations were the number one challenge facing social entrepreneurs across the three regions. Sixty-eight percent of the interviewees (17 out of 25) mentioned this as an obstacle. More specifically, raising investment capital and obtaining government funding were prominently noted as key stumbling blocks. Three non-mutually exclusive strategies or approaches were employed to overcome or mitigate these troublesome funding barriers. One was to diversify funding sources. The second was to employ metrics in promoting the organization and attracting funding. The third pertained to choosing the legal form of the organization— for profit or nonprofit.

The acquisition of external funds is among the fundamental challenges faced by any organization during, and often well beyond, its startup phase. For social and environmental ventures, funding may be particularly difficult for a number of reasons. For one, impact investing—investment that generates both a financial and a social and/or environmental return—is a growing field that between 2014 and 2019 is estimated to reach $500 billion. This, however, is equivalent in size to a mere "one percent of global assets under management in 2008" (Monitor Institute, 2009). This suggests that the average indifferent investor would rather invest in a company whose sole focus is on maximizing profits than invest in a company focused on a double or triple bottom line. Singaporeans, in particular, expect the government to handle social issues, leaving investors and financial markets free to pursue profit maximization (Choo and Wong, 2006). Moreover, risk-averse investors often consider social enterprises speculative and high-risk investments due to their short track record in the market (Social Enterprise Committee, 2007). This investor hesitancy to invest in social enterprises over traditional for-profit businesses can make it difficult for entrepreneurs in Hong Kong, Singapore, and India to raise the needed cash not only to start a social enterprise, but also to later scale up their operations or withstand sudden, unforeseen economic downturns. This is a point several of the interviewed entrepreneurs emphasized.

Because of the difficulty in obtaining funds through investment groups, many social entrepreneurs in all three regions first seek aid from government programs or nonprofit organizations' grants to attain the funding necessary to launch and sustain their enterprises. In Singapore, the government provides some funding for social enterprises, although it is limited in scope and definition. As mentioned, the Singapore government only provides funding to companies that fall within its definition of a social enterprise—an enterprise that helps disadvantaged Singapore citizens, such as ex-offenders, older, less educated citizens, and those who are disabled or recovering from psychiatric illnesses (Government of Singapore, 2011b). Thus, only companies that support those underserved groups can tap into governmental funds earmarked for social enterprises. But even those financial resources are fairly limited. Social enterprises working to ameliorate other social and environmental issues are essentially excluded from government financing. The Green Car Company Ltd (Green Car) in Singapore is one such company that has been unable to obtain government financial support. Green Car's objective is to produce a Singaporean vehicle that provides environmentally friendly, personal transportation. Accordingly, Green Car designed and manufactured its flagship electric vehicle, the SEV-1, a small vehicle with a range of 50 kilometers on a single battery charge. Clarence Tan, owner of Green Car, pointed out that even many of its parts are made from recyclable or recycled materials. Because Green Car has an environmental objective as opposed to a socially oriented mission, it has had to secure private financing.

Even those Singaporean social enterprises that are able to qualify for government funding cannot expect to receive sufficient support to comfortably sustain the business. One example is a technology company, A Good Life Pte Ltd (A Good Life), which developed a mobile phone app called GLO ("Good

Life Offers!") to distribute e-coupons for local businesses. A Good Life aims to help disadvantaged people through its GLO mobile platform by hiring and providing job training for individuals with disabilities. In 2011, GLO had two employees with disabilities, for which it received a small sum of government funding. This subsidy, however, only partially covered the cost of employing the two individuals. According to Tze-Yong Koh, a director at A Good Life, the two individuals were more costly to employ because the company was required to provide additional accommodations for such things as training, transportation, and sick leave. Therefore, the government funding was hardly the determining incentive for providing employment opportunities for those individuals. Ultimately, the company continued to employ them, even after discovering that the subsidies would not cover its additional costs, because of its dedication to its mission.

One successful financial acquisition strategy that social entrepreneurs in any region can pursue is to diversify their sources of funding, a strategy that the Social Enterprise Committee (2007) has identified as a key success factor. Examples of funding sources available for most social enterprises include: private company or corporate donations, government grants, individual gifts, self-generated sales from products or services, strategic partnerships with other organizations, loans, and external investments from public, private, or government investors.

Singapore's Bizlink, India's Sulabh International, and Hong Kong's Senior Citizen Home Safety Association are prime examples of organizations that have mitigated funding barriers through source diversification. Bizlink is a nonprofit organization that helps disabled individuals in Singapore gain independence through employment opportunities. Its mission is to assist Singaporeans with disabilities in "achieving independence, dignity, and integration into the mainstream of society through open and sheltered employment" (Bizlink Centre Singapore Ltd, 2009). Since taking over as CEO, Alvin Lim has transformed Bizlink from a charity into a social enterprise. He accomplished this by adding a commercial component to the organization. Today the enterprise receives revenue from government subsidies, sales to firms that outsource services and production to Bizlink, and general merchandise sales to the public. Sulabh International (Sulabh), an Indian organization with the primary dedication of helping the lowly scavenger caste, receives funding through donations, tuition fees collected from students attending Sulabh schools, and also pay-per-use public toilets located throughout the country. The Senior Citizen Home Safety Association (SCHSA) is an organization that provides services and products to keep senior citizens in Hong Kong safe. Although SCHSA is a nonprofit organization, it is structured and operates much like a conventional business. Founded in 1996 after a wave of cold weather in Hong Kong caused the death of more than 100 elderly citizens living alone and unattended, SCHSA currently benefits over 10,000 elderly people. It generates total annual revenues of approximately HKD 100 million, with 40 percent derived from fees, another 40 percent from government funding, and

20 percent from fundraising. The donations are used to subsidize customers with financial need. By diversifying funding sources, social enterprises such as SCHSA, Sulabh, and Bizlink have found that they can better stabilize and augment their total revenue.

Beyond the deficiency of funding sources, another financial barrier involved the complexities of working within the regulations imposed by government while maintaining a financially sustainable operating model. For many, this means selecting the appropriate legal structure that allows the social enterprise the greatest flexibility in acquiring funding. Specifically, social entrepreneurs must decide whether to form a for-profit or not-for-profit entity. Funding considerations when selecting a legal structure for a social enterprise are:

- ability or ease of raising funds in capital markets;
- access to government funds;
- access to outside grants;
- a climate for charitable donations;
- government/industry restrictions;
- government incentives (such as lower tax rates).

Determination of the appropriate entity structure is a particularly thorny issue in the Indian education sector where governmental restrictions with regard to the legal structure of an organization affects how the organization is permitted to raise funds. With over 200 million school-aged children, India has more school-going children than any other country in the world. Nevertheless, a 2009 report stated that private equity investment in India's education sector was only $180 million. A powerful reason for the dearth of capital in education is that the Indian government mandates educational enterprises in India be established by not-for-profit trusts or the government (Jayashankar, 2010). This mandate has made funding for educational enterprises such as the Hippocampus Reading Foundation highly challenging. Hippocampus (2011), a charitable trust that works to increase literacy among children in disadvantaged communities, is one of India's many social ventures that, because of their nonprofit status, have had difficulty raising needed growth capital in the private sector. Consequently, Hippocampus as well as other educational organizations feel compelled to focus solely on charitable donations and grants to maintain their nonprofit status, yet, in turn, are finding it difficult to sufficiently fund their operations solely through these sources.

Mitu Jayashankar of *Forbes India Magazine* explains an efficacious solution to this funding problem. In a 2010 article she wrote:

A school is a capital-intensive business. In a metro setting, a school for 1,000 children on a 2-acre plot could cost anywhere between Rs. 15 crore to Rs. 25 crore (including land and buildings). The simplest way to raise money is through equity, but no private investor wants to invest money in a not-for-profit trust. This is why the entrepreneurs getting into the business create two legal structures: A trust that runs the school and books all the expenses, and a company that owns all the assets—land, building, management and technology—and leases it to the trust for a fee.

(Jayashankar, 2010)

More and more Indian social entrepreneurs are gravitating toward this twin structure as a solution to their funding requirements.

Creating two entities is not the only option available to social entrepreneurs. Organizations that rely on charitable donations and grants almost exclusively, such as India's Hippocampus, have discovered that there is a positive relationship between accountability and tracking results through the use of metrics and increased funding. Akshara Foundation (Akshara), a public charitable trust in India focused on youth education and literacy, and the previously mentioned SCHSA, the Hong Kong nonprofit organization dedicated to keeping senior citizens safe, have both found that by using metrics to track progress and thereby demonstrate accountability, they are better able to attract funding.

In a 2011 interview John Gautam of Akshara stated that his organization's mission is to ensure that "every child is in school and learning well." It has a vision of universal primary education to be accomplished through innovation and scalable programs. More specifically, Akshara operates five programs— a preschool program, an in-school program, a library program, the Karnataka Learning Partnership, and a capacity learning program—to educate children and fulfill its mission (Dell, n.d.). Akshara measures its progress through a system that tracks both the increasing literacy of the children and the efficiency of its programs. Thus, it can provide quantifiable results to donors and potential donors, making it easier to secure charitable contributions. Since its inception in 2000, it has raised over $8 million, much of this from large corporate sponsors or their charitable foundations, such as Dell Youth Connect, Target Foundation, and Accenture.

The executive director of SCHSA, Timothy Kam Wah Ma, believes that the twin pillars of survival for a social enterprise are strong leadership and adequate funding. Ma explained that he has avoided a monetary shortage by showing a need for and justifying funding requests for his enterprise. The principal way SCHSA justifies its needs is through solid metrics, that is, specific goals coupled with detailed statistics, which Ma believes serve to demonstrate credibility. According to Ma, donors and investors like to see results and progress. The adoption of SMART goals—goals that are specific, measurable, attainable, realistic, and timely (Top Achievement, 2007)—is a useful framework that not only allows an organization to plainly state its objectives with associated timelines and budgets but also enables it to track progress along the way. It can clearly demonstrate to outside funding sources that the venture is well managed. Of course, the measurement needs and requirements of social enterprises vary according to their respective missions. Because of this, a completely standardized metrics system will not work across all social ventures. In *Measuring the Benefit of Social Ventures*, the authors warn that the metrics may change frequently as the business model evolves (Kerr and Powers, 2009). The report *Social Entrepreneurship: Social impact metrics* recommends embedding measurements into daily operations such as administering client satisfaction surveys after the completion of each project, giving quizzes before and after all educational programs or sessions, and creating interactive websites that "track 'drop-outs' at each page so that the site designers can improve usability and reduce drop-outs" (Golden *et al.*, 2010). These suggestions are among the many beneficial ways that metrics can be applied.

In sum, social entrepreneurs in Hong Kong, India, and Singapore tend to have more difficulty raising investment capital than traditional, for-profit businesses due to the majority of investors viewing social ventures as higher risk than traditional businesses. Hence, many social enterprises turn to government aid, charitable donations, or grants when possible. Here, a diverse funding strategy can reduce financial risk by making social enterprises less dependent on a single funding source. Government regulations are important to consider across the three regions, but especially in India. Here, restrictions play a large role in circumscribing funding options. Setting up a for-profit company with a charitable nonprofit sister organization has become a popular way to circumvent government restrictions in the education sector while still taking advantage of available tax breaks and government grants. Finally, implementing a system of performance metrics has helped numerous social enterprises across the three regions attract additional funding.

Talent recruitment and retention

Recruitment and retention of qualified and motivated employees has proven to be another major challenge for many social enterprises in Asia. More than a third of our interviewees stated that talent recruitment and retention was a major challenge. This problem is the consequence of a set of issues including the inability of social enterprises to offer competitive pay, an under-skilled workforce, and the cultural perception that social enterprises do not offer prestigious or stable career paths. Many of the entrepreneurs we interviewed, including Dream a Dream executive director and co-founder Vishal Talreja, stated that nonprofit salaries are often significantly lower than corporate salaries, and therefore, acquiring and retaining talented staff with the requisite skills and experience is an ongoing challenge. We identified four main approaches for minimizing or overcoming the talent recruitment and retention problems our social entrepreneurs face: (1) investing time in employees and building relationships; (2) targeting employees with similar values; (3) replacing human labor with technology where possible; (4) and training employees on the job.

Hiring staff possessing the required skill level, particularly in technical fields, typically requires competitive pay and incentives, which most social enterprises in the startup phase are unable to provide. But even after startup, most social enterprises have difficulty competing with the salaries offered by larger profit-centered entities and, therefore, tend to lose their best talent to the competition. For example, in India, the wages offered by some social enterprises are limited to a mere 20 percent of those offered by comparable profit-oriented companies, according to John Gautam of India's Akshara Foundation. Clearly, this severely limits the pool of talent that social enterprises can draw from.

Competing with prevailing wages, however, is not the only strategy social entrepreneurs can employ in recruiting and retaining talented employees. India's Dream A Dream, whose mission is to empower children by developing life skills and volunteerism, has a staff consisting of many students and retired individuals, which results in frequent turnover amid a constant flow of new talent and expertise. To motivate this educated but transient workforce, Vishal Talreja takes an interpersonal, relational approach to developing talent. The organization seeks to meet the social and emotional needs of its employees by building relationships with staff, investing in employees' professional development, creating a fun and collaborative work environment, and understanding employees' personal motivations for working with at-risk youth.

In similar fashion, Diamond Cab, a Hong Kong taxicab company that provides transportation for the handicapped, takes a largely non-monetary, intangible approach to recruiting and retaining talent. Initially, the company experienced difficulty finding taxicab drivers willing to accept a non-conventional pay structure. Most taxicab drivers in Hong Kong lease a car from a cab company and then race against the clock to cover their costs. This compensation model based on high volume and rapid turnover does not align with Diamond Cab's mission. Diamond Cab's mission is to help wheelchair-bound people become more mobile, and therefore its drivers must share in this vision by assuming time-consuming responsibilities not normally carried out by regular taxicab drivers, such as assisting disabled passengers in safely entering and exiting the cab, securing them in the cab, and providing any special attention that they may require. Consequently, Diamond Cab was forced to deviate from the industry-standard compensation model. Its wages are set on a per-trip or per-day basis depending on the work schedule of the driver. The company's focus during recruitment is on ensuring that a potential employee's values and motivation are aligned with the company's mission. The company seeks out exceptional cab drivers who are willing to accept the company's non-traditional pay plan because they believe in the company's mission. Furthermore, the company specifically targets candidates who are undergoing or have recently completed taxi driver training, because these drivers have not yet become accustomed to the standard taxicab compensation model.

As India's Dream A Dream and Hong Kong's Diamond Cab have demonstrated, there are approaches beyond conventional pay schemes that social enterprises can use to recruit and retain needed talent. These methods include building relationships, investing in employee growth and development, recruiting and targeting groups that align with the organization mission and business model, and providing workers with intangible value and purpose through service that make a difference in their communities.

Even for those few social enterprises that have adequate funding to offer competitive wages, the dearth of competent professionals in the local workforce can be a formidable challenge. For example, the leaders of Arghyam, an Indian social enterprise founded in 2005 by Rohini Nilekani and focused on increasing the widespread availability of safe, clean water in India, believe that the country's educational system has failed to adequately prepare workers to meet the company's special needs. In setting up and operating large-scale systems for clean water access throughout India, Arghyam requires technically skilled workers. The company's frustration in recruiting such qualified individuals has led it to replace people with technology and machinery wherever possible, thereby attenuating its recruitment challenge.

Another successful approach to the problem of finding skilled workers is to provide the needed training in-house. Hong Kong's Happy Grannies and Singapore's Bizlink stand out for their successes in implementing on-the-job training. Happy Grannies is a nonprofit social enterprise in Hong Kong that provides deprived single elders with care and support through ongoing visits and sponsorship. By providing both physical and emotional support, Happy Grannies hopes to fulfill its mission of increasing the awareness of and alleviating problems of the elderly in Hong Kong where the number of under-privileged seniors living on their own and in need of assistance is expected to reach 25 percent of the population by 2033, according to Happy Grannies founder and CEO, Sindy Chow. This nonprofit organization currently faces a shortage of volunteers who have social assistance experience. In consequence, it has enlisted a team of qualified social workers who train volunteers on the proper way to interact with and provide help to isolated senior citizens. The volunteers periodically attend training workshops and receive evaluations with clear feedback on their performance.

Bizlink, the Singapore nonprofit whose mission is to help individuals with disabilities gain independence through employment, also provides on-the-job training as part of its strategy. The organization's operations are divided into three parts: an Employment Placement Program, a Vocational Assessment Program, and a Business Development Program. Its Business Development Program currently has approximately 130 direct hires. Many work in the production workshop completing customer orders, which involves an assortment of structured tasks such as mailing, packaging, shipping, flower arranging, and craftwork. Bizlink's workshop employees are not segregated based on their disabilities; instead, all are mixed together based upon their work abilities. The enterprise's Vocational Assessment Program features a data entry center where employees conduct data entry, cleaning, outsourcing, design, and telemarketing duties. There is a wide range of jobs, and employees are categorized from basic to advanced. As Bizlink employees' skills progress, they are assigned increasingly advanced job tasks.

Ultimately, over a third of social ventures (nine out of 25) interviewed have had difficulty recruiting or retaining qualified workers. These social enterprises have had to overcome difficulties in talent recruitment and retention brought on by their inability to provide competitive wages, a shortage of qualified workers, and cultural perceptions relating to social enterprise. Social entrepreneurships mitigate their talent pool and retention problems by targeting employees with similar values to those of the organizations, investing in employee growth and development, providing on-the-job training, and using technology when possible. Furthermore, some enterprises, such as Singapore's GLO and Bizlink, seek to recruit directly from the target population that the company seeks to aid.

Social resistance

Social resistance—the general public's resistance to changes in social norms, views, or actions—is a third major barrier for social enterprises in Hong Kong, Singapore, and India. Much of the social resistance surrounding social enterprises is perpetuated by these countries' collectivist and hierarchical societies, as well as, in some cases, an aversion to change and risk (Chhokar *et al.*, 2008; Gannon and Pillai, 2010; Hofstede Centre, 2013).

For instance, many of the interviewees stated that risk aversion and approval from family and friends are predominant factors in people's career choices. This was surprising since, according to the Hofstede Centre (2013), Hong Kong, Singapore, and India each has lower than average uncertainty-avoidance ratings, meaning they are able to adeptly tolerate uncertainty, ambiguity, and freedom of opinions. Singapore, in particular, has one of the lowest uncertainty-avoidance rankings out of all countries. However, even though Singapore as a society has a very high tolerance for uncertainty, Singaporeans are more risk averse when it comes to business and careers. According to the Ministry of Finance, as stated in *Culture and Leadership Across the World: The GLOBE book of in-depth studies of 25 societies* (Chhokar *et al.*, 2008), "Singaporeans are generally risk averse, preferring to take safe and professional and managerial jobs rather than to strike out on their own." Much of the aversion to strike out on their own may have something to do with their strong collectivist and hierarchical values (Hofstede Centre, 2013), and not wanting to go against the opinion of the collective group. Parents in India, Hong Kong, and Singapore tend to encourage their children to pursue professional careers in engineering, medicine, or business. The general notion among parents is that successful professionals in the above fields follow a safe and steady career path while achieving a prestigious and respectable status, which is highly important in these cultures. In contrast, social enterprises are perceived to be high risk and unstable organizations. Accordingly, skilled workers with strong traditional values tend to seek work where they believe the risk factors to be low. In a sense, the attitude is similar to investors' concern about investing in social enterprises. Youth are discouraged from becoming entrepreneurs or pursuing employment in a field simply based on their passions. Principled goals such as working for a cause one believes in or contributing to the social good become subordinate to the pursuit of a prestigious career. Consequently, these engrained perceptions, a strong reliance on the opinions and advice of those around them, and aversions to risk leave only a small pool of individuals with the ability and passion for social entrepreneurship.

Social enterprises, such as India's Tata Jagriti Yatra and Singapore's Syinc, are working to transform this pervasive attitude by persuading youth to consider entrepreneurship as the means to raising the quality of life in their communities and creating positive social change. Tata Jagriti Yatra exposes youth to a variety of social issues and provides mentorship opportunities with successful social entrepreneurs. Syinc, a social entrepreneurship that wants to bridge the gap between those with resources and youth with ideas for social change, seeks to attract young people and change negative perceptions through social media such as Facebook and Twitter. The organization refers to itself as a "youth group" whose focus is not on a specific problem but, rather, on providing resources and aid to a target audience—youth and young professionals (Syinc, 2011). The enterprise attempts to educate and connect teens and young adults so that they become change agents in their communities. Tata Jagriti Yatra and Syinc, from two different Asian nations, see influencing youth as the beginning of long-term cultural change and social betterment.

Education and involvement with local communities to foster change and overcome resistance, however, does not have to stop with the youth. To illustrate, solar lighting has had a pejorative image in India as being unreliable, fragile, and of poor quality. This is mainly due to the poor maintenance and upkeep of the solar-powered streetlights installed by the government (Mukerji and Jose, 2010). Technology companies that provide lighting systems for rural communities, such as SELCO Photovoltaic Electric Private Ltd (SELCO) and D.Light, have had to overcome this image barrier in order to facilitate adoption of their products. They have largely accomplished this by establishing relationships at the local level. SELCO is a commercial enterprise that works to provide affordable solar lighting to underserved households and businesses located in rural India. To change the local perception of solar energy, SELCO formed partnerships with and trained local TV and bicycle repair shops to repair and service solar lights. This concomitantly encouraged local entrepreneurship and job creation (Mukerji and Jose, 2010). Like SELCO, D.Light provides solar lighting in rural communities at a reasonable cost to families who previously burned kerosene. To overcome the ingrained social resistance in rural communities to the solar lighting, D.Light has established a network of traveling salespersons who both demonstrate the product and provide a reliable level of customer service on a personal level.

Though not technology-based like SELCO and D.Light, Aashayein, the Indian rural education venture, has also experienced strong local resistance to change. Aashayein discovered that village elders and teachers would try to obstruct its initiatives to provide supplementary education and encouragement of learning if they believed their own influence in the community would be undermined. To address this barrier, Aashayein began to solicit advice from these educators and would give them credit when implementing their programs. Co-opting the company's opponents proved to be an effective strategy for overcoming resistance to their innovative, educational programs.

Indian social enterprises, Sulahb, Aashayein, Dream A Dream, and Mobile and Immersive Learning for Literacy in Emerging Economies (MILLEE)—an organization that develops mobile phone games aimed at improving literacy among children in emerging countries—have learned that they must tailor their strategies to accommodate the existing cultural norms rather than trying to replace them. As suggested above in the case of Aashayein, these enterprises cannot accomplish their goals without the support of the locals. MILLEE ran into cultural resistance while designing its mobile software and gaming products. Results from pilot tests indicated that most Indian children found the educational games confusing. At the time, MILLEE was generating design ideas for its educational games by looking to popular video games and language software for sale in the United States. Because of the confusion among Indian children, MILLEE decided to adjust how it researched and designed its educational games. MILLEE's co-founder, Dr Matthew Kam, explained, "[W]e eventually watched how kids play traditional village games . . . and tried to understand how they were different from contemporary Western video games" (Ramey, 2011). Subsequently, MILLEE began to design games specifically with its Indian target audience in mind by modeling its mobile game applications after traditional Indian games played by the local children. Since then MILLEE has tried to work with children in the local communities as much as possible when designing mobile games in hopes that the games meet the local preferences and tastes. Similarly, one policy Aashayein has adopted to better understand local cultures is to ask its young professionals working in India's urban centers, who are originally from rural areas, to visit their hometowns and act as a liaison for the company. Such steps toward bridging the gap between the social enterprises and the people they try to serve can be highly effective.

Sulabh International (Sulabh) is another example of a social enterprise that has tailored programs to overcome social resistance. Sulabh is the largest nonprofit organization in India with over 50,000 volunteers dedicated to promoting human rights, sanitation and waste management, and social reform. One of Sulabh's key goals is to promote human rights for the scavenger caste, otherwise known as "untouchables." Although some progress has been made, this group still faces heavy discrimination. Sulabh discovered that members of other castes as well as the scavengers themselves have resisted Sulabh's efforts to provide low-cost sanitation systems and schools for them. Some members of the community see Sulabh as being unfair by only helping the untouchable caste and not including other disadvantaged groups. The scavengers, on the other hand, felt their only known livelihood was being taken away from them. Sulabh's response is to provide scavengers with the opportunity for alternative sources of livelihood by offering them adult vocational training as well as primary education for their children. Sulabh's grade and middle schools are free for those who come from the untouchable caste or other disadvantaged backgrounds. These children account for 60 percent of the school's attendees. The remaining 40 percent of students come from the general population, and are charged tuition fees, which constitute one of several revenue streams for Sulabh. Thus, scavengers receive education and training that is also offered to other members of the community with the twin goals of improving social understanding and raising revenue. In this way, Sulabh is working to break deeply held social prejudices against untouchables.

Social entrepreneurs in Hong Kong and Singapore similarly have faced public resistance. In general, both the Hong Kong and Singaporean public expect socially or environmentally beneficial services and products to be priced below comparable products on the market. This mentality stands in stark contrast to that in the United States, where approximately 70 percent of consumers are willing to pay somewhat more for a product that supports a cause, and over 80 percent believe businesses should support nonprofit organizations and charities with financial donations (Do Well Do Good, 2010).

Consider Hong Kong's Diamond Cab, which operates a for-profit taxicab service for the wheelchair-bound. It must provide a public service yet operate in a financially sustainable way, which seems a contradiction to most Hong Kong residents. For Singapore's Bizlink, social perception regarding customer fees is a significant concern. Commercial customers expect to pay less for goods and services from Bizlink because Bizlink is a social enterprise. Most Singaporeans believe that they should not have to pay social enterprises (or charities) for services because providing a social service, not making money, is the mission of these organizations. Similarly, Singapore's Alteration Initiative (Alteration), part of A-Changin Private Ltd, provides a premium alteration service for the general public that concomitantly equips disadvantaged women with garment alteration skills so they can earn an adequate income and enjoy a better quality of life. But the public attitude in Singapore is that they should not pay a premium price for work that is done by workers perceived as "less desirable" and less skilled. To combat this negative consumer mentality, Alteration guarantees that all alterations go through a thorough, rigid quality-assurance process. The company believes that once the customer sees that Alteration does indeed perform high-quality work, the end product will become the main focus and the price will be justified. This strategy appears to be working as the company's recent revenues have been increasing every month. Alteration, Diamond Cab, and Bizlink have learned that providing quality is the key to overcoming consumer prejudices against social products or services.

Socially oriented organizations are not the only enterprises that face price resistance. Déjà Vu Creations provides a prime example of the Hong Kong public's resistance to "green" products. Déjà Vu Creations takes vinyl sheets from promotional banners, typically ones used for only a few days, and transforms them into stylish products, such as purses and handbags. Although it recycles materials that would otherwise go to waste, the message does not translate to market acceptance because customers typically perceive products made from recycled materials as inferior to other products or as "paying more for something made from rubbish." Consequently, the company has learned that it must promote its products solely on their aesthetic and functional qualities, and completely downplay their environmental benefits.

Social resistance to change is prevalent in Hong Kong, Singapore, and India. Although the characteristics of the resistance vary across the three regions, education, local community involvement, and an emphasis on product or service value and quality are three approaches that have been effective in overcoming or reducing social resistance. These findings are tabulated in Tables 2.1, 2.2, and 2.3 at the end of this chapter.

Conclusion

Although similar in many ways, social enterprises typically encounter more trenchant barriers to survival and goal achievement than their strictly for-profit contemporaries. In this study, we found three categories of barriers or challenges common to social entrepreneurs across Singapore, India, and Hong Kong—funding, talent recruitment and retention, and social resistance.

Funding certainly is not a barrier exclusive to social enterprises. Many business firms have trouble raising investment funds and working capital. Social enterprises, however, have funding obstacles that are unique to their genre. Traditional investors typically shun them because they are perceived as being high risk; donors are prejudiced against them because of long-standing cultural beliefs; and government funding tends to be limited and often comes with bothersome restrictions. Recruiting and retaining skilled employees is an ongoing challenge for social entrepreneurs because of their inability to pay competitive wages as well as cultural biases favoring more conventional careers. The third prominent barrier is social resistance. This impediment is evident not only in the aforementioned predisposition toward traditional careers but also in the prevailing perception that goods and services offered by social enterprises are inferior to those offered by conventional commercial firms. Tables 2.1, 2.2, and 2.3 provide a relatively detailed summary of the specific barriers faced by our entrepreneurs and the strategies employed to surmount them.

Additionally, in our research we discerned four general practices that some of the entrepreneurs found very helpful in overcoming challenges and building successful organizations. These practices, which we strongly suspect have broader applicability in the management of social enterprises, are the extensive use of metrics for business analysis and decision making, seeking out strategic partnerships, networking with a range of selected contacts outside of the organization, and utilizing relevant technology. Several of the entrepreneurs emphasized that a good system of metrics is not just a method of attracting outside funding but is also a powerful tool for managing the enterprise. We also learned that strategic partnering can be a key factor in developing a viable business model. For example, several of the social enterprises secured resources such as capital, equipment, and supplies through partnering arrangements, thus lowering their costs. Networking, we discovered, can be a useful source of business advice and a system of word-of-mouth promotion, and in some instances can lead to strategic partnerships. Furthermore, we discerned that new technology can be used to improve organizational efficiency as well as open up new markets (at the bottom of the pyramid, for example) for innovative entrepreneurs.

Finally, an overarching insight gained through our interviews and analysis is that the most successful social entrepreneurs understand that they are operating in a competitive marketplace and consequently need to follow time-tested management and financial principles, and apply sound business judgment. Social enterprises, like their purely commercial counterparts, must have effective business models and efficient operations if they are to compete and prosper. Put simply, without hard-nosed business thinking these hybrid organizations cannot accomplish their social missions. Business skill and knowledge is, in most instances, the crucial success factor for a social enterprise.

To conclude, our study suggests that although there are strong barriers, social entrepreneurship is an emerging sector in the three target Asian regions. Considering the growing awareness of social needs gaps and the increasing presence of social entrepreneurship in academic curricula and research as well as in the business/social marketplace, it will likely become an increasingly significant force in mitigating the pressing social and environmental problems facing the three societies. There are many unmet needs and, therefore, plenty of room for the social enterprise sector to expand. We trust that in some small way this study will contribute to a better understanding of social entrepreneurship in Singapore, India, and Hong Kong, and perhaps even more broadly. We also hope that it will inspire and furnish some guidelines for the next generation of social entrepreneurs.

Acknowledgment

We wish to acknowledge Angela Karaguezian, Stephanie Shapiro, and Karen Hao who helped with the research and made contributions to earlier drafts of this paper.

Table 2.1 Singapore

Organization	Mission	Barriers	Reason for barrier	Method to handle barrier
Alteration Initiative	Provides training and employment opportunities to women in need.	Social resistance	Customers typically do not believe they should pay a premium for a product or service done by a "less skilled" workforce.	Alteration Initiative combats this through training and education, producing products and services of high quality, and implementing a step by step quality assurance process. In addition, costs are kept reasonable through partnerships where Alteration Initiative receives reduced cost machinery, equipment, and supplies.
		Talent recruitment and retention	Many women have not had real jobs before and are lacking in basic workplace skills.	They worked with a high fashion seamstress to assess aptitude of candidates during a four-day workshop. In addition, the founders had significant corporate experience, which helped to build structure and lay a solid foundation.
Bizlink	Provides comprehensive employment services for disadvantaged people, especially those with disabilities, in order for its employees to become more self-sufficient and empowered.	Social resistance/business skills and acumen	Many people resisted using a traditional business model to help the disabled and thought social workers should run the enterprise.	Although unpopular at first, the shift to create diverse revenue streams instead of focusing on charitable donations allowed the organization to be more sustainable. Once appointed, the CEO educated people about the idea of running Bizlink as a business instead of a charity and the benefits of this approach before trying to implement the change. The CEO also implemented key performance indicators, which helped in analyzing progress and proving results.

Company	Description	Factor		
		Volatile market conditions	It does not want to hire people during economic booms and then have to lay them off.	Bizlink outsources work during short-term spikes in demand to similar organizations. This helps Bizlink avoid layoffs. It also uses volunteer organizations to assist with non-financial tasks.
		Social resistance	There is a general mentality among the public that goods and services from nonprofits should be discounted or free since providing social services is in their mission.	Bizlink offers high-quality services and products. It should market its products as superior and comparable to private sector alternatives.
Buy1Give1	Enables businesses to easily and directly donate online to over 600 projects in the Worthy Cause Organizations network.	Government	Buy1Give1 is an international organization working with over 600 projects across 29 countries; however, the government is heavily involved in social causes and wants to support local causes. Buy1Give1 had to find a way to work within existing regulations, while maintaining its global focus.	Buy1Give1 was able to structure the business entity to conform to government regulations, including making certain that 80 percent of charity giving activity remains in country.
		Funding	To build an online donation platform, Buy1Give1 needed skilled IT services; however, the company had a limited startup budget.	Buy1Give1 partnered with Singapore Management University to find skilled IT students. The students built a system in six months, and Buy1Give1 was able to break even by year 3.
The Green Car Company (Green Car)	Focuses on designing, manufacturing and promoting the "All Round Green Car" in order to reduce emissions.	Funding	Green Car is not eligible for government funding.	It secured private financing by creating a model whereby owners of the product are given shares in the company.
		Infrastructure	No publicly metered charging stations.	It continues to develop better batteries to increase range of vehicle. However, additional government investment in infrastructure is needed.

continued . . .

Table 2.1 Singapore—*continued*

Organization	Mission	Barriers	Reason for barrier	Method to handle barrier
A Good Life	Hires and trains disabled persons to maintain operations for its mobile phone app called GLO ("Good Life Offers!"), which distributes e-coupons for local businesses.	Funding	A Good Life had increased costs associated with recruiting, training, and retaining persons with disabilities.	A Good Life receives government funding for employing and training disabled individuals, which helps offset some of the increased costs.
		Talent recruitment and retention	Persons with disabilities typically take longer to train and are not as adept to responding to changes or situations that require responses that lie outside of what they are trained to do. In addition, it tries to retain as many employees as possible, even if it must cut into overhead expenses.	The company could build partnerships with other social enterprises that have experience with persons with disabilities to enhance its training program. A Good Life could also outsource work caused by short-term spikes in demand to other social enterprises that employ physically disabled people, such as Bizlink.
The Asia Centre for Social Entrepreneurship and Philanthropy (ACSEP)	Aims to advance social entrepreneurship and conducts philanthropy research and education on the topic.	Lack of market analysis or preparation in startups	Some social enterprises make the fundamental mistake of not performing an adequate market analysis and fully understanding their business environment.	Companies should analyze the current market and identify competitive challenges, strengths, weaknesses, opportunities, and threats in depth before diving into operations.
		Funding	Many social enterprises have difficulty acquiring and maintaining adequate cash flow for startup expenses and/or daily operations.	Organizations should try to diversify funding sources, with government funding being one of many options available. The government has programs to provide seed funding for social startups if they meet the government requirements.
		Management style	Founders may not have a strong business background or may lack experience in the corporate sector. Many have difficulty balancing how to be both businessmen and social activists.	Management and founders could seek out education in business skills and acumen. Also, the enterprise could hire or consult with business experts to set up and maintain efficient operations with sustaining principles.

O School	Sustains a for-profit performing arts center that generates funds for low-income Singapore youth to complete their secondary school education, while also providing training and employment opportunities for talented youth.	Social resistance	Culturally speaking, it is difficult to gain public acceptance and Singaporeans do not generally accept dance as a lifestyle. Private schools in general are viewed negatively as a last resort.	O School encourages and motivates its students to pursue their dreams and to achieve excellence. O School differentiates itself by being value-centered mission, as opposed to profit driven. Has implemented widespread social changes by placing pressure on both private and public school systems.
		Funding	Little to no investor interest made it difficult to raise capital to start and run the school.	The local church and community provided funds to help launch the social enterprise. To fund daily operations, it produces dancing conventions, which also generates exposure for the business.
		Funding	Rental spaces that met its needs were high cost and out of O School's already tight budget.	It effectively marketed its vision and leveraged relationships with local officials and government representatives to get a low-rent location leased by other NGOs and dance schools.
Syinc	Brings people together to seek innovative solutions for social change while working to enable young people to be change-agents in the community.	Social resistance	Social entrepreneurship is relatively new to Singapore and most social work is charity work. Generating revenue while fighting a social cause is a new concept. Parents do not always support the social change ideas of their children; parents feel their kids should be focusing on their studies.	Syinc is trying to overcome social stigmas through the very nature of its work and by setting the right example. It also uses technology to educate the public, such as its use of web platforms to reach constituents.
		Structure of organization	Syinc feels there is no comparable organization to model. It follows a flat hierarchy with little organization structure as there are few assigned roles.	Syinc plans to get more people involved in the enterprise and delegate out clearer roles and responsibilities going forward.

Table 2.2 India

Organization	Mission	Barriers	Reason for barrier	Method to handle barrier
Arghyam	Focuses on solutions for water and sanitation-related issues in India.	Talent recruitment and retention	Because national water engineering requires highly skilled professionals, it is difficult to recruit enough qualified workers to meet the enterprise's needs.	Arghyam employs robots and other machinery in lieu of human labor whenever possible to reduce the need for human talent.
		Social resistance	The general public feels no need toward responsible water usage. Water is often subject to the tragedy of the commons.	Arghyam focuses on education to overcome this barrier and also partners with those who can act as role models to show the importance of responsible water usage.
Embrace	Addresses infant mortality-related issues among the bottom of the pyramid in India.	Social resistance	Many rural Indians regard Western medicine as too strong and will not use products as directed.	Embrace simplifies directions and labels for products.
		Government	There is a lack of regulation on medical devices in India.	Embrace adopted the international CE (Conformite Europenne) standard as a mark of quality and reliability.
D.Light	Aims to provide reliable and quality solar lighting to those at the bottom of the pyramid.	Social resistance	Rural Indians are skeptical of solar lighting. They also stick to products that are familiar.	It uses a local sales force that demonstrates D.Light's quality and acts as a source of trust.
		Marketing: lack of budget	Costly advertising expenses would cut into maintaining a competitive price and margin.	D.Light used a local sales force, developed a well-engineered product, and gained publicity through product design awards and media attention rather than traditional marketing channels.
		Talent recruitment and retention	Finding talented and qualified job candidates who value and understand D.Light's mission was a challenge for the company.	D.Light offers competitive wages while recruiting extensively and conducting numerous interviews before selecting a candidate.

Organization	Mission	Issue	Challenge	Response
Dream A Dream	Empowers children from vulnerable backgrounds by developing life skills, while also trying to create a society where unique differences are appreciated.	Management	Founders were young and inexperienced in running a business; outsiders and third-party organizations did not take Dream A Dream as a serious operation.	Dream A Dream remained committed to the mission and struck up a partnership with a shelter for at-risk youth. In turn, the shelter championed Dream A Dream and built up its brand image
		Talent recruitment and retention	Dream A Dream was unable to offer competitive wages for skilled talent.	It focused on hiring college students more interested in gaining experience than compensation. It also focused on meeting employees' development and personal needs.
Hippocampus Foundation	Inspires children from disadvantaged communities to read more.	Marketing	Hippocampus only utilizes word-of-mouth marketing and finds that it is challenging to reach children who could benefit from its services.	It should develop partnerships, with social entrepreneurs, nonprofits, and/or NGOs, in order to have access to markets.
		Funding	Hippocampus was having difficulty creating a sustainable and dependable funding stream.	Hippocampus established a strategic partnership to obtain discounted books, which significantly lowered operational costs.
Kriti	Fosters sustainable improvement to quality of life of the poor through education, job creation, and self-sufficiency.	Product quality	Kriti uses waste and recycled inputs in its production of paper products. It was having trouble maintaining high-quality and consistent end products, especially when making products in small batches as orders were placed.	Kriti keeps tighter control and inventory of its stock and inputs needed to manufacture paper products. It also began producing in bulk to increase consistency and quality and decrease a customer's wait-time for products.
		Funding	In order to expand and scale its operations, more cash flow and suitable properties are needed.	Kriti negotiated longer credit lines with suppliers to free up its cash flow, and analyzed and identified ways to increase operational efficiency. Kriti is also collecting funds from consulting fees while looking into venture capitalists, grants, and sponsors.

continued . . .

Table 2.2 India—continued

Organization	Mission	Barriers	Reason for barrier	Method to handle barrier
MILLEE	Makes learning opportunities more equitable around the world through affordable, culturally appropriate technologies.	Social resistance (cultural differences)	Results from pilot tests in India showed that many kids found MILLEE's games confusing.	MILLEE began working more closely with the local communities, and modeling its mobile game applications after traditional Indian games played by the local children.
		Funding	Games are only compatible on some models of mobile phones since current technology does not allow a single application across all mobile platforms. This increases costs for MILLEE.	MILLEE was trying to utilize the most current technology to generate the widest reaching impact and stay updated with technological advances for further development.
SELCO	Promotes solar energy in developing countries.	Social resistance	There was a public perception that solar lighting is unreliable, fragile, and of poor quality.	SELCO took over maintenance of its products as well as solar lighting previously installed by state governments. It trained staff at appliance repair shops on how to maintain solar lights.
		Funding	SELCO launched in 1996 with no external funding.	It developed a partnership with Tata BP Solar, and received solar lights on credit, 1 to 2 systems at a time. It also located financing from USAID, and registered as a commercial company.
		Suppliers	German solar subsidies caused a massive global solar panel shortage and price hike in 2009–2010, leaving SELCO unable to obtain needed solar panels from suppliers/vendors.	It partnered once again with Tata BP Solar in an exclusive relationship, occasionally sacrificing the lowest cost for a reliable supply and flexible ordering schedule and quantities.

Organization	Benefit	Challenge	Description	Response
Aashayein Foundation	Improves the quality of education in rural villages.	Social resistance	Aashayein faces resistance from village elders and teachers. Teachers do not want to compete with new teachers; village elders often feel that their authority is being challenged.	Aashayein gets the elders involved by asking their advice and giving credit to their suggestions and ideas. Aashayein also focuses on enhancing, not replacing, the current curriculum and teachers.
		Talent recruitment and retention	Many Indian families are risk averse, and there is a stigma against failure. In addition, young adults who wish to help society usually do so only on a part-time basis.	Aashayein trains young adults to start their own enterprises. It provides the adults with analytical tools and shows them that failure is not the end, but a part of the learning process.
Sulabh International	Promotes human rights, sanitation and waste management, and social reforms.	Social resistance	Scavengers fear their only livelihood will be taken away if they don't work in waste management.	Sulabh offers education and training so scavengers have new skills to compete in the job market (e.g., cosmetology, manufacturing).
		Social resistance	Those from other castes have alleged favoritism by Sulabh for the enterprise helping one caste and not others.	It opened its education opportunities to others in the community, but maintain a quota to ensure that at least 60 percent of beneficiaries are from the scavenger caste.
		Funding	Obtaining government funding means expansion of reach of benefits, but it also introduces more bureaucracy and allows government a say in the enterprise's operations.	Sulabh could consider allowing government funding for a restricted portion of operations (e.g., funding public toilets), or they could create a separate entity that interacts with government and receives funding.

continued . . .

Table 2.2 India—continued

Organization	Mission	Barriers	Reason for barrier	Method to handle barrier
Tata Jagriti Yatra	Promotes entrepreneurial spirit via an 18-day, 13-city train journey throughout the country.	Social resistance	In general, families are risk averse, and as a result entrepreneurship carries a social stigma.	The program creates a new community of youth with the entrepreneurial spirit. Throughout the program, they are introduced to successful entrepreneurs around India.
		Partnerships	Sponsors and partners were reluctant to participate, fearing the program might not be successful.	The founders approached 70 different organizations before finding Tata as the major sponsor.
Akshara Foundation	Ensures that "every child is in school and learning well."	Talent retention	Due to funding constraints, it has been unable pay comparable market wages.	Akshara has not been able to adequately address this barrier yet.
		Funding	Akshara has had difficulty raising the capital needed to grow or scale operations.	It is trying to diversify its funding sources. For example, it is looking at obtaining corporate grants or fees for services outsourced to other organizations such as Hippocampus.

Organization	Mission	Barriers	Reason for barrier	Method to handle barrier
Happy Grannies	Provides deprived singleton elders with care and support through continuous visits and sponsorship.	Talent recruitment and retention	There is a shortage of qualified and skilled volunteers who are willing to work.	Happy Grannies provides in-house training to volunteers by qualified social workers. The training helps volunteers better serve the elders they work with and, in turn, assists them in their own careers.
		Funding	Being in the startup phase, Happy Grannies relies almost exclusively on its sponsorship program to bring in revenue.	Happy Grannies is focusing on building a strong volunteer base and entrusting volunteers with responsibility, which in turn minimizes labor and operations costs.
		Metrics	Happy Grannies does not collect any data on performance or analyze results.	It is currently working on creating a metrics system to track performance and results in order to identify areas of improvement and to have ability to seek out additional funding sources.
Diamond Cab	Provides taxi transportation services for the wheelchair bound in Hong Kong.	Talent recruitment and retention	The traditional compensation model for cab drivers is based on high volume and turnover, which does not align with Diamond Cab's model.	It recruits employees whose values and motivations align with the company's mission. In the past, it has also created multiple opportunities/press conferences to publicize Diamond Cab and its mission.
		Startup expenses	Taxi company licenses cost a hefty 5 million HKD. In addition, Diamond Cab had to find a small fleet of wheelchair-friendly cabs.	Diamond Cab formed partnerships. It found a wholesaler who shared in its mission and was willing to import Toyota Welcabs. It also located a cab company willing to let Diamond Cab operate under its taxi license.
		Social resistance	In general, public perception is that nonprofit services should cost less than market rate.	To change perceptions about pricing and the value Diamond Cab provides, it reached out to the Director of the Elderly Commission (Dr Leong Che-Hung) to take a ride on Diamond Cab in a wheelchair and try out the enterprise's service.

continued . . .

Table 2.3 Hong Kong—continued

Organization	Mission	Barriers	Reason for barrier	Method to handle barrier
Senior Citizen Home Safety Association (SCHSA)	Provides 24-hour support and caring service to the elderly.	Funding	As a nonprofit, funding exclusively from one or a few sources is risky and often insufficient.	SCHSA is run like a business even though it is a nonprofit. It maintains a diverse revenue stream – 40 percent customer fees, 40 percent government, 20 percent charitable donations.
		Lack of innovation and the repetition of products/ services across companies	When a company or product is successful in Hong Kong, including social enterprises, others try to copy the idea and start similar organizations.	SCHSA focuses on differentiation. It puts a lot of money in product and service research and development from the start, and ensures that it can provide additional services not offered by competitors.
		Government policy and social perception	Some officials believe that instead of subsidizing social ventures, government should use those funds to hire more city employees and tackle the issues itself. Small business enterprises complain that social ventures unfairly get government financial assistance while they don't.	The founder stays active in local boards and commissions and acts as an educational resource and subject matter expert. It educates others about the efficiencies and benefits social ventures can provide to the government and the economy.

Organization	Description	Challenge	Issue	Response
Social Ventures Hong Kong (SVHK)	Provides financial and other support to social purpose organizations and social enterprises.	Social resistance and a lack of innovation in culture	The education system focuses on exams and memorization rather than innovation and creativity. The ideas of social innovation and benefits of social enterprises are still new.	SVHK tries to educate both companies and younger generations about the social enterprise industry and the need for innovation within the culture.
		Funding	Traditional capital investment is hard to obtain since social ventures are new and emerging in Hong Kong. In general, they are perceived as more speculative and risky than traditional for-profits.	SVHK educates investors on the positive impacts of their investment. It also aims to target larger investors and groups. SVHK sees a lot of optimism among the younger generation, who may be future investors in social enterprises in the long term.
Déjà vu Creations	Specializes in reusing waste materials by transforming them into stylish products.	Funding	As a recent startup, initial funding was obtained solely through personal funds and prize money from social enterprise and business contests.	It is moving toward product sales as the enterprise's main revenue stream and also diversifying where products are sold (online store, Facebook, local retailers, and trade shows).
		Social resistance	Recycled products are not looked at favorably by the typical consumer.	Products are targeted toward making a fashion statement, while prices are kept low and competitive.

References

Agazzi, I. (2012) *India's Economic Growth Leaves Human Development in the Dust*, Global Issues, May 23. Available online at www.globalissues.org/news/2012/05/23/13772 (accessed April 20, 2013).

Bizlink Centre Singapore Ltd (2009) *About Us*. Available online at www.bizlink.org.sg/ (accessed June 15, 2011).

Bornstein, D. (2005) *How to Change the World: Social entrepreneurship and the power of the new ideas*, New York: Penguin Books.

Brock, D.D., Steiner, S., and Kim, M. (2008) "Social entrepreneurship education: is it achieving the desired aims," *USASBE Conference Proceedings*, January.

Central Intelligence Agency (2012a) *The World Factbook: Singapore*, Central Intelligence Agency, March 12. Available online at www.cia.gov/library/publications/the-world-factbook/geos/sn.html (accessed March 24, 2012).

Central Intelligence Agency (2012b) *The World Factbook: India*, Central Intelligence Agency, October 4. Available online at www.cia.gov/library/publications/the-world-factbook/geos/in.html (accessed October 15, 2012).

Central Intelligence Agency (2012c) *The World Factbook: Hong Kong*, Central Intelligence Agency, March 20. Available online at www.cia.gov/library/publications/the-world-factbook/geos/hk.html (accessed March 24, 2012).

Chen, T.-P. (2012) "Hong Kong's wealth gap gets larger," *Wall Street Journal*, June 19. Available online at http://blogs.wsj.com/chinarealtime/2012/06/19/hong-kongs-wealth-gap-gets-larger/ (accessed October 15, 2012).

Chhokar, J.S., Brodbeck, F.C., and House, R.J. (2008) *Culture and Leadership Across the World: The GLOBE book of in-depth studies of 25 societies*, New York: Taylor & Francis Group.

Choi, D. and Gray, E. (2010) *Values-centered Entrepreneurs and their Companies*, New York: Routledge.

Choo, S. and Wong, M. (2006) "Entrepreneurial intention: triggers and barriers to new venture creations in Singapore," *Singapore Management Review*, 28(2): 47–64.

Dees, J.G. (2001) *The Meaning of Social Entrepreneurship*, Center for the Advancement of Social Entrepreneurship, May 30. Available online at www.caseatduke.org/documents/dees_sedef.pdf (accessed May 16, 2013).

Dell (n.d.) *Akshara Foundation—Building an Early Foundation for Long-term Learning*. Available online at http://content.dell.com/us/en/corp/d/corp-comm/cr-youthconnect-akshara.aspx (accessed June 15, 2011)

Department of Statistics Singapore (2012) *Singapore in Figures 2012*, Statistics Singapore. Available online at www.singstat.gov.sg/pubn/reference/sif2012.pdf (accessed September 9, 2012).

Deutsche Bank Research (2010) "The middle class in India: issues and opportunities," *Deutsche Bank Research*, February 15. Available online at www.deutschebank.co.in/jcr/pdfgen/pdf/The_middle_class_in_India.pdf (accessed December 10, 2013).

Do Well Do Good (2010) *The Do Well Do Good Public Opinion Survey on Cause-Marketing Summary Report*. Available online at http://dowelldogood.net/wp-content/uploads/2011/03/DWDG_Cause_FINAL.pdf (accessed August 1, 2011).

Economist, The (2008) "Battling the Babu Raj," March 6.

Forbes India (2012) *How India's HNI Philanthropists are Solving Social Problems*, Forbes India, August 1. Available online at http://forbesindia.com/blog/the-good-company/how-indias-hni-philanthropists-are-solving-social-problems/ (accessed August 1, 2012).

Gannon, M.J. and Pillai, R. (2010) *Understanding Global Cultures: Metaphorical journeys through 29 nations, clusters of nations, continents, and diversity*, vol. 4, Thousand Oaks, CA: Sage.

Golden, K., Hewitt, A., and McBane, M. (2010) *Social Entrepreneurship: Social impact metrics.* MaRS, February. Available online at www.marsdd.com/news-insights/mars-reports/social-entrepreneurship-social-impact-metrics/ (accessed August 1, 2011).

Government of Hong Kong (2012) *Support to Social Enterprises in Hong Kong—Source of Start-up Funds*, Social Enterprises, April 13. Available online at www.social-enterprises.gov.hk/en/support/t_funds.html (accessed October 15, 2012).

Government of Singapore (2011a) *ComCare Enterprise Fund (CEF)*, EnterpriseOne, June 18. Available online at www.enterpriseone.gov.sg/en/Government%20Assistance/Grants/Social%20Care/gp_mcys_cef.aspx (accessed September 2, 2012).

Government of Singapore (2011b) *Government Assistance: Grants*, EnterpriseOne, August 2. Available online at www.business.gov.sg/EN/Government/Government Assistance/TypeOfAssistance/Grants/SocialCare/ (accessed August 2, 2011).

Hardgrave, R.L. and Kochanek, S.A. (2008) *India: Government and politics in a developing nation*, Andover: Cengage Learning.

Hippocampus Reading Foundation (2011) Website, http://hrfindia.org (accessed June 17, 2011).

Ho, P.-y.A. (2010) *The Incubation of Social Entrepreneurship in Hong Kong*, Resource Center Pacific Ocean Asia NPO, June 14. Available online at www.parc-jp.org/solidarityeconomy/about/taiwan20100614/Po-ying%20Amy%20HO,%20The%20Incubation%20of%20Entrepreneurship%20in%20Hong%20K.pdf (accessed October 15, 2012).

Hofstede Centre (2013) *National Cultural Dimensions.* The Geert Hofstede website, April 1. Available online at http://geert-hofstede.com/national-culture.html (accessed April 13, 2013).

Hong Kong Industrialist (2007) "The future of Hong Kong's population," *Hong Kong Industrialist*, January: 12–19.

IRAS (2012) *IRAS: Tax rates and exemption schemes*, Inland Revenue Authority of Singapore, February 12. Available online at www.iras.gov.sg/irasHome/page04.aspx?id=410 (accessed May 14, 2012).

Jayashankar, M. (2010) "The business of schools," *Forbes India Magazine*, April 8. Available online at http://forbesindia.com/printcontent/12062 (accessed March 18, 2012).

Kerr, G. and Powers, L.C. (2009) *Measuring the Benefit of Social Ventures*, a background paper. Available online at www.logicaloutcomes.net/wp-content/uploads/2010/07/Measuring-benefit-of-social-ventures-2010.pdf (accessed August 1, 2011).

Kriti Team (2011) *About Us*. Available online at http://krititeam.blogspot.com/search/label/about%20us (accessed May 13, 2011).

Lim, H. (2007) *International Infrastructure Development in East Asia: Towards balanced regional development and integration*, Jakarta Pusat, Indonesia: Economic Research Institute for ASEAN and East Asia.

Monitor Institute (2009) *Investing for Social and Environmental Impact: A design for catalyzing an emerging industry*, Monitor Institute, January. Available online at http://monitorinstitute.com/downloads/what-we-think/impact-investing/Impact_Investing_Exec_Summary.pdf (accessed October 15, 2012).

Morris, S. (2007) *Singapore's Quest for Water Self-reliance*, Inventory of Conflict & Environment (ICE) Case Studies, May 9. Available online at www1.american.edu/ted/ice/singapore.htm (accessed December 10, 2013).

Morrison, T. and Conway, W.A. (2006) *Kiss, Bow, or Shake Hands*, Fairfield, OH: Adams Media.

Mukerji, S. and Jose, P. (2010) *SELCO: Solar lighting for the poor*, New York: UNDP, Growing Inclusive Markets.

New York Times, The (2012) "World news: Hong Kong," *The New York Times*, September 9. Available online at http://topics.nytimes.com/top/news/international/countriesandterritories/hongkong/index.html (accessed October 15, 2012).

Ramey, C. (2011) *MILLEE: English literacy through games on the third screen*, Mobile Active, February 15. Available online at www.mobileactive.org/millee-learning-english-through-games-small-screen (accessed April 13, 2011).

Saad, I. (2011) "Singapore fertility rate falls to record low," *Channel NewsAsia*, January 17. Available online at www.channelnewsasia.com/stories/singaporelocalnews/view/1105160/1/.html (accessed March 24, 2012).

Segran, G. (2008) "Social entrepreneurship emerging in India but needs are massive," INSEAD Knowledge, December 26. Available online at http://knowledge.Insead.edu/csr/social-entrepreneurship/social-entrepreneurship-emerging-in-india-1898 (accessed October 15, 2012).

Seth, S. and Kumar, S. (2011) "Social entrepreneurship: a growing trend in Indian business," *Entrepreneurial Practice Review*, 1(4): 4–19. Available online at www.entryerson.com/epr/index.php/jep/article/viewFile/66/49 (accessed October 15, 2012).

Singh, Y. and Pollock, T. (2011) "Interview: The future of social entrepreneurship in India," SocialEarth, August 8. Available online at www.socialearth.org/interview-the-future-of-social-entrepreneurship-in-india (accessed October 15, 2012).

Social Enterprise Committee (2007) *Report of the Social Enterprise Committee*. Singapore: SEC.

Srivastava, M. and MacAskill, A. (2012) "India's poor starve as politicians steal their food," *BloombergBusinessweek*, September 6. Available online at www.businessweek.com/articles/2012-09-06/indias-poor-starve-as-politicians-steal-their-food (accessed October 15, 2012).

Syinc (2011, May 26) *Current Programs*. Available online at www.syinc.org/ (accessed June 15, 2011).

Top Achievement (2007) *Creating S.M.A.R.T. Goals*. Available online at www.topachievement.com/smart.html (accessed August 1, 2011).

World Bank (2011) *India Country Overview—September 2011*, World Bank—India, September. Available online at www.worldbank.org.in/WBSITE/EXTERNAL/COUNTRIES/SOUTHASIAEXT/INDIAEXTN/0,,contentMDK:20195738~pagePK:141137~piPK:141127~theSitePK:295584,00.html (accessed September 5, 2011).

3 Corporate social responsibility in emerging markets

Corporate India's engagement with local communities

Ramendra Singh and Sharad Agarwal

India is a diverse nation with 28 states, seven union territories and a phenomenal population of over 1.2 billion people. The interplay of this diversity and demographic factors rightly place it in the coterie of emerging world economies. The 2003 Goldman Sachs global economics paper, "Dreaming with BRICS: path to 2050," suggests that India is one of the leading BRICS countries and has the potential to outperform Japan to become the third largest economy in the world by 2032. However, despite the rapid economic growth made in India, much remains to be done by corporate India with regard to linking markets with the larger society. It is particularly challenging, as it has to accomplish this while meeting the ever-increasing expectations from stakeholders on the corporate social responsibility (CSR) front.

According to the World Business Council for Sustainable Development (2000), CSR is "the commitment of business to contribute to sustainable economic development, working with employees, their families, and the local community." In India, there has been a gradual realization by firms that expanding their scope and ambit of social responsibility is the pertinent need of the hour. The Indian government is also mulling over a new Companies Bill in the Indian Parliament; clause 135(5) of the same bill prescribes that every company with a net worth of at least Rs 5,000 million ($1 is approximately Rs 55), or turnover of at least Rs 10,000 million, or a net profit of at least Rs 50 million, will have to spend 2 percent of its three years' average profit on CSR activities (*The Indian Express*, 2012). Despite impressive economic growth during recent decades, India continues to face a number of socio-economic challenges. India contains the largest concentration of people living below the World Bank's international poverty line of $1.25/day.

Given that almost a third of the country's population lives in poverty and penury, CSR provides Indian corporations with a readily available and highly impactful opportunity to prove and establish the legitimacy of their actions by moving beyond charities and rural developmental activities. The firms can be innovative in producing and marketing affordable products and services for the massive population at the "bottom of pyramid." This will embrace the notion of both compassionate capitalism and inclusive business as proposed in Western business academia. More objectively, it will tend to counterbalance, to some extent, the impact of the huge negative externalities that commercial activities tend to create in the developing societies they operate in. Also, new business models emerging out of these innovative hybrid partnerships may give rise to unforeseen fortuitous results that will give a boost to economic growth in this emerging market.

In this chapter, we discuss the contemporary understanding of CSR practiced by companies operating in India, through their CSR initiatives, novel implementation approaches, and stakeholder issues and concerns. We present the finding of our research on the top 200 Indian companies using content analysis. Through this discussion and explanation, we explain the current CSR orientation of companies in India. The text gives insights into the current practices of the top 200 companies in India, the social issues that are often ignored, and the needs to be addressed by these organizations. More importantly, the chapter addresses the concern regarding corporate entities getting maximum return on their social investments, and at the same time ensuring that they are able to garner substantial visibility and positive publicity from the societies that they operate within.

CSR's role in making economic growth more inclusive refers to the process of growth that ensures equal access to available opportunities for all segments of the society irrespective of their individual circumstances. Since India's GDP has been growing annually at an average of about 6 percent, the concept of inclusive growth becomes even more pertinent for the political establishment and the privileged sections as they strive to accommodate everyone on the high-growth bandwagon.

Methodology

To investigate the landscape of CSR activities in India, we collected data regarding the CSR policies and practices of the top 200 public listed companies in India, which are categorized in the "A" category by the Bombay Stock Exchange (BSE) of India (NB: the sample deliberately excludes multinational companies such as Coca-Cola and IBM, which do of course operate in India and might also have substantial CSR initiatives in the country, but are not listed on the BSE). We decided to take this sample of the top 200 companies as it contains a good/healthy mix of industries cutting across sectors. The list of 200 companies used in our sample is shown by industry type in Table 3.1. We used content analysis to generate the underlying themes in our data since content analysis is a "technique for making inferences by objectively and systematically identifying specified characteristics of messages" (Holsti, 1969: 14). Content analysis has been widely used in corporate social and environmental responsibility research (Gray *et al.*, 1995). Given that CSR literature suggests that organizations increasingly use CSR activities to position their corporate brands in the eyes of the consumers and other stakeholders through their annual reports (Sweeney and Coughlan, 2008) and websites (Maignan and Ralston, 2002), we collected data using these public sources.

Table 3.1 List of the top 200 companies included for this study by industry type

Industry type	Company name
Manufacturing/Engineering/ Construction (n=47)	ABB Lmited
	Acc Ltd
	Adani Enterprises Ltd
	Alstom Projects India Ltd
	Ambuja Cements Ltd
	Areva T&D India Ltd
	BGR Energy Systems Ltd
	Bharat Electronics Ltd
	Bharat Heavy Electricals Ltd
	Cairn India Ltd
	Century Textiles & Industries Ltd
	Container Corporation of India Ltd.
	Crompton Greaves Ltd
	D B Realty Ltd
	DLF Ltd
	Engineers India Ltd
	GMR Infrastructure Ltd
	Godrej Properties Ltd
	Grasim Industries Ltd
	Great Eastern Shipping Company Ltd
	Gujarat State Petronet Ltd
	Havells India Ltd
	Hindustan Construction Company Ltd
	Housing Development & Infrastructure Ltd
	IL&FS Transportation Networks Ltd
	Indiabulls Real Estate Ltd
	IRB Infrastructure Developers Ltd
	IVRCL Infrastructure & Projects Ltd
	Jaiprakash Associates Ltd
	Jaypee Infratech Ltd
	Jet Airways (India) Ltd
	Larsen & Toubro Ltd
	MMTC Ltd
	Mundra Port & Special Economic Zone Ltd
	Nagarjuna Construction Co. Ltd
	Opto Circuits India Ltd
	Pipavav Shipyard Ltd
	Punj Lloyd Ltd
	Reliance Natural Resources Ltd
	Shipping Corporation of India Ltd
	Shree Cements Ltd
	Siemens Ltd
	Suzlon Energy Ltd
	UltraTech Cement Ltd
	Unitech Ltd
	Videocon Industries Ltd
	Voltas Ltd

continued . . .

Table 3.1 Continued

Industry type	Company name
Banking/Finance (n=37)	Allahabad Bank
	Andhra Bank
	Axis Bank Ltd
	Bajaj Finserv Ltd
	Bajaj Holdings & Investment Ltd
	Bank of Baroda
	Bank of India
	Canara Bank
	Central Bank of India
	Corporation Bank
	Federal Bank Ltd
	HDFC Bank Ltd
	Housing Development Finance Corporation Ltd
	ICICI Bank Ltd
	IDBI Bank Ltd
	IFCI Ltd
	Indiabulls Financial Services Ltd
	Indian Bank
	Indian Overseas Bank
	IndusInd Bank Ltd
	Infrastructure Development Finance Company Ltd
	Kotak Mahindra Bank Ltd
	LIC Housing Finance Ltd
	Mahindra & Mahindra Financial Services Ltd
	Oriental Bank of Commerce
	Power Finance Corporation Ltd.
	Punjab National Bank
	Reliance Capital Ltd
	Religare Enterprises Ltd
	Rural Electrification Corporation Ltd
	Shriram Transport Finance Company Ltd
	State Bank of India
	Syndicate Bank
	UCO Bank
	Union Bank of India
	Vijaya Bank
	YES Bank Ltd
Petroleum/Petrochemical (n=10)	Aban Offshore Ltd
	Bharat Petroleum Corporation Ltd
	Essar Oil Ltd
	Hindustan Oil Exploration Company Ltd
	Hindustan Petroleum Corporation Ltd
	Indian Oil Corporation Ltd
	Mangalore Refinery and Petrochemicals Ltd
	Oil and Natural Gas Corporation Ltd
	Oil India Ltd
	Reliance Industries Ltd

continued . . .

Table 3.1 Continued

Industry type	Company name
Automobile/FMCG/Auto Ancillary (n=28)	Aditya Birla Nuvo Ltd
	Apollo Tyres Ltd
	Ashok Leyland Ltd
	Asian Paints Ltd
	Bajaj Auto
	Bosch Ltd
	Castrol India Ltd
	Colgate-Palmolive (India) Ltd
	Cummins India Ltd
	Dabur India Ltd
	Exide Industries Ltd
	Godrej Consumer Products Ltd
	Hero Honda Motors Ltd
	Hindustan Unilever Ltd
	ITC Ltd
	Jain Irrigation Systems Ltd
	Mahindra & Mahindra Ltd
	Marico Ltd
	Maruti Suzuki India Ltd
	Motherson Sumi Systems Ltd
	Nestle India Ltd
	Procter & Gamble Hygiene & Healthcare Ltd
	Sintex Industries Ltd
	Tata Global Beverages Ltd
	Tata Motors Ltd
	Thermax Ltd
	Titan Industries Ltd
	TVS Motor Company Ltd
Power Generation/Gas Distribution (n=18)	Adani Power Ltd
	CESC Ltd
	GAIL (India) Ltd
	GVK Power & Infrastructure Ltd
	Indraprastha Gas Ltd
	Jaiprakash Power Ventures Ltd
	JSW Energy Ltd
	Lanco Infratech Ltd
	Neyveli Lignite Corporation Ltd
	NHPC Ltd
	NTPC Ltd
	Petronet LNG Ltd
	Power Grid Corporation of India Ltd
	Reliance Infrastructure Ltd
	Reliance Power Ltd
	SJVN Ltd
	Tata Power Company Ltd
	Torrent Power Ltd

continued . . .

Table 3.1 Continued

Industry type	Company name
Fertilizer/Chemical/ Forging (n=24)	Bharat Forge Ltd
	Bhushan Steel Ltd
	Coromandel International Ltd
	Godrej Industries Ltd
	Hindalco Industries Ltd
	Hindustan Copper Ltd
	Hindustan Zinc Ltd (Vedanta Group)
	Jai Corp Ltd
	Jindal Saw Ltd
	Jindal Steel & Power Ltd
	JSW Steel Ltd
	National Aluminium Company Ltd
	National Fertilisers Ltd
	NMDC Ltd
	Rashtriya Chemicals & Fertilizers Ltd
	Sesa Goa Ltd
	Shree Renuka Sugars Ltd
	Steel Authority of India (SAIL) Ltd
	Sterlite Industries (India) Ltd
	Tata Chemicals Ltd
	Tata Steel Ltd
	United Phosphorus Ltd
	United Spirits Ltd
	Welspun Corp Ltd
Pharmaceuticals/ Healthcare (n=14)	Aurobindo Pharma Ltd
	Biocon Ltd
	Cadila Healthcare Ltd
	Cipla Ltd
	Divi's Laboratories Ltd
	Dr Reddy's Laboratories Ltd
	Fortis Healthcare Ltd
	GlaxoSmithKline Pharmaceuticals Ltd
	Glenmark Pharmaceuticals Ltd
	Jubilant Life Sciences Ltd
	Lupin Ltd
	Piramal Healthcare Ltd
	Ranbaxy Laboratories Ltd
	Sun Pharmaceutical Industries Ltd
Entertainment/Hospitality/ Retail (n=6)	Dish TV India Ltd
	EIH Ltd
	Indian Hotels Company Ltd (TAJ Hotels)
	Pantaloon Retail (India) Ltd
	Sun TV Network Ltd
	Zee Entertainment Enterprises Ltd
Computer (s/w & h/w) (n=10)	Educomp Solutions Ltd
	Financial Technologies (India) Ltd
	HCL Technologies Ltd
	Infosys Technologies Ltd

continued . . .

Table 3.1 Continued

Industry type	Company name
	MphasiS Ltd
	Oracle Financial Services Software Ltd
	Patni Computer Systems Ltd
	Tata Consultancy Services Ltd
	Tech Mahindra Ltd
	Wipro Ltd
Telecommunications (n=6)	Bharti Airtel Ltd
	GTL Infrastructure Ltd
	Idea Cellular Ltd
	Mahanagar Telephone Nigam Ltd
	Reliance Communications Ltd
	Tata Communications Ltd

We made an exhaustive list of all CSR areas in which the companies work and methodologies employed by them for carrying out the same, as reported by them in these public sources. We coded the areas of work for CSR by these companies into seven broad categories: "Education," "Health," "Community welfare," "Entrepreneurship development," "Environment," "Market place," and "Rural development." These areas of societal development work are not related to the core business of the companies examined and are pursued by them on a voluntary basis as there is no statutory requirement for any of the corporations to pursue such activities. These categories are depicted in Table 3.2 and further explained in detail in the section on "Domains of CSR activities of Indian corporations." The methodologies adopted to carry out CSR activities are coded in eight categories: through self-run foundations; NGOs, charitable trusts, etc.; government bodies; direct company involvement; healthcare, for example donating tablets, etc.; providing special budgets for CSR; employee involvement; and the public private partnership (PPP) model. These categories are explained, with examples, in later sections of the chapter.

The face of India's corporate social responsibility

In 2008, Tata Motors, a major Indian automobile company, was forced to shift its manufacturing project for the *Nano* model from Singur in West Bengal to Sanand in Gujarat due to agitation by farmers and other community members whose lands were being acquired for the above-mentioned project (in Singur). This agitation led to Tata motors suffering losses of more than Rs 10,000 million (1 US $ = 55 INR approx). Probably if the company had recognized its social responsibility from the very beginning, these losses would not have occurred and it would possibly have led to mutual benefits for both the company and the surrounding community. In another instance, Hindalco Industries Ltd, an Indian aluminum conglomerate, was forced to stop bauxite

Table 3.2 Areas of work by companies in India

Activities	Explanation
Education	The companies working in the area of promoting education, e.g. girl education, providing scholarships, etc.
Health	The companies working in the area of healthcare for the needy and deprived, e.g. rural health, preventing HIV/AIDS, etc.
Community welfare	The companies working for the welfare of various sections of the society, e.g. philanthropic donations, promotion of inclusive growth, etc.
Entrepreneurship development	The companies working toward promotion of entrepreneurial activities or assisting people to set up their own enterprises to earn their livelihood, e.g. skill development, imparting technical know-how, provision of startup capital, etc.
Environment	The companies stating a policy of minimizing negative environmental impact or positively benefiting the natural environment as a part of their business practice, e.g. financial firms such as banks restricting access to capital to industries contributing to the depletion of the ozone layer.
Market place	The companies working in issues related to their core markets and having an accompanying impact on their business, e.g. provision of micro-finance in villages, etc.
Rural development	The companies carrying out activities for the development of rural areas/tracts, e.g. carrying out agricultural development activities, providing street and solar lights in rural areas, etc.

mining operation in Mali Hill in south Odisha's Koraput district due to agitation by the local tribal community. The locals were contending that the water sources, on which they are dependent for their survival, would dry up if mining was undertaken in the pristine area. The locals were also demanding the immediate cancellation of the mining lease granted to Hindalco (Mohanty, 2012).

The above examples explicitly indicate that in industrializing societies firms need to connect/build rapport with local communities and foster/maintain relationships with concerned stakeholders. These stakeholders include farmers, whose land may have been acquired for industrial purposes, landless laborers, who used to work on the land where factories stand today, and other members of the population directly or indirectly adversely impacted by the process of industrialization. All these stakeholders, more often than not, constitute the local community around the manufacturing and operating facilities of these corporations. Industries such as mining, energy, infrastructure, automobiles, etc., which need large areas of land for their operations and, thus, necessarily cause displacement of thousands of people from their native places, have started facing resistance from local communities, which, in some sense, feel themselves deprived of the fruits/benefits of the current growth processes.

Similar incidents of outrage/anguish from local community members are being reported across the country, prodding corporations to consider local community members as important stakeholders and include/accommodate them in their growth story, and the growth story of the nation in the long run. The prospect of not being able to amalgamate the social and business object-ives amiably may prove to be too costly. This is an aspect for which corporate firms have been perceived to have not shown sufficient accountability to society.

Legacy of CSR by Indian businesses

Businesses in India have been aware of their social responsibilities since ancient times, because for many decades community-led businesses dominated by certain communities such as the Jains or Marwaris were known for their dona-tions and charitable contributions toward various schools, colleges, drinking water facilities for travelers, guest houses (*dharamshalas*), etc. along key trade routes and such centers are a legacy of their contributions. In modern times, the larger Indian corporations have adopted structured approaches to CSR activities, which range from having their own foundations for CSR activities, to simply donating to government agencies or the Prime Minister Relief fund for developmental activities. Many of the practices adopted by corporations in India have simply been rip-offs of Western notions of charity or CSR.

Based on the frameworks provided by Kolk (2000) and Chahoud *et al.* (2007), the journey of Indian CSR can be divided into four phases. The first phase was predominantly determined by culture, religion, and family traditions of the owners of the businesses. The CSR of businesses in this phase was limited to building temples and providing relief in times of crisis such as famine or epidemics. The corporations during this phase were responsible only to their owners and managers. The second phase (1910–60) was largely influenced by Mahatma Gandhi's theory of trusteeship, which referred to establishing an equitable economic order through a proper scheme of distribution of the accumulated wealth to all members of the society. The theory of trusteeship does not recognize the hereditary inheritance of wealth and refers to transition or transformation of wealth and property from individual ownership to com-munity (Sapru, 2008). Among others, industrialists such as Jamnalal Bajaj and G.D. Birla were his followers. Gopinath (2011) quotes Birla's words:

> It has been the policy of the House of Birla not to build up business with a view of accumulation of capital but to develop unexplored lines, harness the underdeveloped resources of the country, promote know-how, create skilled labor and managerial talent, spread education, and above all, add to the efforts of the leaders of the country who have been strug-gling to build a new, independent India, free from want, the curse of unemployment, ignorance, and disease.

These words of Birla, who then owned one of the largest industrial houses, reflect the commitment of corporate leaders toward society in those times. The corporations were responsible to their owners, managers, and employees. With the emergence of public sector units (PSUs) and ample legislation on labor and environmental standards, the third phase (1960–80) was dominated by the paradigm of the "mixed economy." The organizations also became responsible to the environment besides their owners, managers, and employees. After the globalization of the Indian economy in 1990, Indian firms faced tough competition from foreign firms to survive in the domestic markets. Along with an opportunity to expand globally, they were now required to comply with the global standards and adopt better management practices, and to become efficient in their production processes. However, Arora and Puranik(2004) mention that with the increased profitability of these Indian companies their ability and willingness to give also increased. Chahoud *et al.* (2007) termed this fourth phase (1980/90 until the present) of Indian CSR as being a "confused state." The history of CSR in India is summarized in Table 3.3.

Hindustan Unilever Ltd (HUL), for example, follows a four-pronged strategy for CSR activities, which is influenced by Carroll's (1991) Pyramid of Corporate Social Responsibility. At the top of this strategy is pure philanthropy, which encompasses those corporate actions that are in response to society's expectation for businesses be good corporate citizens. This includes actively engaging in acts or programs to promote human welfare or goodwill (Carroll, 1991). HUL places "sustainable living" at the core of its business model, and mentions it as its duty and an opportunity to address the social issues of availability of pure drinking water, sanitation in rural areas, energy conservation, etc. On the second rung comes the social investments that relate to the socially responsible projects of the HUL foundation, which Carroll (1991) refers to as "ethical responsibilities" and which can be explained as ethical behavior beyond mere compliance with laws and regulations. On the third rung come commercial initiatives that blend commercial objectives with social responsibility; this includes the introduction of products such as "Pureit," which is described as the world's most advanced range of in-home water purifiers. This product is a solution to water-borne diseases, which are

Table 3.3 Evolution of CSR among Indian companies

Phase 1	Phase 2	Phase 3	Phase 4
1850–1914	*1910–60*	*1950–90*	*Since 1980/90*
Pure philanthropy and charity during industrialization; corporation is responsible to owners and managers only.	CSR as social development during the independence struggle; corporation is for owners, managers, and employees.	CSR under the "mixed economy paradigm"; corporation is responsible to owners, managers, and other target environments.	CSR in a globalized world in a "confused state"; corporation is responsible to owners, managers, other target environments, and public at large.

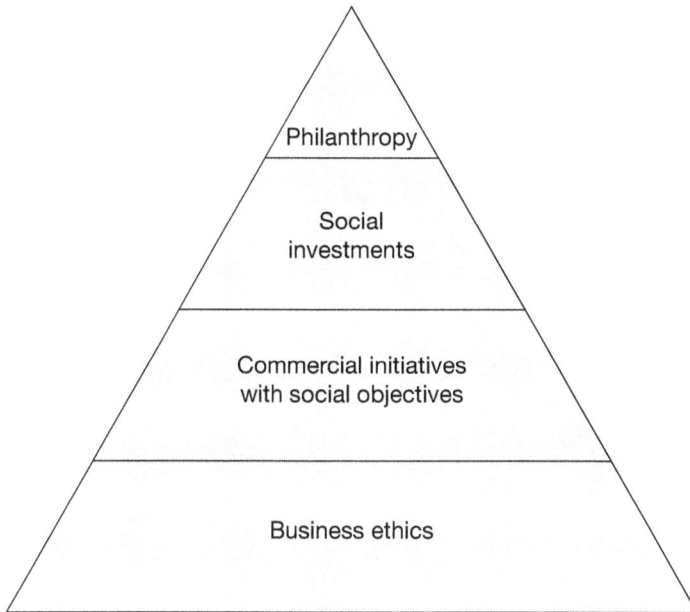

Figure 3.1 A pyramidical representation of CSR adopted by corporate India.

a great challenge in the developing world as diarrhea alone leads to over two million deaths and four billion episodes of disease every year worldwide. On the bottom rung in the CSR model of HUL lies the pure business strategy that attempts to marry business objectives with an ethical outlook, which Carroll (1991) refers to as "economic responsibility" and is the organization's commitment to being reasonably profitable, maintaining a strong competitive position and a high level of operating efficiency, and constantly being defined as a successful enterprise. This is best shown through a pyramid, as in Figure 3.1.

CSR methodologies in India

Based on our study, we present the chart in Figure 3.2, which depicts the major approaches used by top Indian corporations to pursue their CSR activities. The data were collected from the information provided by the corporations on their websites, and official communications such as annual reports and sustainability guidelines.

In our sample of the top 200 Indian corporations, 64 have their own dedicated foundations to carry out their CSR activities. Foundations are not-for-profit organizations created for serving society through various activities such as education development, etc. In India, foundations are generally registered as charitable trusts for the purpose of social development through

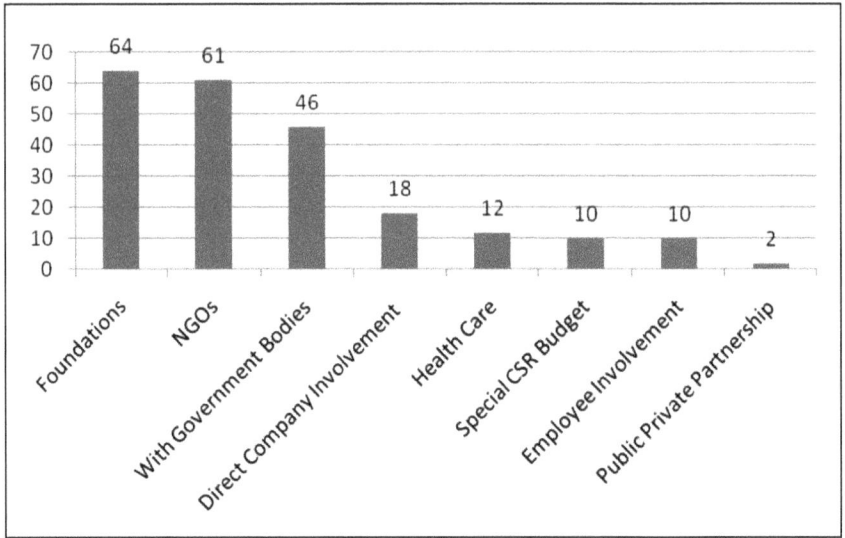

Figure 3.2 Methodologies adopted by firms in India for its CSR.

Note: Numbers in the chart denote the number of companies out of 200 companies in our sample.

poverty eradication programs, healthcare development programs, etc. Foundations are generally formed after an individual or a corporation donates a certain sum of money for a cause, which reflects the long-term dedication of the top management of the corporations toward the development of society. The corporations work on a voluntary basis, without any legal compulsion to do so. For example, DLF Foundation, belonging to India's largest realty firm, DLF, runs initiatives in rural areas that aim toward a wide-ranging impact on local communities in terms of both income and living standard improvement by building village roads and improving road connectivity with mainstream road/highway networks. The foundation also provides help in improving basic amenities such as sewage disposal, water supply, provision of drains, and electrification (DLF Foundation, 2009). The aforementioned Hindustan Unilever Ltd (HUL), an Indian FMCG (fast-moving consumer goods) major, promotes the Unilever Foundation, set up two years ago to work toward improving the lives of the poor in local communities, and simultaneously nurtures markets of the future. The Unilever Foundation is a key initiative taken by HUL to achieve its ambitious goal of helping more than one billion people to improve their health and well-being and, in turn, create a sustainable future (Unilever Foundation, 2012). Therefore, CSR works through foundations of firms not only to achieve the compliance objectives but also to build markets for the future, where no markets exist today.

In our study it was found that most of the corporations in India carry out their CSR activities through their own trusts. As another example, Bharti

Foundation, promoted by Bharti Airtel Ltd, a leading integrated telecommunications company with operations in 20 countries across Asia and Africa, ranked among the top five global mobile service providers in terms of subscribers. Registered under the Registration Act 1908 with charitable status, it helps underprivileged children and young people to realize their potential by supporting programs that bring about sustainable changes through education and training opportunities to the youth to make them employable (Bharti Foundation, 2012).

Out of the 200 Indian companies in our sample, 62 of the companies in India work with NGOs, charitable trusts, and other like-minded organizations to achieve their objectives of carrying out development in the society in which these organizations operate. For example, Jet Airways, India's leading airline, with the widest domestic network and operations in 24 international destinations across four continents, works with several NGOs to carry out its CSR activities. Jet Airways has an in-flight collection program, the "Magic Box," in association with the NGO Save the Children India (STCI) (Jet Airways Community Services, 2012). The company has also engaged the services of Shraddha Charitable Trust—a registered NGO that trains and provides post-school employment to their mentally challenged and autistic young wards. Every year, Jet Airways, together with various NGOs, organizes one or two "Flights of Fantasy" for underprivileged children. The partnership with several NGOs helps the company to work for the welfare of the underprivileged children, on whose potential hinges the future of the country.

Of the 200 companies sampled, 46 work in collaboration with different government agencies for carrying out their CSR activities. For example, Essar Oil is a fully integrated oil company with refining capacity of 18 million metric tonnes per annum in India and over 1,400 Essar-branded oil retail outlets across India. Essar's CSR is guided by the E3 model: entrepreneurship, education, and environment (Essar Foundation, 2012). This corresponds with the United Nations' Millennium Development Goals, also endorsed by the Government of India. The company focuses on neighborhood CSR activities to make a positive impact on the communities around Essar Oil plants that include participating families who have contributed their land to its plants, and other communities that live in the immediate vicinity. Communities not in the vicinity, but whose socio-economic and lifestyle factors are influenced by Essar's activities, are also helped through its association with National Development Programs. The company also plans to supplement and support various schemes and programs run by government institutions and developmental agencies in India.

Of the 200 companies sampled, 18 were involved directly in CSR activities. For example, Havells India Ltd, a $1.3 billion organization and one of the top five lighting companies in the world, provides mid-day meals to around 350 government schools in the Alwar district of Rajasthan, covering 30,000 students per day (Havells, 2012). Havells has a spacious kitchen with modern equipment and utmost care is taken in terms of hygiene while preparing and serving food. This initiative increased the number of children attending school regularly, and helps to alleviate hunger. The company has acquired land for constructing a larger kitchen with all the modern facilities to serve freshly cooked food to 50,000 students in the area. Through its CSR activities, the company claims to contribute to social and environmental causes on a regular basis.

Of the 200 companies sampled, 12 pursue their CSR by provisioning healthcare facilities for the backward sections of society. For example, GlaxoSmithKline Pharmaceuticals Ltd, one of the oldest pharmaceutical companies in India, having a turnover of Rs 26,990 million and employing over 3,500 people, has as a mission statement "to improve the quality of life by enabling people to do more, feel better and live longer." The company, as part of its CSR activities, provides money, medicines, time, and equipment to nonprofit organizations to help improve health and education in underserved communities (GlaxoSmithKline-India, 2012).

Ten companies in our sample maintain special funding for CSR activities and also keep provisions of reserve funding for CSR for the next financial year, so that the CSR activities of the company can be planned and carried out strategically throughout the year. For example, Oil and Natural Gas Corporation Ltd (ONGC), a state-owned, Fortune Global 500 company ranked 413, and contributing 77 percent of India's crude oil production and 81 percent of India's natural gas production, defines its role in CSR by emphasizing the transformation of the organization from "philanthropy" to "stakeholder participation." Effective in the financial year 2009–10, the company decided to allocate 2 percent of the net profit of the previous fiscal year as its CSR budget. Among other activities, the company's key achievements include its ONGC PURA—Providing Urban amenities in Rural Areas—as envisioned by former Indian President, Dr A.P.J. Abdul Kalam. ONGC plans to have ONGC PURA in each state where ONGC produces oil and gas, including in states with a possibility of future availability of isolated gas. As a start, the Tripura PURA project has already been in execution mode (Upwanshi, 2012). The company also won the Golden Peacock Award for Excellence in Corporate Social Responsibility in Emerging Economies 2006, awarded by the World Council for Corporate Governance, UK.

Ten companies in our sample also report involving their employees directly to pursue their CSR activities with local community members. For example, HCL Technologies Ltd is an India-based global IT service provider with revenue of more than US $2.5 billion and a market capitalization of more than US $5 billion with 82,400 plus employees. As a part of its CSR activities it has a unique program named "Power of One," which refers to every HCLite spending a day in the community and experiencing the power of giving. The project in total had 922 volunteers, 43 leaders, more than 2,000 beneficiaries, and 7,376 hours of community service on one single day (HCL, 2012). Major activities implemented included slum cleaning and beach cleaning. These activities are carried out in collaboration with Exnora International, an

NGO. Some of the other activities included infrastructure improvement for Sollamangalam Government Higher Secondary School, Chennai; preserving natural resources at the Vandalur Zoo, Chennai; preparing food for Akshay Patra corporation schools of Vrindavan; learning from the disabled at Noida Deaf Society, Delhi; working with medicinal plants at the Foundation for Revitalization of Local Health Traditions (FRLHT), Bangalore; and so on.

Two companies in our sample of 200 Indian companies, Ranbaxy Laboratories Ltd and Educomp Solutions Ltd, mention practicing public private partnership (PPP) as a model to carry out their CSR activities (IndiaCan, 2012; Ranbaxy, 2012). Ranbaxy Laboratories Ltd is India's largest pharmaceutical company with global sales of US $2.1 billion. The company claims that corporate social commitment and public service are deeply embedded in the culture of the company. Ranbaxy Community Healthcare Society (RCHS), an independent body run by the company, is devoted to the health of the disadvantaged. RCHS provides multiple well-equipped mobile healthcare vans and an urban family welfare centre, which benefit over 200,000 people, in certain identified areas in the states of Punjab, Haryana, Himachal Pradesh, Madhya Pradesh, and Delhi. Ranbaxy entered into a PPP with the Punjab State Government, to deliver healthcare services in identified districts of Punjab.

Educomp Solutions Ltd is the largest education company in India with revenues of Rs 13,509 million during 2010–11. The company has the vision to "apply innovative solutions to solve critical problems relating to 'Quality of Education' and 'Access to Education' for all." Educomp has adopted 18 technical institutes (ITIs) altogether in Punjab, Haryana, Rajasthan, and Uttar Pradesh under the PPP scheme (IndiaCan, 2012) and is motivated to train and prepare the students to excel in life. These two examples of CSR through the PPP model are contrasting, since Ranbaxy is an example of pure CSR, while Educomp resembles CSR via the social entrepreneurship model.

Domains of CSR activities of Indian corporations

Corporations in India perform a diverse range of activities under the CSR umbrella. These activities are primarily oriented toward the welfare of different stakeholders as identified by respective corporations. India being a developing nation, a substantial proportion of the population lives in utter poverty and the government finds it extremely difficult to meet even the basic developmental needs of society, such as primary healthcare, minimal education facilities for children, drinking water, and sanitation facilities in rural areas, etc. Corporations through their CSR activities aim to bridge this gap by being agents in promoting the inclusive growth of society (as based on the demands from society and provisions from the government). As already mentioned in this chapter, the CSR activities of the selected companies are coded as "Education," "Health," "Community welfare," "Entrepreneurship development," "Environment," "Market place," and "Rural development" and the numbers of companies working in each of these areas are depicted in Figure 3.3.

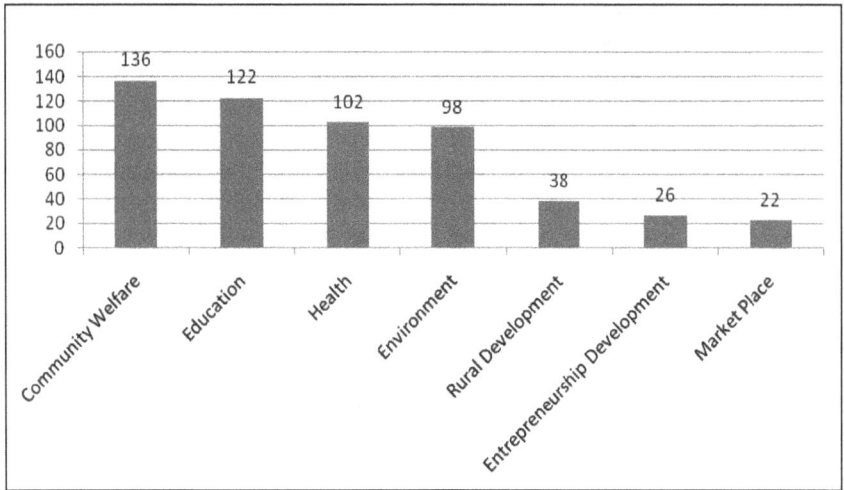

Figure 3.3 CSR activities (number of companies) practiced by Indian corporations.

In our sample, 136 of the companies were found to work in the area of community welfare, for example by philanthropic donations and promoting inclusive growth. The companies working in this area include Oil India Ltd, National Thermal Power Corporation Ltd (NTPC), and Nagarjuna Construction Ltd. Out of these 136 companies, 122 companies worked for the cause of education, which included girl education and the provision of scholarships to deserving students, for example Procter & Gamble Hygiene & Healthcare Ltd, Ultra Tech. Cement, Tata Steel Ltd, and ONGC.

Of the companies in our sample, 102 worked for the cause of health of weaker sections of society; activities included providing medical facilities in rural areas, preventing HIV/AIDS, distributing medicines, operating charitable medical hospitals, etc. Companies working for the cause of health included Tata Global Beverages Ltd, TVS Motors Ltd, and Ranbaxy Laboratories Ltd. A similar number, 98 companies, worked for the cause of the environment, either through their policies of minimizing negative environmental impact, or positively benefiting the natural environment as a part of their business practices, for example financial institutions refusing to lend to industries contributing toward the depletion of the ozone layer and forcing industries to reduce their carbon emissions. Examples include Hindustan Unilever and the National Hydro Power Corporation Ltd (NHPC).

In our sample, 38 companies worked for the development of rural areas, through agricultural development activities and providing streetlights in rural areas. The companies in this segment included National Mineral Development Corporation Ltd (NMDC), Nestlé India Ltd, and Jain Irrigation Systems Ltd. Twenty-six companies worked for entrepreneurship development by promoting entrepreneurial activities or helping people to set up their own enterprises through imparting technical expertise, providing startup capital, and so on; examples include the Oriental Bank of Commerce, Indian Bank, and Voltas Ltd. Twenty-two companies worked for the development of their market places as part of their CSR activities, that is, on issues that have an impact on their businesses, for example being ethical in their operations and paying genuine taxes to government. These included United Spirits Ltd and Rural Electrification Corporation Ltd. Two percent of the 200 companies also reported their activities as being related to their workplace development as part of their CSR activities; these companies are Aban Offshore Ltd, Shipping Corporation of India Ltd, Shree Cements Ltd, and Shree Renuka Sugars Ltd. These companies report promoting safety of their employees as part of their CSR activities (safety mostly came under the broader umbrella of safety–health–environment, followed by many companies in our sample).

Case study: CSR achievements of Coal India Ltd

To exemplify in more detail and to understand the nature of involvement of corporations with local communities, we take as an example a case study on the CSR activities of India's leading public sector corporation, Coal India Ltd (CIL henceforth). CIL is the world's largest producer of coal, with an annual turnover of Rs 699,520 million and profit after tax of Rs 212,726 million (after adjustments) in 2011–12 (after transferring Rs 2,312 million to the CSR reserve fund), and employee strength of more than 371,000 employees. CIL mentions on its website that it formulated a CSR policy in 2010, keeping in line with the Government of India guidelines, which suggests that CSR may be followed more as compliance, or at least compliance has a large influence on its CSR activities. The main areas of focus in its CSR activities include education, water supply, healthcare, social empowerment, employment generation, infrastructure support, and financial assistance to NGOs (Press Information Bureau, Government of India, 2012).

A five-year (2007–12) impact assessment of CIL's CSR activities suggests the extent to which the corporation engaged with local communities. CIL spends 5 percent of the retained earnings of the previous year (or a minimum of Rs 5/- per ton of coal production of the previous year) on its CSR activities. Out of the total CSR budget, 15 percent and 8 percent are being collected separately for undertaking developmental works for Scheduled Cast and Scheduled Tribes populations respectively (Parliament of India, Rajya Sabha, 2012). An analysis of the CSR budget and actual expenditures on CSR suggest that CIL is not fully utilizing the budgets allocated for CSR. For example, in 2011–12 only 57 percent of the sanctioned budget of Rs 238.2 million was actually spent on CSR activities (Rs 135 million). While CSR budgets have increased from Rs 72.5 million in 2008–9 (CAGR growth of 33.1 percent), yet the CSR budget utilizations have only been an average of 55 percent during this period. In addition, during 2011, CIL faced criticism from the Indian accounting watchdog, Comptroller and Auditor General of India (CAG), for inadequate fund allotment toward CSR, which was less than 1 percent of Rs 310,623.6 million net profit earned during 2004–10. The CAG in its report stated: "The budget allocation of Rs 211.80 crore [crore = 10 million] for community and peripheral development during the period 2004–10 was only 0.7% of the aggregate net profit of Rs 31,062.36 crore of CIL over the same period" (Press Trust of India, 2011).

The company's involvement with local communities is confined to 15 km of its areas of operation, whether its coalmines or headquarters. A breakdown of the cumulative CSR expenditure during 2008–12 on CSR activities suggests that almost 50 percent of it was spent on infrastructure projects such as building rural roads, water supply amenities, and community centers. Almost 14 percent was spent on healthcare and education each, and the remaining funds on other development works. A meager 1 percent was spent on self-employment generation activities. This breakdown suggests that CIL's CSR projects are supplementing government projects on infrastructure development (e.g., Rs 71 million was used only for building roads), rather than being used for capacity-building among poor people at the bottom of the pyramid in India. As an example, CIL conducted 40 training programs in 2011–12 to train poor people in areas such as motor driving and computer education. As an example of CSR in healthcare, CIL adopted girl students from poor families and spent Rs 12 million on their health and education. Other than this, health check-up camps were organized that benefited 1,856 girls. All-in-all it seems CIL, due to its public sector ownership, has treated its CSR merely as compliance, rather than as a strategy for making a socio-economic impact on the poor sections of the Indian society.

Implications and conclusions

This chapter considered the CSR practices of 200 major corporations operating in India and gave a glimpse of the areas in which the Indian companies work as part of their CSR practices based on a multitude of approaches adopted by them. Most companies in India engage with local communities in the vicinity of their areas of operations, and the beneficiaries of CSR activities are generally the local population. Most often we found that most benefits of such local engagement go to people who are displaced or affected by the operations of the companies, such as when a new manufacturing plant is being built. For example, a pharmaceutical company organizes a medical camp for the poor near its manufacturing facilities, or a power plant takes an initiative of planting trees in the areas near its facilities. In the case of CIL also, we found that 2012–13 CSR targets for the company include training people who have been displaced since their lands were acquired by the company for its operations. In that sense, CSR activities of most firms were found to be more of compensation in kind, rather than being compliance to the regulatory guidelines. In the case of most private sector firms, especially MNCs, we found that they have a four-pronged strategy for CSR that ranges from ethics in pure business to pure philanthropy, with social objectives sandwiched in between. We found that most MNCs and private enterprises operating in India go beyond CSR as a compensation model, or CSR as a compliance model, and view it as a future market development model. CSR as a model of future market development is conspicuous by its absence in the segment of public sector companies, since these companies do not have to engage in competitive marketing practices, and have assured markets, or a strong government patronage.

The managers of Indian companies try to claim the legitimacy of their operations to the population in the vicinity of their plants, while the products are sold across the country, with consumers and shareholders spread across the world. The companies should try to develop scalable models of CSR that can be extended across the nation using local NGOs in each geographical area, a very helpful resource yet at a low cost. Scalable models will be helpful in expanding the socio-economic impact of CSR activities of corporations. Larger socio-economic value creation can then be equated as a proxy for legitimacy that goes beyond local communities in the near vicinity of the business operations. But taking a more holistic view of CSR is vital since currently, in our sample of companies, we observe that most firms have adopted the same sectors for CSR (e.g., healthcare or education), and then they spend CSR budgets on a project-to-project basis (creating some health camps, adopting a village, building a road, maintaining a facility, and so on). Such project-to-project variations in CSR initiatives are seemingly devoid of a strategy, and also show a lack of synergy with business operations. An attempt to align their business strategy with CSR strategy will help firms to leverage their CSR expenditures. We suggest taking a return on investment (ROI) approach may help, where returns can be calculated in terms of socio-economic value creation, and investments calculated as the opportunity costs for society. Therefore, we suggest a directional change in perspective and that Indian corporations take in planning and strategizing their CSR operations.

The Indian corporations through their CSR activities, along with governmental support, can go a long way to address the issues faced by the distressed sections of society. In light of the CSR bill, ready to be passed by the Indian legislature, we may observe a revolution in the developmental activities of backward sections of Indian society through the CSR activities of Indian corporations. However, it's about time that firms operating in India started to look at CSR as a strategy to create socio-economic impact and not merely view it as regulatory compliance, or as compensation for society.

References

Arora, B. and Puranik, R. (2004) "A review of corporate social responsibility in India," *Development*, 47(3): 93–100.

Bharti Foundation (2012) Available online at www.airtel.in/wps/wcm/connect/Bharti Foundation/bhartifoundation/home/pg_bhartifoundationhome (accessed October 5, 2012).

Carroll, A.B. (1991) "The Pyramid of Corporate Social Responsibility: toward the moral management of organizational stakeholders," *Business Horizons*, (34)4: 39–48.

Chahoud, T., Emmerling, J., Kolb, D., Kubina, I., Repinski, G., and Schlager, C. (2007) "Corporate social and environmental responsibility in India: assessing the UN Global Compact's role," German Development Institute. Available online at www. die-gdi.de/CMS-Homepage/openwebcms3.nsf/(ynDK_contentByKey)/ENTR-BMDUB/$FILE/Studies%2026.pdf (accessed August 10, 2012).

DLF Foundation (2009) Available online at www.dlffoundation.in/dlf/wcm/connect/ dlf_foundation/DLF_foundation/Top_Links/home/ (accessed October 8, 2012).

Essar Foundation (2012) *Guiding Principles*. Available online at www.essar.com/ section_level1.aspx?cont_id=VEKh2+iXDaE= (accessed October 8, 2012).

Goldman Sachs (2003) "Dreaming with BRICS: path to 2050," Global Economics Paper No. 99. Available online at www2.goldmansachs.com/ideas/brics/book/ 99-dreaming.pdf (accessed November 6, 2012).

GlaxoSmithKline-India (2012) *Corporate Social Responsibility*. Available online at www.gsk-india.com/corporate-index.html (accessed October 8, 2012).

Gopinath, C. (2011) "Trusteeship as a moral foundation for business," Bombay Sarvodaya Mandal. Available at www.mkgandhi-sarvodaya.org/articles/trusteeship4. htm (accessed August 10, 2012).

Gray, R., Kouhy, R., and Lavers, S. (1995) "Corporate social and environmental reporting: a review of the literature and a longitudinal study of UK disclosure," *Accounting, Auditing and Accountability Journal*, 8(2): 47–77.

Havells (2012) "CSR initiatives." Available online at www.havells.com/Csr-Initiatives. aspx (accessed October 10, 2012).

HCL (2012) "Power of one." Available online at www.hcltech.com/socially-responsible-business/repay-society/power-one (accessed August 10, 2012).

Holsti, O.R. (1969) *Content Analysis for the Social Sciences and Humanities*, Reading, MA: Addison-Wesley.

IndiaCan (2012) "CSR activities." Available online at www.indiacan.com/csr-activities.asp (accessed August 10, 2012).

Indian Express, The (2012) "New Cos Bill should ensure 2% spend on CSR: house panel," August 14. Available online at www.indianexpress.com/news/new-cos-bill-should-ensure-2-spend-on-csr-house-panel/987886/2 (accessed September 10, 2012).

Jet Airways Community Services (2012) *About Us*. Available online at www. jetairways.com/EN/IN/AboutUs/CommunityServices.aspx (accessed October 5, 2012).

Kolk, A. (2000) *Economics of Environmental Management*, Harlow: Financial Times Prentice Hall.

Mohanty, H. (2012) "'Tribals' protest halts Hindalco's bauxite mining at Mali Hill," *Business Standard*, August 14. Available online at www.business-standard.com/ india/news/tribals-protest-halts-hindalcos-bauxite-mining-at-mali-hill/483176/ (accessed September 10, 2012).

Parliament of India, Rajya Sabha (2012) "Question number 2645, answered on 30.04.2012." Available online at http://164.100.47.4/newrsquestion/ShowQn.aspx (accessed October 20, 2012).

Press Information Bureau, Government of India (2012) "Coal India Ltd sets aside Rs 553 crores for CSR activities," May 14. Available online at http://pibmumbai.gov.in/ scripts/detail.asp?releaseId=E2012PR3257 (accessed October 20, 2012).

Press Trust of India (2011) "CIL draws flak from CAG for inadequate CSR spending," *Business Standard*, September 7. Available online at www.business-standard. com/india/news/cil-draws-flakcag-for-inadequate-csr-spending/146188/on (accessed October 20, 2012).

Ranbaxy (2012) *Corporate Social Responsibility*. Available online at www.ranbaxy. com/socialresposbility/socialcommitment.aspx (accessed August 10, 2102).

Sapru, R.K. (2008) *Administrative Theories and Management Thought*, 2nd edn, New Delhi: Prentice-Hall of India.

Sweeney, L. and Coughlan, J. (2008) "Do different industries report Corporate Social Responsibility differently? An investigation through the lens of stakeholder theory," *Journal of Marketing Communications*, 14(2): 113–24.

Unilever Foundation (2012) Available online at www.hul.co.in/aboutus/foundation/ (accessed October 5, 2012).

Upwanshi, A. (2012) "ONGC corporate social responsibility," CSR World. Available online at www.csrworld.net/ongc-corporate-social-responsibility.asp (accessed August 12, 2012).

World Business Council on Sustainable Development (2000) "Corporate social responsibility: making good business sense," January. Available online at www. wbcsd.org (accessed August 14, 2012).

4 CSR development and local community in Japan

Satoshi Mizobata, Olga Bobrova, and Kyoko Fukukawa

Studies of corporate social responsibility (CSR) tend to draw attention to issues of globalization, which relates to the transnational status of corporations, the standardization of professional CSR discourse, and the perceived increase of the global impact of operations. At the same time, however, CSR can be examined from the angle of local community, as a developing socio-structure with its own unique set of representatives who bring forward initiatives in connection with companies operating in the region. Stakeholders representing local community have a choice of which company to cooperate with. It is likely in the near future we will begin to see growing competition between companies for the right to work with local stakeholders as partners. Such a trend is evident in the Japanese context, and is particularly pertinent following the Great East Japan Earthquake 2011, which devastated the lives of whole communities up and down the coastline of the Tōhoku region and led to the Fukushima nuclear disaster, which raised both local and international alarm.

Following the earthquake, there has been increased pressure on companies to conduct CSR activities in line with the remedial operations rebuilding towns and villages, with the view to returning normalcy to whole communities. The close business–society relationship in Japan is well documented (Dore, 1973; Fukukawa and Manghani, 2013). Banks, for example, have long maintained a relationship with the community, including local SMEs. Yet, the earthquake provided highly visible opportunities for corporations to engage in community. In this chapter, based on the published statements of key Japanese business societies (and other sources), we consider the recent development of CSR in Japan, and the specific role of the local community. Ronald P. Dore (1973) stressed the specific community character and social function of Japanese corporations, as being remarkably different from those in the USA and Europe. In part, then, we consider here how these distinctive features have gone on to influence CSR development in Japan. In particular, we examine the basic features of local community in Japan and the role of business associations promoting CSR, and provide examples of partnerships between corporations and their local stakeholders, as well as considering the constraints on CSR development.

One assumption made of CSR in Japan is that it comes to intervene "when the government cannot manage the public policy issues" (Fujii and Shintani, 2008: 5). In this respect we might think more readily of the significance of philanthropy for Japanese companies as a starting point in making a social contribution to local communities. A distinct feature of company engagement following the earthquake of 2011 is high levels of philanthropic and charitable contributions made by companies to those affected. In one survey of 225 Japanese companies listed on the Nikkei Stock Average Index, the findings show high levels of "donations to the suffers (90%) and aid supply (58%)," as well as "business service with no charge (43%) and charity campaign towards customers (29%)" (Takaura, 2013: 201). However, drawing on the work of Porter and Kramer (2011), who advocate a shift from CSR to CSV—creating shared value, Takaura (2013) notes it is not only the giving of aid that has been significant, but also a growing desire and expectation for companies to engage within the local context in order to create shared value. A criticism made of Japanese companies in the aftermath of the earthquake was that not enough effort was made to align core business with social benefit for those who suffered; though of the listed companies examined, there is nonetheless some evidence of attempts "to restore the suffered communities through social business (3%) or employment (3%)" (Takaura, 2013: 201). Regardless of the actual levels of engagement in evidence, we can discern an important shift in the debates about the understanding and implementation of CSR in Japan. Echoing broader conceptual debates, a key idea being raised is the pursuit of social responsibility *through* a company's core business, rather than through the mere gesture of contributing aid.

CSR in Japan

Japanese CSR is frequently framed as an institutional import from the USA and Europe (Ebashi 2009: 3–7), and certainly much of the terminology has been adopted without the need of translation. Yet, the concept of CSR in various forms has long been a point of discussion for Japanese business associations. The Japan Business Federation, Nippon Keidanren, formerly referred to a like-minded notion in 1973 and thereafter developed guidance in such spheres as business ethics, contribution to society, and environmental protection. During the tail end of the twentieth century Japanese businesses' cooperation with local communities and other stakeholders was developing, but not in a systematic way. We might say, every company in Japan was looking for its own unique way of conducting social responsibility. By 2004, greater coherence was emerging. Keidanren issued a report, *Basic Concepts for the Promotion of CSR* (Keidanren 2004a), which considered global trends such as globalization and innovation of information technology, changes in consumer behavior patterns, evaluation of investments, change of consciousness of employees, and legalization processes. The report raised a question of the promotion of voluntary CSR and actually updated the *Charter of Corporate Behavior* (Keidanren, 2004b) as a guideline for CSR.

In response to the demands of ISO, the Japanese government and the Japanese Standard Association established the CSR Standardization Committee in 2002. Keidanren, however, stressed the importance of CSR promotion by the private sector to operate on a voluntary basis. According to Keidanren, in 2004 the importance of CSR was equally underlined in the USA, where attitudes were generally moving against the need for ISO regulations. Also, in Europe there were no new regulations regarding CSR. To begin with, then, there was a movement against ISO regulation. Keidanren was against standardization in order to preserve the voluntary nature of CSR, allowing each company to develop practice in its own way (Keidanren, International Affairs Bureau, 2004: 34–6; Fukada, 2004: 58–9). It can also be argued, many companies were against the legalization and standardization of CSR due to financial reasons, as well as due to concerns to hold to traditional company philosophies.

Nonetheless, the situation gradually altered. In 2005, in a report titled *Tools Promoting CSR* (Keidanren, 2005), the following six key areas were associated with the CSR concept: (1) business ethics and compliance; (2) information; (3) safety and quality; (4) human rights and labor environment; (5) environmental protection; and (6) contribution to society. Notably, activities contributing to the development of local communities were represented by all sorts of local voluntary activities (opening of public facilities, support of local NGOs, street-cleaning campaigns, philanthropy, and other volunteer activities), assistance in organizing local events, and support of local elementary schools. Thus, by the time ISO26000 was approved in Japan in 2010, there was marked interest in CSR, with leading companies having launched voluntary, dedicated CSR schemes (see Fukukawa and Teramoto, 2009).

With the introduction of ISO26000, Keidanren has altered its stance, to hold a positive attitude toward ISO. It amended the *Charter of Corporate Behavior*, making the following declaration:

> While the presence of corporations is indispensable for the economic development of society in terms of their capacity to generate income and employment, corporations should realize the great impacts they have on society as well as the environment and take the initiative to discharge their CSR.
>
> (Keidanren, 2010)

The charter issued ten key principles relevant to the regional community. These covered disclosure of corporate information, respecting the rights of employees, environmental issues, community involvement activities, and confronting anti-social forces and organizations that pose a threat to the order and security of civil society (Keidanren, 2010). Keidanren's view was to harmonize a Japanese CSR standard with global standards, and to broaden its scope based on changes in view of the current economic and social situation.

The aftermath of the 2011 Great East Japan Earthquake gave Keidanren further cause to reconsider its policy recommendations, and led to the publication of a statement on the building of a "resilient society" (Keidanren, 2012). The statement inevitably evoked the idea of strong business–society relations, but also, importantly, it was articulated through both an international and national business perspective:

> Building a resilient society that is more robust against natural disasters is indispensable and is also a major premise for recovering international trust and attracting investment. Keidanren shall contribute to building a more resilient society with the world's highest level of disaster prevention by fully utilizing the private sectors' technology and the wisdom.
>
> (Keidanren, 2012)

Thus, from March 2012, companies became obliged not only to take preventive measures toward natural disasters, but also to implement a course of action in response to the consequences of such occurrences, with the view to securing full recovery within affected areas. Action in this case refers to the collaboration of companies, state, and local communities, involving the sharing of information and infrastructure facilities among government officials and citizens (Keidanren, 2012). In light of such a statement to secure the notion of a "resilient society," and given that Japan is at high risk of suffering the consequences of earthquake and associated events, the development of socio-economic systems resistant to natural disasters has become a central pillar of CSR among Japanese companies.

The Japan Association of Corporate Executives, Keizai Doyukai, has also held a long-term interest in CSR. In fact, adopting the slogan "companies are organs of society" as far back as 1956, Doyukai has long declared the importance of a socially orientated self-consciousness among executives. In the 1970s, the association concentrated on issues of lack of trust between companies and local communities as caused by environmental pollution and defective products. In March 2003, Doyukai explicitly stressed the importance of CSR in the *15th Corporate White Paper*. Since then it has regularly published its own self-assessment report, *CSR of Companies*. Doyukai's formulation of the concept of CSR is that it is not limited to the idea of obeying laws or being involved in charity activity, but is in fact more about the impact a company has on society *through* its business activity. If such activity is of "value," both company and society can develop sustainably.

Recent formulations of CSR as based on value creation echo the view taken by Doyukai when they situate CSR as part of core business activity, so as to cover a range of issues relating to health, an aging society, natural disasters, barrier-free society, security, food safety, etc. (Keizai Doyukai, 2008a). Based on this view, Doyukai went on to propose a *New Style of Japanese Management* (Keizai Doyukai, 2008b), which is considered more adept at connecting with a global business community; in addition, the creation of value through CSR activities is argued to have the potential to enhance international competitiveness (Fukukawa and Teramoto, 2009: 139). Such a formulation, then, is to be viewed as "offensive" CSR (Keizai Doyukai, 2008a), which fundamentally is based on the practice of CSR *through* core business activity; a form of CSR aiming to fulfill both commercial objectives and the beliefs and needs of local communities; and a measure of CSR based on the idea that companies possess goodwill to create value by improving the existing society.

It is important to acknowledge a bias in an account of CSR from the viewpoint of business society. While business circles have been proactive in formulating and adopting a view on CSR, and despite such formulations clearly referring to the interests of local community, it does not directly reflect the local community (a point that will be developed further in the next section). In Japan, for example, relations with non-profit organizations (NPOs) and non-governmental organizations (NGOs) are relatively weak, and more generally, the structure of collaborative relations of stakeholders within the local community is underdeveloped (Umeda, 2006: 101). However, from the year 2000 onwards, having been influenced by the environmentalist movement, local communities started acting as more prominent stakeholders; as such, changes in CSR practices became explicit. In particular, the aftermath of the Great East Japan Earthquake stressed the importance of local communities and raised matters to a new level; many parties concerned underlined the importance of functions of the local community authorities (including Keidanren, as acknowledged with the quote above from its statement, "Toward a more resilient society" (March 5, 2012). With respect to measures for dealing with disasters, the emerging consensus was that companies should not only act to maintain their business and secure infrastructure, but should actively promote CSR activity. In light of which, local communities, as stakeholders (albeit formerly possessing only passive and limited rights), became impossible to ignore.

The earthquake of 2011 demanded a reconsideration of the relations between companies and local communities in respect to CSR, not least because many companies suffered direct damages of infrastructure. The restoration of services and infrastructure—as an act of survival for all involved—became the most important component of CSR practice in the Tōhoku region. In short, recovery of local communities was inseparable from the recovery of companies and supply chains. It is perhaps no surprise, then, in a new report, *CSR in the Global Era* (Keizai Doyukai, 2011), published after the earthquake and attuned to the broader agenda of globalization, Doyukai explicitly pitches CSR as an alliance of local authorities and local communities, and in conjunction, based on the business activity of companies.

Japanese business society

CSR has developed in Japan in relation to global trends, yet retains its own distinctiveness, marking it out as different from that of Western Europe and the USA. Japan's distinctive civic society, the tradition of business philosophy, and quality of markets may explain some of these differences. Having considered the view of Japanese business society in the previous section, it is evident that a key difference of CSR relates to Japan's specific corporate system, and model of corporate governance (Aoki, 1995; Dore, 2006). While managers in US and European companies have responsibility mainly to shareholders and to the employees, the managers in Japanese corporations have responsibility jointly to employees in a "quasi-community company" (Dore, 2006: 202), so that the corporation is regarded as a collective of its employees, and a structured community striving for the same purpose by prescriptive means.

An understanding of business–society relations in Japan needs to take into account the structure of local community, inequality among regions, and the distinctive communal character of the Japanese corporate system. So-called "castle towns" (see below) and industry clusters are two main examples of the country's typically strong business–society relations. Nonetheless, the local community has traditionally had only weak influence on corporations. Companies have typically played a paternal role in local society, which has not necessarily lent itself well to a dialogical relationship. Through the historical development of CSR, the status of local communities and other stakeholders in relation to companies has been relatively weak (due in part to the fact that CSR in Japan emerged with a specific focus on attending to environmental damage). Companies were also more focused on addressing matters of business ethics following the expansion of philanthropic activity and the reform of corporate governance, aimed at tackling the aberrations of corporate scandals. Companies, as taxpayers and job-creators, have come to hold dominant and favorable positions in the regions in which they operate, and have tended to expect preferential treatment by the local communities. The nuclear power industry, for example, has established "company towns," whereby a town is entirely tailored to the needs of a power station. In these cases, a company would identify itself with a local community (and ensure safety, etc.), yet would not have necessarily viewed members of the local community as stakeholders.

In some cases, *jōkamachi* (business castle towns), or company towns, have actually replaced or at least reconfigured a local community. In Japan there are many company towns, typically associated with specific industries, such as textiles, paper manufacturing, automotive industry, metallurgy, mining, the energy sector, among others. The nuclear power plant accident at Fukushima in 2011 brought into the spotlight the constitution of a company town, demonstrating the fact that many citizens and related industries are integrated and dependent upon the central business of the town. The sustainability of companies here overlaps and strongly depends on whether the local community will continue to exist safely or not. This strong linkage partially explains the requests for governmental aid in forms of subsidies for business that may be characterized as a form of assistance to local communities through companies.

Industrial clusters of the "Silicon Valley" mold represent industrial and research bases that include local companies and scientific institutions. They can be regarded as another example of the relations between companies and local communities. It is important to note, the industrial activity of a company upon entering a region (and its community) is not limited to the region's borders. As the case with the Japanese *keiretsu* and sub-contracting system shows, a particular region (and its local community) is in fact embedded in a wider supply chain and therefore is linked with other regions (other local communities). This situation became obvious in 2011 with both a devastating flood in Thailand and the Great East Japan Earthquake. These natural disasters led to parts of the supply chain being cut off, forcing many Japanese companies to reorganize their intra-firm division of labor and so making apparent their dependence on local communities of different regions.

There are also cases where many independent companies (mostly small and medium-sized enterprises—SMEs) concentrate in a particular region and exercise their competitive advantages. The coming together of independent companies (i.e., not affiliated to big corporations or parent companies) often results in a common sharing of information and socially common infrastructure being facilitated in the local community. Some typical examples of these are Higashi Osaka City and Ota Ward of Tokyo, where there is a concentration of SMEs in the machinery and metallurgical manufacturing sectors. From the late 1990s the creation of networks of innovative SMEs has been actively promoted through governmental policy on industrial accumulation of companies, revitalizing the local area, introducing venture capital, and focusing on international competitiveness. In 2011, the Ministry of Economy, Trade and Industry (METI) initiated an industrial cluster project to strengthen the competitiveness of Japanese industry, explicitly stipulating that industrial accumulation should become the pulling power of regional economies; and which was partially implemented in the IT, biotechnology, and environmental sectors. Simultaneously, a scientific technology promotion policy launched the so-called intellectual clusters, examples of which relate to biotechnology in Sapporo and a software cluster in Hamamatsu (Nagayama, 2010).

Elsewhere, in response to external environmental conditions such as the shift of industrial sites of big enterprises or stagnation in the industry, there are other examples of the establishment of relations between companies and local communities in the 2000s. In Arita city (Saga prefecture), which is known for its production of consumer goods such as pottery and furniture, there was an initiative to establish a local brand. In Suwa city (Nagano prefecture), a machinery equipment cluster emerged specializing in the manufacturing of precise and minute equipment. And in Beppu (Oita prefecture), the tourism industry developed together with the regeneration of the city. These are examples of what the Japanese describe as an *aratana* community, meaning "new community"—a term originally used by Shibayama (2012: 11) to denote a form of community associated with the sharing of a sense of crisis, and involving autonomous organizations, open communities, and interactive relations among various stakeholders. The communities in this context have come together around the restoration of regional industries, which can be seen as initiatives of local communities supported by companies (Shibayama, 2012).

As cases relating to the development of CSR, these examples of company towns and clusters can be seen as determined by regional economics and social structures. Government policy and initiatives cannot be detached from local community. Traditionally, local finance and local public administration have been strongly supervised by the central government in Japan, which can affect local communities through financial support, public policy and industrial policy, and the engagement of individual politicians. Regardless of the specificities of a local community, companies cannot ignore the idea of CSR as contributing to local community; as such, CSR must be based on the harmonization of integrated interests of various stakeholders with respect to regional and sub-regional conditions. Over a long period of time the relationship between local communities and companies might be described as companies being blended into the communities. However, as society becomes more complex and bureaucratic, this relationship results in a more fragmented and administrative experience. Arguably, the advent of the earthquake—and its totalizing effects on individuals, communities, and corporations—prompted an opportunity for rediscovery and new means of engaging collectively.

CSR for local communities

The local community is generally regarded as an important stakeholder for a company. Being engaged with a local community the company takes certain social responsibilities, acknowledges its impact on the regions where it operates, and may get various benefits. Carroll and Buchholtz write that "stakeholder engagement may be seen as an approach by which companies implement the transactional level of strategic management capability" (Carroll and Buchholtz, 2009: 86). Or, perhaps more practically, we can consider the definition used by the United Nations Environment Programme (UNEP): "stakeholder engagement can be described as an organization's efforts to understand and involve stakeholders and their concerns in its activities and decision-making processes" (Stakeholder Research Associates Canada, 2005: 6).

One particular example of social cohesion and development between local community and business is in the finance sector. In Japan, local financial institutions not only provide finance, tax payments, and secure employment, but also constitute a relationship with the local community in the sphere of science and education, culture, social welfare, street cleaning, and beautification, and actively publish environmental reports for public awareness and debate (Furue, 2011: 23).

The government recommended at the beginning of the 2000s that local financial institutions should contribute to the development of local community for their long-term survival. Moreover, financial and social problems existing in the community give rises to a demand for CSR activities from local financial institutions. The importance of the collaboration with the local communities here might be explained by a willingness to eliminate social problems, prevent huge debts and bank transfer scams, and strengthen environmental protection.

94   *Satoshi Mizobata* et al.

According to Furue (2011: 25), local financial institutions "by including CSR in their business activities, pursue the type of CSR based on both resolving problems of the local community and improvement of the company's value"; and again, significantly, the argument here is based on CSR as part of core business activities with a view to long-term gains. Furue (2011: 26–8) suggests that positive estimated results from such practices are the company's image enhancement (increase of customers' satisfaction), secure employment of skilled workers, and improvement of the motivation of employees.

Financial services can yield new social value when working within communities. In Japan they present an interesting example of local CSR development. In the sphere of environmental protection, for example, there are so-called "eco-businesses" advocating eco-friendly, energy efficiency financing and socially responsible investments (SRI). Shiga Bank has developed its own environment assessment system and provides financing at beneficial interest rates to eco-friendly and earthquake-proof housing projects. Further examples include a new grant-in-aid (subsidy) system initiated by local communities (working with the Senshyu Ikeda Bank), and measures by Nigata 4th Bank, which offers special interest rates for reconstruction and revival works following the Mid Nigata Prefecture Earthquake.

Other community measures—initiated by Ouita Bank, Gamagori Credit Association, Fukuoka Bank, Tama Credit Association, and others—include improved access to bank branches for the elderly and disabled, as well as the provision of employment for those with special needs (Furue, 2011). In addition, cooperative-type financial institutions, by implementing their businesses in local communities, considerably strengthen their CSR practices through strong adherence to the local communities. Business matching and additional services for the clients of Shinkin Depository, assistance to debtors of Labor Depository, and promotion of agriculture in regions by the Agricultural Cooperative are typical examples. Companies and financial institutions regard local customers within the aged population and those ecologically aware as key stakeholders. Again, these examples relate to CSR as part of core business.

Of course, it is not just the local financial institutions who engaged with infrastructural restoration following the 2011 earthquake in Tōhoku region. Many companies prefaced their CSR reports with a direct reference to the Great East Japan Earthquake and detailed a range of activities, such as participating in street cleaning works, improvement of city infrastructure, providing assistance to the education process, elaborating measures to tackle the disaster consequences and exchange information, and organizing cultural and charity events. Moreover, though not directly connected to CSR measures, the establishment of industrial accumulative bases to pursue goals of the up-coming new industries in local communities has in part been related to the restoration process. Needless to say, the active participation of local SMEs in the creation of these new industries is indispensable (Niki, 2012).

Conclusion

This chapter charts developments in Japanese CSR, reflecting trends in corporate governance and the socio-economic system tied to the local level. In Japan, both Keidanren and Doyukai espouse CSR as a distinct Japanese style of management and point to its strengths (both the *Charter of Corporate Behavior* and *Value-creative CSR* can be characterized as products of the Japanese-style management system). In contrast to European society, where NGOs play a clear role in promoting CSR and civil society, Japanese CSR emerged not from within, but rather was imported from the "outside" and its restrictive role is—at least early on—quite prominent. Various factors have determined this specificity, but two are worth noting.

First, stagnation of the Japanese economy for the last 20 years and deflation sharpened the sensitivity and response of companies in bearing severe costs related to CSR. In turn, the emergence of "offensive CSR" (Keizai Doyukai, 2008a) and the inclusion of CSR into a company's management strategy are notable outcomes. One common measure of the scale of CSR engagement relates to environmental reporting. A questionnaire conducted by the Japan Finance Corporation in July 2010 (Matsubara, 2011; Takeuchi, 2011) shows that two-thirds of the companies (from its sample of 6,828 Japanese firms) had undertaken environmental measures, of which half implemented these on a voluntary basis; 23 percent of companies implemented no measures due to lack of rules and regulations and other reasons. Close to 60 percent of those respondents who engaged in active environmental measures stated that companies introduced eco-friendly measures in order to decrease costs; while only 40 percent gave CSR as the reasoning behind the measures. It is also interesting that around only 10 percent of respondents cited pressure from customer expectations—note that respondents gave multiple responses, and so each of these factors could yield combined pressure for change. Nonetheless, the responses suggest reduction of costs and competitiveness as an overridingly strong factor (Matsubara, 2011: 73); while environmental concerns from the company's customers and suppliers can still point to the fact that CSR involves intra-company networks and easily spreads among related companies. Implementing environmental measures can undoubtedly bring positive results, such as cost reductions, the improvement of a company's image, and the strengthening of employee motivation. However, obstacles such as the non-transparency of results and effects, heavy expenses compared with merits, additional costs for systems of certification, and lack of information can lead to significant questions over the sustainability of these measures in the future.

Second, despite the fact that, after a disaster such as the earthquake of 2011, the importance of NGOs/NPOs is reconsidered along with the nature of ties within the local community, the dependence of local communities on the government remains very strong in Japan and sometimes is regarded as an obstacle to closer cooperation with business. One example to note relates to the perceived failure of the government to tackle the consequences of the nuclear accident in 2011. The role of government arguably overrides that of corporations, thereby hindering opportunities to establish relationships with local communities. In broader terms, it can be argued that the social environment as a driver to promote CSR among companies is still relatively weak. Nevertheless, as this chapter has sought to show, CSR activities within local communities have evolved in various spheres and the measures adaptive to the communities have taken on a long-term character, as linked to the core business of companies. Of course, this is not to suggest there are no conflicts of interest among companies, community, and some specific stakeholders, only that there are signs of shifting patterns and trends.

In many cases, CSR is now a built-in part of management strategy and generally reflects a company's interests, such as reduction of costs and consolidation of a company's positive image. Nonetheless, while Japanese CSR was eventually brought on stream through a process of legalization and standardization based on global rules, the originality of Japanese business ethics considerably influences the concept of CSR that continues to reveal the strong impact of tradition and path-dependency. Japanese CSR in many cases is deeply rooted in a company's philosophy and mission statements. In examining the Japanese context it is soon evident that while it is difficult to impose partnership with the local community by simply importing new institutional practices, the traditions of local communities—and the events that befall them—have the potential to develop and strengthen CSR for all involved.

References

Aoki, M. (1995) *Evolution and Diversity of Economic Systems*, Tokyo: Toyokeizaishin-pousha.

Carroll, A. and Buchholtz, A. (2009) *Business and Society: Ethics, sustainability and stakeholder management*, 8th edn, Mason, OH: South-Western Publishing.

Dore, R. (1973) *British Factory—Japanese Factory*, Berkeley, CA: University of California Press. Translated (in Japanese) by Yamanouchi, Y. and Nagayasu, K. (1987), Tokyo: Chikuma.

Dore, R. (2006) *For Whom Companies Exist*, Tokyo: Iwanami Shoten (in Japanese).

Ebashi, T. (ed.) (2009) *CSR*, Tokyo: Hoseidaigaku (in Japanese).

Fujii, T. and Shintani, D. (2008) *CSR in Asia and CSR in Japan*, Tokyo: Nikkagiren (in Japanese).

Fukada, S. (2004) "Dramatically increasing international dialogue," *Keizai Trend*, 9: 58–9 (in Japanese).

Fukukawa, K. and Manghani, S. (2013) "Transformations and translations of Japanese business-society," in MacIntosh, M. (ed.) *The National Transition*, Sheffield: Greenleaf Publishing.

Fukukawa, K. and Teramoto, Y. (2009) "Understanding Japanese CSR: the reflections of managers in the field of global operations," *Journal of Business Ethics*, 85: 133–46.

Furue, S. (2011) *CSR Strategy of the Local Financial Organizations*, Tokyo: Shinhyouron (in Japanese).

Keidanren (2004a) *Basic Concepts for the Promotion of CSR*, February 17. Available online at www.keidanren.or.jp/japanese/policy/2004/017.html (in Japanese) (accessed April 6, 2013).

Keidanren (2004b) *Charter of Corporate Behavior*, May 18. Available online at www.keidanren.or.jp/japanese/policy/cgcb/charter2004.html (in Japanese) (accessed April 6, 2013). The original was adopted on September 14, 1991, and the last one was revised on September 14, 2010.

Keidanren (2005) *Tools Promoting CSR*, October 4. Available online at www.keidanren.or.jp/japanese/policy/csr/tool.pdf (in Japanese) (accessed April 6, 2013).

Keidanren (2010) *Charter of Corporate Behavior*. Available online at www.keidanren.or.jp/japanese/policy/cgcb/charter2010.html (accessed April 6, 2013).

Keidanren (2012) "Toward a more resilient society," March 5. Available online at www.keidanren.or.jp/en/policy/2012/013_summary.pdf (accessed April 6, 2013).

Keidanren, International Affairs Bureau (2004) "Trends of CSR in foreign countries," *Keizai Trend*, 7: 34–6 (in Japanese).

Keizai Doyukai (2008a) *Social Changes through Value-creative CSR*, May 28. Available online at www.doyukai.or.jp/policyproposals/articles/2008/pdf/080529b.pdf (in Japanese) (accessed May 20, 2013).

Keizai Doyukai (2008b) *Creating a New Style of Japanese Management*, July. Available online at www.doyukai.or.jp/en/policyproposals/2008/pdf/080702a.pdf (accessed May 20, 2013).

Keizai Doyukai (2011) *CSR in the Global Era*, April 4. Available online at www.doyukai.or.jp/en/policyproposals/2011/pdf/110404a.pdf (accessed April 6, 2013).

Matsubara, N. (2011) "Activities of environment problems in SMEs," *Journal of Japan Finance Corporation*, 11(May): 65–91 (in Japanese).

Nagayama, M. (2010) "New industrial cluster and regional advancement," in Yoshida, K. and Inouchi, N. (eds) *Regional Advancement and Small–Medium Enterprises*, Kyoto: Minerva (in Japanese).

Niki, K. (2012) *Do Not Make Unprofitable CSR*, Tokyo: Nihon Keizai Newspaper Co. (in Japanese).

Porter, M.E. and Kramer, M.R. (2011) "The big idea: creating shared value: how to reinvent capitalism—and unleash a wave of innovation and growth," *Harvard Business Review*, January–February: 2–17.

Shibayama, K. (2012) "Autonomous organizations as creating externality," *Journal of the Japan Finance Corporation*, 14(February): 1–24 (in Japanese).

Stakeholder Research Associates Canada (2005) *The Stakeholder Engagement Manual, vol. 1: The guide to practitioners' perspectives on stakeholder engagement*, Cobourg, Ontario: Stakeholder Research Associates, UNEP, and AccountAbility.

Takaura, Y. (2013) "The post-March 11 CSR in Japan: a survey on philanthropic activities of 225 Japanese companies listed on the Nikkei Stock Average Index to reconstruct the communities affected by the Great East Japan Earthquake 2011," *Journal of Japan Society for Business Ethics Study*, 20: 201–12.

Takeuchi, E. (2011) "Activities of environment problems in SMEs," *Journal of Japan Finance Corporation*, 12(August) (in Japanese).

Umeda, T. (2006) *How to Investigate Corporate Ethics*, Tokyo: NHK (in Japanese).

5 Exploring the potential of social entrepreneurship in developing countries

Fara Azmat

Using a case study of Waste Concern – an initiative of social entrepreneurs in Bangladesh – this chapter aims to deepen our understanding of social entrepreneurship and how it can lead to sustainable development in developing countries in the South Asian region (which includes India, Pakistan, Bangladesh, Sri Lanka, Nepal, Bhutan and the Maldives). Bangladesh, a country in South Asia, has all the characteristics of a developing country such as low per capita income, an agro-dominated economy, poor infrastructure, prevalence of poverty, a lack of adequate facilities for health, education and sanitation, political instability and environmental pollution (World Bank, 2009). Due to its sharing of similar economic, social, political and environmental contexts of developing countries, this chapter uses Bangladesh to justify the 'developing countries' context, particularly those in the same geographic region of South Asia. In this chapter, the term 'developing countries' is therefore used to refer to developing countries in South Asia.

Entrepreneurial actions can lead to both economic and social goals by reducing poverty and improving social indicators such as health and well-being, education and self-reliance (Patzelt and Shepherd 2010). Research further suggests that in developing countries, social entrepreneurs, through their innovative and creative strategies, are transforming social problems into manageable problems (Seelos and Mair 2005). The concept of social entrepreneurship appears to have been attracting a lot of attention recently; however, it has existed for quite some time with differing initiatives in an attempt to address social problems (Thompson *et al.* 2000; Alvord *et al.* 2004). The recent interest in social entrepreneurship can be explained by the fact that social entrepreneurs recognize opportunities in innovative ways and their intended outcomes are multifaceted, ranging from reducing poverty to promoting education or feeding the hungry, compared to initiatives of traditional entrepreneurs (Murphy and Coombes 2009: 333). Social entrepreneurs, like other entrepreneurs, also create value through innovation and creativity; however, they differ from business entrepreneurs as they focus on both social and economic goals rather than just economic goals.

Fowler (2000) describes social entrepreneurship as the creation of viable socio-economic structures, relations, institutions, organizations and practices that yield and sustain social benefits. Austin *et al.* (2006: 2) further broadly conceptualize social entrepreneurship as an 'innovative, social value creating activity that can occur within or across the non-profit, business, or government sectors'. In addition to the aspects of innovation and value creation, the definitions of social entrepreneurship mostly focus on economic and social goals and therefore refer to a double bottom line, rather than a triple bottom line, which has an additional focus on preserving the natural environment (Patzelt and Shepherd 2010). Although the definitions of social entrepreneurship emphasize that the double bottom line places social and economic aspects on an equal footing, most existing definitions imply that social entrepreneurship relates to exploiting opportunities for social change and improvement 'rather than traditional profit maximization' (Zahra *et al.* 2009: 521).

Social entrepreneurs share a passion for pursuing social issues, yet there remain major differences among them in terms of how they discover social needs, pursue social opportunities and make an impact on the broader social system (Zahra *et al.* 2009). Consequently, social entrepreneurship has been described as having multiple meanings, leading to three main approaches (Alvord *et al.* 2004). The first approach mainly views social entrepreneurship as combining commercial goals with social impacts; that is, using business skills and knowledge to create enterprises that carry out social purposes (Emerson and Twersky 1996). The second approach, on the other hand, views social entrepreneurs as focusing on innovative initiatives that place greater emphasis on social gains rather than economic gains (Dees 1998). The third approach (Alvord *et al.* 2004) views social entrepreneurship as a catalyst for social transformation by producing small changes in the short term, which, in turn, lead to bigger changes in the long term. For the purpose of this chapter, social entrepreneurship is defined as including all the three approaches, that is, combining commercial and business goals, focusing on innovative approaches and acting as a catalyst for social transformation. Further, social entrepreneurs in this chapter are defined as having a focus on a triple bottom line – economic, social and environmental aspects – rather than emphasizing a double bottom line that represents economic and social gains.

The chapter is organized as follows: first, a discussion on the 'bottom of pyramid' is provided to give a sense of the opportunities and challenges it offers for businesses. Next, the potential of social entrepreneurs in promoting sustainable development at the bottom of pyramid is explored in the context of developing countries. This is followed by a case study of Waste Concern in Bangladesh. This case study demonstrates the potential of social entrepreneurs in contributing to sustainable development by alleviating poverty and promoting environmental sustainability in Bangladesh, despite facing multiple obstacles. This is followed by a discussion on the case study, highlighting the factors that differentiate social entrepreneurs from mainstream entrepreneurs. The chapter concludes with avenues for further research.

The bottom of the pyramid and social entrepreneurs

Since its initial articulation (Prahalad and Hammond 2002; Prahalad and Hart 2002), the concept of bottom of the pyramid (BOP) has attracted both interest and controversy as a means for poverty alleviation through innovative business strategies (London 2007). The BOP 'represents the poor at the base of the global socio-economic ladder, who primarily transact in an informal market economy' (London 2007: 11). The population includes four billion low-income people around the world, who survive on incomes below US $3,000 per annum in local purchasing power (World Resource Institute 2007). The BOP involves the world's poorest population, yet it is increasingly being seen as an important emerging market that remains untapped and that businesses apparently cannot afford to ignore. Despite their relatively poor income, the BOP population collectively has substantial purchasing power constituting a US $5 trillion global consumer market (World Resource Institute 2007).

The BOP proposition has attracted a lot of interest, with the argument that the poor who lie at the bottom of the economic pyramid are potential customers, and provide a vast, untapped and unexploited opportunity (Karnani 2009: 2). The BOP proposition is based on the argument that by tapping the vast BOP markets through designing and developing customized products, MNCs can simultaneously make money and also curtail poverty (Jaiswal 2008). For example, Prahalad and Hart (2002: 14) argue that 'pursuing strategies for the bottom of the pyramid dissolves the conflict between proponents of free trade and global capitalism on one hand, and environmental and social sustainability on the other'. However, recent research also indicates that the BOP approach is associated with unrealistic expectations (Karnani 2011). Karnani (2011) further argues that the BOP is misunderstood and that solutions to date have not met true needs of the population as it comprises poor people – who have very little disposable income to purchase anything other than basic needs and cannot be treated as traditional customers. In order to help the population at the BOP level, Karnani (2011) challenges conventional thinking about poverty and proposes an eclectic approach to poverty reduction that emphasizes the need for business, government and civil society to partner together to create employment opportunities for the poor. In this context, the discussion in this chapter is timely as it provides insights into the potential of social entrepreneurs to partner with government and businesses in developing countries to fulfil the needs of the poor while making profit and producing environmental benefits.

While the BOP proposition has received considerable attention, much emphasis has been placed on how dealing with the BOP population has the potential to lead to economic and social benefits. However, whether these benefits translate into environmental benefits as well or whether dealing with the BOP population can also lead to environmental benefits remains under-researched, thus presenting a major gap in the literature. For example, research on the BOP is mainly focused on who is in the BOP (Hammond *et al.* 2007) and how BOP ventures need new market entry strategies, and on how to explore business development (Hart and London 2005). Also, much of the focus of the BOP literature has been on large multinational companies; individual social entrepreneurs have not attracted much attention, despite having the potential to create economic, social and environmental impacts at the BOP level. This is mainly because social entrepreneurs have the potential to come up with creative and innovative solutions to address the problems (Zahra *et al.* 2009), and change the systems that create and sustain poverty (Seelos and Mair 2005), with less likelihood of being discouraged by contextual constraints (Haugh 2005).

The role of social entrepreneurs in promoting sustainable development

The BOP approach has contributed to shifting the view about the poor as being 'customers' rather than being 'recipients of charity' (Seelos and Mair 2007). However, the social, cultural and institutional characteristics of the BOP make it a unique market. Due to their low socio-economic status, BOP populations are highly dependent on informal or subsistence livelihoods. They also have low levels of education and awareness of their rights, which limits their access to market information as well as financial services. In addition, they are dominated by the informal economy and are not integrated into the global market economy (Azmat and Samaratunge, 2013). As they are economically, culturally and socially deprived, they are vulnerable (Karnani 2009), implying that traditional products, services and management processes will not work and need to be changed or tailored to meet their specific needs. Some examples of products and services specifically designed for the BOP that have been successful to some extent include soaps and shampoos provided by Hindustan Lever in India in small sachets, single use or other packaging strategies that lower prices, and microcredit services offering small loans to people who have no financial assets in Bangladesh. This implies that businesses, in order to be profitable while catering to the needs of the poor, need to come up with innovative strategies as well as radically rethink the whole supply chain (Prahalad 2004). This therefore indicates the opportunity for involving social entrepreneurs at the BOP level in developing countries due to their potential to come up with innovative strategies to address social and economic problems.

Research suggests that social entrepreneurs generally have a more positive outlook than the population as a whole and, therefore, are less likely to be discouraged by contextual constraints (Haugh 2005). Haugh (2005: 4) further contends that in the context of financial limitations, bureaucracy and inflexibility of the market – common in developing countries, market opportunities fail to attract mainstream entrepreneurs; however, 'in these conditions, social enterprises perform a residual function and are instrumental in garnering resources and capitalising sub-market opportunities'. Consistent with this,

Seelos and Mair (2005) also report that in the context of developing countries where the government and market structures are not effectively developed, social entrepreneurs come up with innovative initiatives that not only expand and grow on an impressive scale but, at the same time, also promote sustainable development by addressing a wide range of human, social, economic and cultural problems. Similarly, Austin *et al.* (2006) also argue that market failure creates differing entrepreneurial opportunities for social entrepreneurship.

The BOP approach establishes a business case for companies by rethinking strategies and models, acquiring and building new resources and capabilities and forging local partnerships (Seelos and Mair 2007). Social entrepreneurs can leverage existing capabilities and local partnerships to build markets to cater to the poor and be profitable at the same time. By building on existing capabilities and partnerships, social entrepreneurs utilize their potential to come up with innovative strategies to address the economic and social problems with environmental sustainability, thus leading to sustainable development. This is supported by Murphy and Coombes (2009: 332), who contend that 'social entrepreneurial discoveries allow economic, social, and environmental resources to reinforce one another in novel ways'.

Developing countries present a number of contextual challenges for businesses in terms of stability, crime, corruption, lack of access to finance, bureaucracy, weak legal institutions and poor infrastructure (Sinha and Fiestas 2011). Research suggests that social entrepreneurs are not discouraged by these challenges (Haugh 2005); however, they are likely to start their initiatives on a small scale by producing small changes in the short term. With the passage of time, these small changes act as a catalyst for social transformation, which, in turn, leads to bigger changes in the long term (Alvord *et al.* 2004), which is consistent with the third approach of social entrepreneurship as mentioned earlier.

The following section discusses the case study of Waste Concern in Bangladesh, which demonstrates how social entrepreneurs are contributing to sustainable development by alleviating poverty and promoting environmental sustainability, despite the contextual constraints.

The case of Waste Concern

With the motto, 'Waste is a Resource', Waste Concern, a social business enterprise in Bangladesh comprising both 'for-profit' and 'not-for-profit' components, was founded by two entrepreneurs in 1995. Overcoming hurdles such as rigid bureaucracy, lack of access to finance and other resources such as land and information, and the prevalence of corruption and poor infrastructure – common in developing countries – that emerged from the unique contextual realities in Bangladesh, Waste Concern has been successful not only in disposing of waste in an environmentally friendly way but also in creating economic and social gains as is discussed below.

Bangladesh is geographically slightly smaller than the state of Iowa in the United States, yet is one of the most populous countries in the world, with 160 million people residing in 143,998 km^2 (CIA Fact Book 2011). Bangladesh is particularly interesting as a case study because it faces a myriad of problems, with the combination of population, poverty, environmental degradation, a depleting resource base and poor governance all creating developmental challenges. Bangladesh is interesting to analyse because, despite weaknesses in governance and the complex problems it has been facing since its independence in 1971, it has been growing 5–6 per cent per year since 1996 (CIA Fact Book 2011), with remarkable achievements in the social indicators in terms of life expectancy, female schooling, contraceptive adoption and so on (World Bank 2007; Mahmud 2008). As a result of this growth, the poverty reduction rate is estimated to be 2 per cent per annum (DFID, 2010). This is, no doubt, a remarkable achievement, yet having roughly 30 per cent of the population still under poverty line (World Bank 2012) also suggests that, despite decades of assistance provided by international development agencies such as the World Bank and the Asian Development Bank, Bangladesh has been unable to eliminate extreme poverty. These mixed results of strengths and weaknesses have led to the emergence of the concept of the 'Bangladesh paradox', referring to the economic resilience despite many problems as discussed (World Bank 2007). Although this situation creates challenges for development, at the same time it also provides possible opportunities for involving social entrepreneurs in addressing the problem of poverty at the BOP level.

In terms of population, Dhaka, the capital city of Bangladesh, is the eleventh-largest city in the world, with 12.3 million people. The city is projected to be the fourth-largest city in 2015, with the population growing at the rate of 1.56 per cent per year (Sinha and Enayetullah 2010; CIA Fact Book 2011). The increase in population is also associated with an increase in the generation of waste. The urban population in Bangladesh is reported to generate, on average, 14,000 tons of waste per day (Rahman 2010), creating a major challenge for waste management. Dhaka City Corporation (DCC), a public sector agency responsible for managing waste, can only collect 50 per cent of the waste. Due to a lack of adequate financial and non-financial resources, DCC is not even capable of disposing of the collected waste in a hygienic way. The problem is compounded by the fact that Dhaka has only one official landfill site (Sinha and Enayetullah 2010). The remaining waste is often piled up in the streets and in unmanaged landfill sites. It is reported that around 70–80 per cent of the waste generated in Dhaka is composed of organic materials, which are biodegradable and generate greenhouse gases polluting the environment (Sinha and Enayetullah 2010). The accumulation of waste on the streets and in unmanaged landfill sites leads to various social and environmental impacts. These range from the spread of disease, insufferable odour and leakage of pollutants into water sources, to greenhouse gas emissions. In addition, the waste also exposes the 'waste pickers', who are mostly women and children at the extreme end of the BOP, to toxic and other hazardous substances (Seelos and Mair 2007).

In this context, Waste Concern has been assisting with the problem of managing waste effectively by recycling waste into organic fertilizer. In this process it is reducing poverty and creating jobs at the BOP level as well as producing carbon credits to sell in the international market (Waste Concern 2011). Despite initial problems with bureaucracy, a lack of resources and technology, and the absence of a conducive policy for recycling, over the years since its foundation, Waste Concern has managed to overcome these constraints and has been able to create a system that not only allows the community to dispose of waste effectively but also improves their economic and social standards with positive environmental impacts. It is interesting to note that Waste Concern has not only been successful in decoupling economic growth from environmental pressure, but has also taken the whole concept to the next level by making a positive impact on the environment through very simple, cost-effective, flexible but innovative strategies. As a result, the Waste Concern model has been replicated in a number of countries, such as Nepal, Pakistan, Sri Lanka and Vietnam, and was expected to be replicated in ten African cities by 2012 (Waste Concern 2011). The successful replication of this model in South Asian developing countries further confirms Bangladesh as an exemplar of developing countries, particularly in the South Asian region.

The Waste Concern model

The main concept of Waste Concern is to recycle and convert the organic matter in urban waste into organic composts and fertilizer without emitting greenhouse gases, thus earning carbon credits to sell in the international market. Waste Concern hires the poor and marginalized – particularly women – to collect organic kitchen waste from households within the community and vegetable market and deliver it to the composting plants, where the waste is converted. The resulting high-yield, lower-cost organic compost is sold to rural farmers via fertilizer companies, while the emission reduction is sold to the international market (Waste Concern 2012). This process of converting waste into resources is cheap, simple and has a number of benefits that spans across economic, social and environmental areas as discussed below.

Economic gains

Waste Concern, operating in different cities all over Bangladesh, is acting to alleviate poverty at the BOP level in a number of ways. It is providing job opportunities for the population at the BOP by employing them as waste collectors and employees in the compost plant. The plant recycles the organic waste into organic fertilizers or compost without any greenhouse gas emissions. While the carbon credits are sold in the international market and cover the entire cost of the project, the organic compost/fertilizer is used in rural areas with a number of benefits. It is reported that in the period 2001 to 2006 the compost plants reduced 17,000 tons of greenhouse gas, created jobs for 986 urban poor and saved a landfill area extending 33.12 acres and 1 metre deep (Ashoka's Citizen Base Initiative 2007).

In the process of recycling waste, Waste Concern is also creating an urban–rural symbiosis by producing organic compost from the waste generated in urban areas which is used by farmers in rural areas. This organic fertilizer reduces the need for chemical fertilizers by at least 30 per cent and also leads to increased yields and improved food security, which again indirectly contributes to poverty reduction in the rural areas. Further, the recycling of waste into organic fertilizers is not only solving a major urban problem of waste management but is also contributing to food security – a major challenge in the context of Bangladesh. Finally, the effective management of waste also leads to poverty reduction by improving human rights at the BOP level by offering improved access to the basic rights to life and health. In addition to reducing poverty at the BOP level, Waste Concern is helping the DCC to manage waste effectively. According to the Waste Concern website (2012), in the period of 2001 to 2006, 124,400 tons of waste were processed, producing 31,100 tons of compost that benefited about 2.9 million people. The total value of the compost sold in the local market in that period was US $1.10 million, and a further US $1.24 million in foreign currency was saved by avoiding the import of chemical fertilizers (Waste Concern 2012).

Social gains

In addition to economic benefits, Waste Concern is addressing social problems in a number of ways that relate to poverty alleviation. First, it creates jobs at the BOP level, particularly focusing on waste pickers at the lower end of the BOP, and provides these employees with facilities such as health insurance, day-care centres and free meals – people who otherwise would be engaged in illegal social activities (Azmat 2013). Second, it is playing a role in the empowerment of the poor, particularly women, who are employed by Waste Concern at a reasonable wage rate. Third, the improved food security in rural areas due to the use of organic fertilizers also leads to better social outcomes. Finally, the manufacture of compost from the recycling of waste that would otherwise be left lying in the streets also decreases the spread of various diseases.

Environmental gains

Considering waste as a resource, Waste Concern is recycling the organic waste into organic fertilizers or compost without any greenhouse gas emissions, thus creating carbon credits for sale in the international market. In addition, the organic compost is not only cheaper than chemical fertilizers but is also environmentally friendly, as it does not drain the soil of nutrients the way chemical fertilizers do, thus leading to better productivity and higher yields (Waste Concern 2011). Further, the disposal of waste leads to cleaner streets, preventing the spread of diseases and pollution.

Discussion

The case of Waste Concern exemplifies that sustainable development in developing countries is possible with no trade-off between poverty reduction and environmental sustainability. The contextual constraints of developing countries, in terms of poor access to finance and other non-financial resources, as well as the struggle with bureaucracy, can all act as challenges to start something new and innovative. In this case, despite the contextual constraints, the social entrepreneurs were able to overcome the challenges and come up with an innovative approach to recycle waste, benefiting society and the environment, while making profit at the same time, thus presenting a win-win outcome in all aspects. This case, therefore, supports the findings of Haugh (2005) that social entrepreneurs generally have a more positive outlook and are less likely to be discouraged by environmental constraints.

Consistent with earlier findings (Leadbeater 1997; Austin *et al.* 2006), social entrepreneurs in this case responded to the problem by filling the market gaps left by the traditional private and public sectors. As mentioned earlier, around 50 per cent of the waste in Dhaka remained uncollected and was left in the streets as the government agency, DCC, did not have enough resources to collect and dispose of it effectively. The gap left by DCC, in this case to dispose of waste effectively, failed to attract the traditional private sector due to contextual constraints and the lack of innovative ideas. Considering waste as a resource, Waste Concern filled this gap left by the public and private sectors.

This case study further highlights certain factors that differentiate social entrepreneurs from mainstream entrepreneurs and are supported by earlier research. Social entrepreneurs in this case identified new opportunities to manage waste effectively, which had failed to attract mainstream entrepreneurs. Through their positive outlook, and unlike mainstream entrepreneurs, these entrepreneurs were not hindered by the contextual constraints described in earlier findings (Haugh 2005; Austin *et al.* 2006). Rather, they leveraged existing capabilities and partnerships to cater to the poor (Seelos and Mair 2007) through their positive outlook. Further, their innovative initiatives have multidimensional outcomes (i.e., economic, social and environmental), which also resonate with earlier findings (Seelos and Mair 2005; Austin *et al.* 2006). Finally, the fact that they started initially with a small initiative, which later expanded and grew in scale as a result of its huge success, also concurs with earlier findings (Alvord *et al.* 2004; Seelos and Mair 2005).

The concept of Waste Concern, as mentioned, is innovative and unique in a number of ways. The beauty of the model lies in the fact that it is simple and utilizes locally available resources such as low-cost composting plant that can be adapted to both urban and rural areas and can be implemented on a small, medium or large scale, based on needs. The model is also a classic example of a successful integrated governance approach, with a partnership between the public sector (the DCC), the private sector (Waste Concern) and the community. Research suggests that prior approaches to poverty reduction have not been effective, partly because they emphasized one sector – the government – taking on the primary responsibility in most cases despite the synergy that can be created by involving each sector – government, business and civil society – to work together in an integrated way (Karnani 2011). The concept of integrated governance is defined as including both better integration between government (inter and intra) and collaboration with other actors to increase efficiency and improve transparency (Azmat *et al.* 2009). It is emphasized that networks in integrated governance draw their strength from the comparative advantages of the resources, capabilities and knowledge of the actors involved (Wright 2000; Steets 2003). In recent years, networked or integrated governance has gained importance as governments worldwide are increasingly turning to opportunities for working jointly with other sectors such as businesses and civil societies to create synergies and to be efficient and effective (Szirom *et al.* 2002). Although integrated governance is yet to emerge as a functional model in developing countries, in terms of efficiency, transparency, effective coordination and provision of sustainable development (Azmat *et al.* 2009), this case provides evidence that integrated governance linking the state, the private sector and the community can lead to a functional model. As this case shows, the integrated partnership approach between the DCC, Waste Concern and the community is leading towards sustainable development by the pooling and sharing of resources, capacities and knowledge of each of the players involved.

The success of Waste Concern in the context of Bangladesh has been huge and acknowledged by international agencies such as the United Nations Economic and Social Commission for the Asia and the Pacific (UNESCAP), United Nations Development Program (UNDP) and Asian Development Bank, who are assisting in replicating the model to other Asian and African countries. Waste Concern has been effective in confronting the persistent problem of poverty, involving communities, creating awareness of waste recycling, promoting environmental sustainability and making profits at the same time.

Conclusion

This chapter strengthens and deepens our understanding of social entrepreneurship in promoting sustainable development in Bangladesh, a developing country. Through the case study of Waste Concern, the chapter illustrates that social entrepreneurs can come up with innovative strategies, such as the concept of 'turning waste into resource', to cater to the poor in developing countries, and radically rethink different ways to address problems. Their unique and innovative strategies also have the potential to achieve economic and social development with environmental sustainability, thus leading to sustainable development. The chapter also reinforces earlier findings that social entrepreneurs differ from mainstream entrepreneurs in their positive approach and are not hindered by contextual constraints (Haugh 2005), such as lack of financial and non-financial resources, bureaucracy, inappropriate technology, lack of support and inflexibility. As this case shows, the social entrepreneurs, instead, took advantage of market opportunities that had failed to attract mainstream entrepreneurs. Through their innovative approach and creative thinking they overcame the hurdles, thus acting as catalysts for sustainable development by contributing to economic, social and environmental gains.

As Bangladesh has the characteristics of a typical developing country in the South Asian region, with its large population, low per capita income and an agriculture-dominated economy (World Bank 2009), the case provides insights for academics and policy makers as well as practitioners, particularly in developing countries in South Asia in a similar geographical context, into the possibility of addressing social and environmental obligations while making profits through social entrepreneurship. The findings also reinforce earlier suggestions (Seelos and Mair 2007) about the need for innovative ways of addressing social problems rather than the traditional efforts, such as development aid, donations and charity, in developing countries. Social entrepreneurs, through their innovative approach, have the potential to play a positive role in sustainable development and reducing poverty, even within the difficult contextual constraints of developing countries.

This chapter has some limitations that prompt future research on the topic. Most of the information concerning Waste Concern – although credible and reliable – is sourced from the Waste Concern website due to lack of academic research on this topic. The lack of academic research and access to data is a methodological concern that may create a challenge for fellow researchers who intend to undertake a similar investigation. The lack of academic research further highlights the need for empirical research on this social enterprise and its impact on economic, social and environmental aspects as well as social inclusion efforts. Further research is needed to explore other social enterprises in other developing countries in order to come up with generalizable findings. In addition, research could also explore the strategies and motivation that drive social entrepreneurs to grapple with the inevitable contextual constraints, and also how they identify the market opportunities left unutilized by the private sector, to provide a better understanding of social entrepreneurs and their success, particularly in developing countries.

References

Alvord, H.S., Brown, D.L. and Letts, W.C. (2004) 'Social entrepreneurship and societal transformation: an exploratory study', *Journal of Applied Behavioral Science*, 40(3): 260–82.

Ashoka's Citizen Base Initiative (2007) 'Concerned scientist – with a cause – waste concern? Available online at www.citizenbase.org/node/3006 (accessed 18 June 2012).

Austin, J., Stevenson, H. and Wei-Skillern, J. (2006) 'Social and commercial entrepreneurship: same, different, or both?', *Entrepreneurship Theory and Practice*, 30(1): 1–22.

Azmat, F. (2013) 'Sustainable development in developing countries: role of social entrepreneurs', *International Journal of Public Administration*, 36(5): 293–304.

Azmat, F. and Samaratunge, R. (2013) 'Exploring customer loyalty at Bottom of the Pyramid (BOP) in South Asia', *Social Responsibility Journal*, 9(3): 379–94.

Azmat, F., Alam, Q. and Coghill, K. (2009) 'Integrated governance: a prerequisite for sustainable market-orientated development in Bangladesh', *International Journal of Public Administration*, 32(10): 829–51.

CIA Fact Book (2011) *The World Fact Book*. Available online at www.cia.gov/library/publications/the-world-factbook/geos/bg.html (accessed 6 June 2011).

Dees, J.G. (1998) 'Enterprising non profits: what do you do when traditional sources of funding fall short?', *Harvard Business Review*, 76: 55–67.

Department for International Development (DFID) (2010) 'Bangladesh key facts'. Available online at www.dfid.gov.uk/Where-we-work/Asia-South/Bangladesh/Key-facts/ (accessed 6 June 2011).

Emerson, J. and Twerksy, F. (eds) (1996) *New Social Entrepreneurs: The success, challenge and lessons of non-profit enterprise creation*. San Francisco, CA: Roberts Foundation, Homeless Economic Development Fund.

Fowler, A. (2000) 'NGDOs as a moment in history: beyond aid to social entrepreneurship or civic innovation?', *Third World Quarterly*, 21(4): 637–54.

Hammond, A.L., Kramer, W.J., Katz, R.S., Tran, J.T. and Walker, C. (2007) *The Next Four Billion: Market size and business strategy at the base of the pyramid*, Washington, DC: World Resources Institute and International Finance Corporation.

Hart, S.L. and London, T. (2005) 'Developing native capability: what multinational corporations can learn from the base of the pyramid', *Stanford Social Innovation Review*, 3(2): 28–33.

Haugh, H. (2005) 'A research agenda for social entrepreneurship', *Social Enterprise Journal*, 1(1): 1–12.

Jaiswal, K.A. (2008) 'Fortune at the bottom of the pyramid: an alternate perspective', *Innovations*, 3(1): 85–100.

Karnani, A. (2009) *The Bottom of the Pyramid Strategy for Reducing Poverty: A failed promise*, DESA working paper No. 80 ST/ESA/2009/DWP/80, New York: United Nations Department of Economic and Social Affairs.

Karnani, A. (2011) *Fighting Poverty Together: Rethinking strategies for business, governments and civil society to reduce poverty*, New York: Palgrave Macmillan.

Leadbeter, C. (1997) *The Rise of Social Entrepreneurship*, London: Demos.

London, T. (2007) *A Base-of-the-Pyramid Perspective on Poverty Alleviation*, working paper, Ann Arbor, MI: William Davidson Institute/Stephen M. Ross School of Business.

Mahmud, W. (2008) 'Social development in Bangladesh: pathways, surprises and challenges', *Indian Journal of Human Development*, 2(1): 79–92.

Murphy, P. and Coombes, M.S. (2009) 'A model of social entrepreneurial discovery', *Journal of Business Ethics*, 87: 325–36.

Patzelt, H. and Shepherd, D.A. (2010) 'Recognizing opportunities for sustainable development', *Entrepreneurship Theory and Practice*, 35(4): 631–52.

Prahalad, C.K. (2004) *The Fortune at the Bottom of the Pyramid: Eradicating poverty through profits*, Upper Saddle River, NJ: Wharton School Publishing.

Prahalad, C.K. and Hammond, A. (2002) 'Serving the world's poor, profitably', *Harvard Business Review*, 80(9): 48–57.

Prahalad, C.K. and Hart, S.L. (2002) 'The fortune at the bottom of the pyramid', *Strategy + Business*, 26: 54–67.

Rahman, H.M. (2010) *Growing Inclusive Markets: Waste Concern: Decentralised community-based composting through public private partnership*, Bangladesh: UNDP.

Seelos, C. and Mair, J. (2005) 'Sustainable development: how social entrepreneurs make it happen', *Working Paper Series*, 611: 1–14, Barcelona, Spain: IESE Business School.

Seelos, C. and Mair, J. (2007) 'Profitable business models and market creation in the context of deep poverty: a strategic view', *Academy of Management Perspectives*, 21(4): 49–63.

Sinha, M. and Enayetullah, I. (2010) 'Innovative ways to promote decentralized composting by Waste Concern in Bangladesh', paper presented at the C40 Cities Climate Leadership Group Waste Workshop, London, 22–24 March.

Sinha, S. and Fiestas, I. (2011) *Literature Review on Constraints to Investment in Developing Countries*, final report, London: Department for International Development (DFID).

Steets, J. (2003) 'Networks: engaging governance? The case of Transparency International', paper presented at the United Nations Interregional Workshop on Engaged Governance, Colombo, Sri Lanka, 9–11 December.

Szirom, T., Lasater, Z., Hyde, J. and Moore, C. (2002) *Working Together: Integrated governance*, report prepared for the Institute of Public Administration of Australia, Sydney.

Thompson, J., Alvy, G. and Lees, A. (2000) 'Social entrepreneurship: a new look at the people and the potential', *Management Decision*, 38: 328–38.

Waste Concern (2011/2012) Available online at www.wasteconcern.org/ (accessed 7 July 2012).

World Bank (2007) *Bangladesh Strategy for Sustained Growth*, Poverty Reduction and Economic Management Unit, Bangladesh Development Series, Washington, DC: World Bank.

World Bank (2009) *Country Data Report for Bangladesh 1996–2009*, Washington, DC: World Bank.

World Bank (2012) *World Development Indicators*, country data report for Bangladesh, Washington, DC: World Bank.

World Resource Institute (2007) *The Next 4 Billion: Market size and business strategy at the base of the pyramid*, Washington, DC: WRI.

Wright, D. (2000) 'Subsidiarity in public governance: issues and implications for stakeholders', in Collins, P. (ed.) *Applying Public Administration in Development: Guideposts to the future*, Chichester: John Wiley and Sons.

Zahra, A.S., Gedajlovic, E., Neubaum, O.D and Shulman, M.J. (2009) 'A typology of social entrepreneurs: motives, search processes and ethical challenges', *Journal of Business Venturing*, 24: 519–25.

6 Corporate social responsibility in Pakistan

Corporate engagements in the local community and their social impact

Ashique Ali Jhatial, Nelarine Cornelius and James Wallace

Corporate social responsibility (CSR) is a mechanism for aligning company policies and practices within the socio-economic, cultural and environmental challenges facing society and, in particular, communities. Though the majority of empirical research on CSR has been conducted in Western companies, there is growing interest in CSR in transitional and developing economies, as well as Western firms working in developing countries.

The focus of our study is CSR in Pakistan, a country that emerged as an independent nation on 14 August 1947 after previously being under British colonial rule for two centuries. Since then, the country has experienced interludes of democratic and military governments. Religious norms and postcolonial civil-military and landed elites play a powerful role in the country's institutions. Pakistan is a distinctive environment where government organizations are often run within traditional, legal and administrative frameworks. Nonetheless, the country has vibrant multinational and private sectors along with widespread networks of social enterprises and non-government organizations (NGOs). However, Pakistan also faces many challenges, including political and civil instability and widespread poverty. In this chapter, we evaluate CSR activities in commercial organizations in Pakistan. We consider also the views of NGOs, often a delivery mechanism for the CSR activities of firms. We undertake in-depth interviews with senior executives in commercial organizations and NGOs. Additionally, we consider the effectiveness of Pakistan government regulation that sets minimum standards of CSR disclosure. We draw conclusions regarding the rhetoric and reality of CSR action generally, and the distinctive character of some of the forms of CSR activity found in Pakistan given cultural values and norms. Finally, we consider if CSR activity in Pakistan provides the basis for sustainable social impact at the local community level.

CSR: Western perspectives

In Adam Smith's *The Wealth of Nations*, it is argued that as a result of the activities of firms, society gets goods and services, government is paid tax, employees receive pay and entrepreneurs earn profits (Lantos, 2001). However, Adam Smith's thesis also raised concerns over the morality of unfettered capitalism.

In Victorian Britain there are long-established examples of socially responsible corporate activity focused on the welfare of local communities. These include those of philanthropists such as Sir Titus Salt, who established the town of Saltaire in 1851 for his factory workers and their families near Bradford, UK. In the United States, John H. Patterson of National Cash Register (NCR) seeded the fledgling industrial welfare movement and the philanthropist, John D. Rockefeller, set a precedent for charitable corporate activity during the nineteenth century. However, CSR as we understand it today is most often associated with Howard Bowen's work, *Social Responsibilities of the Businessman*, in which he asserts that CSR concerns 'the obligation of businessmen to pursue those policies, to make those decisions, or to follow those lines of actions, which are desirable in terms of the objectives and values of our society' (1953: 44; see also Carroll's 1979 and 1994 reviews of the conceptual and definitional evolution of corporate social responsibility, tracing its modern history from the 1950s). However, it could be argued that CSR activity is more consistent with more traditional high-profile philanthropic 'gift giving' activity than genuine, strong and direct engagement with the needs of local communities. More recently, authors such as Garriga and Mele (2004) and Haigh and Jones (2006) highlight that inter-organizational factors, competitive dynamics, institutional investors, end-users, government regulators and NGOs all influence the CSR choices that corporations make.

Clearly, some scholars have asserted that the only responsibility of a firm is to its shareholders (Friedman, 1970). However this position, from the neoclassical school of economics, more commonly known as the 'shareholder model', has been criticized. An alternative position regarding the firm's responsibility to society is stakeholder theory. In his groundbreaking book, *Strategic Management: A stakeholder approach*, Freeman (1984) identified and modelled the relationships between the stakeholders of a corporation. He described and recommended methods by which management can give due regard to the interests of stakeholders holistically, including the interests of communities. Today, many blue chip corporations such as Microsoft and Apple invest in healthcare, education projects and poverty reduction programmes, along with philanthropic works in developing countries, with substantial impact at the community level.

In the West, CSR may therefore be regarded as a voluntary duty of companies, associated in particular with financial success. However, strong economic performance is no longer a preserve of the West. Many countries in the developing world have shown an upward economic trajectory and performance over the last 40 years (IMF, 2006). Nonetheless, social provision by national government is often limited in many developing economies, including the BRICS (the strongest emerging economies), due to a limited national budget and marked social and economic pressures. Additionally, social provision may be compromised as a result of corruption, malpractice, poor governance, human rights violations, unskilled labour and high rates of poverty. As a result, there are greater chances of unrest in society, instability in governments, communal and ethnic violence and extremism, all of which can discourage foreign direct investment. Many of these countries are also experiencing acute environmental crises (UNDP, 2006). Additionally, global-ization, economic growth, investment and business activity are likely to have the most dramatic social and environmental impacts, both positive and negative (World Bank, 2006). Further, an increasing body of empirical research focuses on understanding governments' roles in developing countries in regulating and facilitating the CSR environment across business organizations (Jamali and Mirshak, 2007; Jamali and Sidani, 2011). Thus, developing countries present a distinctive set of CSR challenges that are often different from those of developed nations.

In this chapter, our focus is on CSR in a non-Western context, specifically Pakistan, and we explore the importance placed by organizations on local need, rather than more broad-based, philanthropic-type activity. In particular, we attempt to ascertain the extent to which firms either 'follow' Western practices or undertake CSR in a manner informed more by non-Western, traditional, local cultural norms and values.

CSR in developing countries: contextual factors

It is important to recall that the social responsibility of powerful institutions is long-established, and it could be argued, for example, where the role of religious organizations remains strong, that religious organizations are regarded as an important sector for social provision for the poor (Visser and Macintosh, 1998). Therefore, religious sensibilities may inform views on what comprises 'acceptable' social responsibility. Nevertheless, many discussions in the extant literature on CSR in developing countries draw strongly on indigenous cultural traditions of philanthropy, business ethics and community welfare. According to Crane and Matten (2007), adopting an ethical stance is much more respected and practised in Europe than in the United States. However, corporate sectors in developing countries often consider ethics as the least important factor in the CSR agenda. Similarly, Crane and Matten (2007) suggest that philanthropic responsibility in Europe tends more often to be mediated via sectoral codes of conduct and legal frameworks, while in the United States social responsibility is more likely to be undertaken through discretionary acts of successful companies or rich individuals. In this respect, some scholars have argued that developing countries have more in common with the American model, as philanthropy generally gets a higher priority as a manifestation of CSR (Arora and Puranik, 2004; Fig, 2005; Ahmad, 2006; Amaeshi *et al.*, 2006; Weyzig, 2006). Developing countries' legal responsibilities, corruption, tax evasion and good governance generally have a lower priority than in developed countries. Further, many developing countries are behind the developed world in terms of incorporating human rights and other issues relevant to CSR into their legislation (Mwaura, 2004). There appears consensus among scholars that companies in developing countries most often avoid paying taxes to the government, which contradicts their CSR claims of good conduct (Christensen and Murphy, 2004). However, in the case of national emergency or catastrophic circumstances, public and private companies in developing countries are likely to generate significant financial support in worst-affected areas (for example, in the major earthquake of 2005 and the flooding in 2010 and 2011 in Pakistan).

Pakistan and CSR

It has been argued that CSR is passing through an evolutionary stage in Pakistan (Ahmad, 2006; Naeem and Welford, 2009; Ali *et al.*, 2010; Khan and Lund-Thomsen, 2011) and that there are common variations in the way CSR is perceived. Some consider CSR as compliance with state laws, paying taxes and employee welfare; others focus on corporate philanthropy (Jaseem, 2006; Naeem and Welford, 2009). Pakistan is a multicultural nation with many social divisions in the society, which has struggled with the enduring threat of terrorism since 9/11. Pakistan was ranked twelfth in the index of 20 'failed states' based on criteria such as uneven development, and the fragile state of the economy and public services. These 20 unstable states have been characterized as being on the brink of failure to perform basic state functions as well as being susceptible to the outbreak of civil unrest. About one-third of Pakistan's 176.7 million people are below the poverty line, unable to bear the cost of basic food, clothing and shelter. Economic growth, estimated at 3.67 per cent, remains insufficient to significantly and rapidly reduce poverty. Pakistan lags behind its commitment under the Millennium Development Goals, particularly in the areas of education and health. Half of all Pakistani men and two-thirds of all women are illiterate. Insufficient primary care remains another major obstacle; for example, one in 11 children die before their fifth birthday and 14,000 mothers die in childbirth annually.

CSR in Pakistan has been encouraged through professional bodies. The Asian Institute of Management (AIM) pioneered CSR activities by establishing the Asian Forum on Corporate Social Responsibility. The forum meets annually and recognizes and awards Asian companies that promote health, take care of the environment, help to reduce poverty and support education. In 2006 and 2007, Unilever Pakistan received an award for support and improvement of education and best workplace practices, and, in 2006, Engro Chemicals Ltd was the winner in the concern for health category. Thus, corporate efforts to implement CSR in Pakistan are rewarded where they help to develop well-being and community stability at the grass roots. However, it could be argued that what these awards encourage is the high-profile, philanthropic activity with limited account of the impact and sustainability of CSR actions at the local level.

Some research has identified that government and private firms lack initiatives and investments in providing training, skill-development education, volunteering, healthcare and community empowerment, poverty reduction and similar programmes for people at work and their families. Hameed (2010) identified that government and private sector businesses in Pakistan lack coherent CSR programmes and offer limited socio-economic disclosure, and that the impact of much CSR activity is questionable. Similarly, Ahmad (2006) found there was often a gap between the rhetoric and reality of CSR policy and actual practice. Indeed, Naeem and Welford (2009) suggest that some multinationals and private listed companies in Pakistan fail to address key aspects of CSR such as anti-corruption, gender equality, child labour, poverty reduction, human rights, education, health and community giving and the formal representation of workers in trade unions. Seeing the lack of corporate efforts in community development with limited disclosures, the federal government's Commissioner of Companies issued a General Order No. S.R.O. 983(I)/2009 on 16 November 2009 making it obligatory for companies to provide descriptive as well as monetary disclosures of CSR engagements undertaken during each financial year (Government of Pakistan, 2009). The CSR areas for information disclosure include corporate philanthropy, energy conservation, environmental protection measures, community investment and welfare schemes, consumer protection measures, welfare spending for under-privileged classes, for example poverty reduction, industrial relations, employment of special persons, occupational safety and health, business ethics and anti-corruption measures, national-cause donations, contributions to the national exchequer and the rural development programme.

In other words, the government has incorporated CSR into the formal reporting structure of firms operating in Pakistan. However, although an important development for the enhancement of CSR accountability, the General Order does not provide a clear mandate for accountability at the level of community impact. Today, how do firms in Pakistan account for their CSR policies and practices, and what are the views of senior managers on the robustness and impact of CSR activity? To answer these questions, we attempt to obtain a more explicit and nuanced understanding of how government CSR accountability policies have affected the way companies engage in local communities in the following empirical investigation.

In order to further investigate CSR policy, practices and impact in Pakistan, we undertook an exploratory, empirical study. We randomly selected five companies each from government-owned enterprises (nationalized organizations that operate on commercial lines) and privately owned and multinational organizations; we evaluated their websites in order to examine how these firms account for their CSR engagements and their anticipated social impact.

Organizational websites and online documents were probed extensively in order to assess firm compliance with the federal government's General Order of information disclosures on CSR engagement, as well the socio-economic and environmental development aspects achieved through corporate engagement, and the extent to which organizations engaged with local communities. The website information was content analysed from a broadly constructivist perspective, building on a method that the authors have developed previously for website analysis (Wallace and Cornelius, 2010; Trueman *et al.*, 2012). This analysis was used to scope the interview schedule, and it is the interview findings that are the primary focus for reporting in this chapter. We employed constructivist grounded theory techniques (Charmaz, 2006) and the constant comparative method (Silverman, 2000) to analyse the empirical website and interview data.

In the interviews, senior executives and middle-level managers from government sector organizations were interviewed and probed on a number of current and past CSR engagements of their respective organizations. We were especially interested in, first, the level of local community engagement undertaken via CSR activities and also the extent to which these CSR practices followed Western practices or drew on local cultural norms and values. Additionally, we conducted interviews with senior managers of community-based non-governmental organizations (NGOs). This was done in order, first, to test the veracity of the assertions made and views put forward by firm managers and, second, as a proxy voice for local communities, as part of a larger-scale project. However, the focus of this chapter is on firms.

Eleven participants were male and seven female. The participants included senior executives and seven were in the middle level of management across the business sectors. A total of 18 interviews were conducted (see Table 6.1). Analysis focused on CSR contributions that the corporate sector undertakes for the local community in areas that directly have lasting impact and reduce poverty such as education, healthcare, skills-based training to enable and empower youth to enter into the job market, infrastructure development (drinking water, improving village infrastructure, construction of schools, roads,

Table 6.1 Personal information of respondents

Business sector	Management position		Gender		No. of participants
	Top-level management	*Middle-level management*	*Male*	*Female*	
Government	2	2	3	1	4
Private	3	1	3	1	4
Multinationals	2	3	3	2	5
NGO/SEs	4	1	2	3	5
Total	11	7	11	7	18

healthcare clinics etc.), environment (tree plantation etc.), relief and assistance in the event of natural disasters, human rights, women's empowerment and employees' welfare.

The website analysis revealed that most of the organizations provided a clear account of the range and scope of CSR activities undertaken. Many of the organizational websites evaluated addressed a mixture of community development activities, along with disaster relief, health, education and skills development, women's development, water security and employee welfare (the latter often referred to as internal CSR). Thus, provision was a combination of civil society provision and the provision of public goods (such as hospital and school provision), often viewed traditionally as primarily the duty of the state in developed economies. However, though statements were made about the anticipated impact of CSR activity (and thus companies complied with the Pakistan government's General Order), the actual local community-level impact was more difficult to discern from the online information provided. The evidence gathered reveals that many of the corporate engagements in the local community relate to specific areas such as education, healthcare and emergency relief work, which seem more like philanthropic initiatives rather than comprehensive CSR programmes, and were concentrated in the four areas of community education; community healthcare; community development and enabling youth; and response in national emergencies. However, the interviews provided more nuanced information and an indication of, first, the main areas of CSR activity engaged in by firms and, second, that less 'high-profile' activities that impacted at the local level within these four areas were within the purview of firms, but were regarded more as part of their *religious* duties.

Community education

> Our company has a long history of supporting the local community in education by providing schools with buildings, furniture, equipment and students with stationery, textbooks and paying their tuition fees and transport service. The company has also established a Computer Training Centre and Library (CTCL) in 2010 in the Sui area of Balochistan to train hundreds of youth in information and communication technology.
>
> (Senior Manager, Pakistan Petroleum Ltd)

UNESCO (2012) figures confirm an adult literacy rate in Pakistan of 56 per cent in 2005–10 and World Bank Development Indicators show public expenditure on education as only 2.4 per cent of GDP in 2010 (World Bank, 2010). Consequently, there is strong motivation for the private sector to shoulder the responsibility of educating the local communities they work in. For example, government companies such as Pakistan International Airlines Corporation (PIAC) established the Model Secondary School in 1980 to provide good-quality education to the children of the company's employees.

Similarly, Pakistan State Oil (PSO) supports several educational access programmes at university level. In partnership with the Heritage Foundation and the Citizens Foundation, PSO built several schools in areas struck by an earthquake in 2005. Pakistan Petroleum Ltd (PPL) established the Sui Model School and Girls College in 1957 to provide education for children of the company's employees and local community. Precisely, PPL boasts of its CSR obligation, which it has continually fulfilled for the community for five decades by delivering quality education.

Another government enterprise, Engro Corporation, was the first Pakistani company to become a signatory of the UN Global Compact (UNGC) and adopted the Global Reporting Initiative (GRI) framework for measuring and reporting corporate performance on economic, social and environmental parameters. Since then, the corporation has been publishing annual sustainability reports. CSR operations of Engro address a variety of socio-economic needs of local communities. For instance, the corporation invests in the construction and repair of schools, and the provision of furniture, textbooks, stationery and other teaching and learning materials (EngroCorp, 2011).

Similarly, multinationals in the country keep pace with national firms. Procter & Gamble (P&G) Pakistan partners with the Rural Education and Development Foundation (READ) to build seismic-compliant schools in the earthquake-affected areas of Kashmir and north Pakistan to provide access to good-quality education for underprivileged children (Procter & Gamble, 2011). In the same way, Shell Pakistan plays a central role through structured social investment programmes. Company initiatives focus on encouragement of youth through scholarship programmes, including those from traditionally disadvantaged communities for engineering and business graduates. A senior official (male) pointed out that 'In 2008, the company spent some $148 million on investing in community projects on education, skills development, social cohesion, health, environment, safety-related issues, enterprise development and capacity-building.'

Likewise, national private sector organizations also seem interested in investing in community education. Tapal, in collaboration with NGOs, for example The Citizen's Foundation (TCF), constructed its own primary school campuses in rural Sindh with a special focus on girls' education and recruiting female teachers to encourage female participation in education and employment. Another private company, the Karachi Electric Supply Corporation (KESC), invests in child education to contribute to the development of 'a generation of responsible citizens'. The company also invests in renovating, upgrading and adopting government schools. Another private organization, the Shafi Gluco Chem Group of companies, participates in the education of underprivileged children. The Group has set up several schools and colleges to provide underprivileged communities with primary through to college-level education. Hundreds of thousands of students across Punjab and Sindh are enrolled in such schools and colleges.

Community healthcare

> Our company helped Chipa Welfare Association in the purchase of a fully equipped air-conditioned ambulance and the company also funded the procurement of equipment, fixture and utilities for an operating theatre in the civil hospital Karachi and PSO is also associated with Al-Mehrab Tibbi Imdad (AMTI) to look after terminally ill patients.
>
> (Senior Manager, PSO)

Government enterprises and private companies engaged in community health-care focus on preventive, promotional and curative services. Interestingly, provision was historically initially for employees and their families, with this expertise extended eventually to local communities. PIAC, in collaboration with hospitals, diagnostic labs and medical institutions, provides employees with a comprehensive medical package. In 1959, PIAC established a medical division to supply wide-ranging medical coverage to employees and their dependants. PIAC also supports the Al-Shifa Trust, which provides relief and rehabilitation services to children suffering from cerebral palsy and other motor disorders. Similarly, other government enterprises such as PSO provide financial assistance to the National Institute of Cardiovascular Diseases in Karachi and supports financially the Marie Adelaide Leprosy Centre (MALC) in running a Leprosy Centre in Gawadar, Balochistan province. What charac-terizes these CSR activities is that they are mediated via community-based NGOs.

Likewise, PPL established a dispensary in 1956 to provide basic healthcare facilities for the company's employees. This was upgraded to a hospital in 1962 and a 24-hour emergency and accident service was made available to benefit employees and the local community. PPL also operates mobile dispensary services for remote and marginalized communities in operational areas of the company in Balochistan. A senior medical officer gave more details of health initiatives undertaken by the company. She noted that the company contributes to MALC for the treatment and rehabilitative facility for leprosy patients in the country. Moreover, the company arranged a training programme on obstetric care and life-saving skills for midwives in collaboration with the Royal College of Obstetricians and Gynaecologists (RCOG), UK, for com-munity midwives. The company also funded the construction of a 50-bedded community hospital and donated Rs 10 million for the purchase of medicines. Similarly, Engro has introduced occupational healthcare programmes such as industrial hygiene, occupational medicine and regular monitoring to reduce risks employees are exposed to. A senior official of the marketing department noted that the company's charitable arm, the Engro Foundation, has been active in creating local community access to basic services, for example education, health, water and sanitation, and infrastructure. Women and children are a priority area of Engro's community investments. Several projects were established by Engro that provided specialist healthcare for poor communities, such as specialized clinics dealing with snakebites, thalassaemia treatment, reproductive and maternal health, and eye and kidney diseases.

Similarly, healthcare provision offered by multinational corporations (MNCs) is extensive. P&G Pakistan's community development programmes look innovative and focus on providing customers and the general public with updated knowledge through awareness campaigns by visiting homes and schools and through media tools. P&G claims to have improved the lives of more than 19 million Pakistanis to date through its product-related programmes. For example, P&G's Pampers Hospital Education Programme aims at equipping new mothers with key babycare information; as a result 3.3 million mothers across the country have benefited since 2000. Pampers Mobile Clinics reached some 5.3 million mothers at their doorsteps. The Safeguard Sehat-o-Safai School Education Program, since 2004, has reached over seven million children in schools and raised awareness of hygiene. The Always Agahi Program reached some six million young girls with guidance on feminine hygiene. They were also made aware of the physiological and psychological changes they go through while growing up. Likewise, GlaxoSmithKline (GSK) Pakistan supports various health programmes at the grass roots level. GSK, in collaboration with the Pakistan National Forum on Women's Health (PNF) and Pakistan Nursing Council (PNC), supports the development of quality nursing education. The company also supports the Concern for Children Trust (CFC) for promoting preventive and primary healthcare for children since 1997. The company also supports better management of Parkinson's disease. Shell Pakistan actively plays a central role in creating awareness and precautions for HIV. The company also supports eye treatment and over one million patients receive free medical attention annually through a chain of nine hospitals throughout the country. Tapal organized free medical camps for unprivileged people across Sindh for the treatment of eye, ENT (ear, nose and throat), heart and skin problems.

Community development and enabling youth

Most of the firms studied in this chapter support the economic empowerment and financial inclusion of low-income or disadvantaged groups in communities where they operate. The companies claimed to work collaboratively with a range of partners (government, NGOs, international donor organizations and community-based organizations) to reach out to the needy. CSR initiatives included support for the development of community leadership and community knowledge-building, vocational training and humanitarian relief activities. For example, PIAC supports the Boy Scouts Association (PIA-BSA), with a mission of training and developing members through youth training programmes. Trained scouts have taken active part in a number of health, cleanliness, literacy, tree plantation, drug prevention and blood donation drives and also participated in the management of sports events. The PIA-BSA has also started a cricket academy where hundreds of youths have received cricket coaching from PIA's renowned test and first-class cricketers. A senior member of the human resource management department added that the BSA performed outstandingly in the aftermath of the earthquake in 2005 and the flooding in 2010 and 2011. Similarly, CSR initiatives from the government enterprise PSO for the local community seek to enrich the lives of the needy and poor in collaboration with NGOs. PSO supports projects addressing women's empowerment, special needs children's welfare, sports development and relief activities. Women's empowerment projects focus on reproductive health, education and vocational training, and attempt to uplift the under-privileged sections of society. The company supports several institutes dealing with the education and vocational training of special needs children (e.g., deaf, dumb, blind, etc.) across the country. PSO has always been at the forefront of promoting various sports, such as the International Squash Championship 2007 and the Asian Football Confederation (AFC) 2007. Among other economic contributions, companies take an active part in natural calamities, for example the earthquake of 2005 and the flooding of 2010 and 2011.

Likewise, the government enterprise PPL believes in empowering marginalized members of the local community through skill development training to enable youths to enter the job market. The company has invested heavily in engaging people in earning livelihoods through sustainable sources of income. A senior manager elucidated by saying that:

> Since the company is engaged in exploration and production of hydrocarbons in remote areas, the company focuses on developing infrastructure and civic amenities not only for its own employees but also for local communities. The company has supplied gas and water to nearby towns of company operations and built roads, culverts, schools and hospitals. In national emergencies such as the 2005 earthquake and the 2010 and 2011 floods, PPL donated in cash and kind.

Similarly, the Engro Foundation provides a single platform for community engagement activities and social investments to create large-scale social impact. The Foundation supports a range of partnerships with government, non-profit organizations and other industry players, to enhance the scale of social investments and ensure sustainability of CSR initiatives, focusing on eliminating social problems and promoting local arts and culture.

For local community and youth development, P&G introduced sustainable innovations that improve the environmental profile of products and operations and focus on improving children's lives. The company has initiated several programmes to improve the lives of children, teens and young mothers through health and hygiene awareness, education and female empowerment, and has improved the lives of about five million Pakistanis. Shell projects of social investment are linked to road safety, local enterprise development and securing safe and reliable access to energy. Shell works with other companies to help set standards for the transport industry, pooling skills and resources, and influencing governments to improve the safety of the roads and to raise standards for the vehicles on the roads. Shell Tameer (which means to build) encourages young people to start a business and the company provides counselling, training and technical assistance on entrepreneurship. For Siemens Pakistan, sustainability and corporate responsibility constitute a strategic, management-driven task that integrates business, environmental and local community interaction to create sustained tangible and intangible value. The company's CSR engagements are grounded in the development of community health, education, culture and sports. Siemens runs several CSR initiatives, including an apprenticeship training programme, a workers' education assistance programme, internships, gold medal awards and the Siemens student award. KESC has initiated an attraction for the local community through inspiring youth for sporting activities by training, mentoring and coaching to harness their talents and engage them in positive activity. The KESC Football Team is an affiliated unit of the Pakistan Football Federation (PFF) and supports the KESC Football Youth Development Project.

Response in national emergencies

Natural disasters are also considered as main obstacles to poverty alleviation and economic growth. GSK has provided medicine in national emergencies across the world, not only in Pakistan (2005, 2010 and 2011), but also Haiti (2010), Southeast Asia (2009), El Salvador (2009), Myanmar (2008) and China (2008).

In the recent past, due to environmental factors, especially climate change, natural disasters have hit Pakistan regularly. An earthquake struck Khyber Pakhtunkhwa (KP) and Azad Jammu and Kashmir (AJK) on 8 October 2005, which was considered to be a big tragedy for the nation. Still the memories of that misfortune were fresh and rehabilitation work in progress when monsoon rains in 2010 and 2011 affected much of the nation across KP, Punjab, Sindh and many parts of Balochistan. The floods caused by heavy rainfall deteriorated living and sanitation conditions in the affected areas: over 14 million people were in need of assistance. The Asian Development Bank and World Bank estimated that the cost of recovery and reconstruction following these storms was US $10 billion.

The unpreparedness and limited resources on the part of government meant that private firms and government enterprises played a very active part in addressing these national emergencies. Siemens Pakistan launched the 'Light for Life' programme after the devastating earthquake of 2005. Contributions from Siemens in the regions and head office had poured in under the umbrella organization, the Siemens Caring Hands Foundation. In continuation of flood relief efforts, Siemens Pakistan installed five water filtration plants in villages affected by the floods in 2010 and 2011. Each water filtration plant can purify 10,000 litres of water every day and provide over 8,000 people with clean water. KESC launched a massive flood relief campaign exclusively managed by employees. KESC Care Camps in Sindh were established to provide humanitarian aid to over 30,000 displaced people and provided some 3,000 tents. The camps provided medical treatment, preventive care, emergency evacuation, food, shelter, safe drinking water and other basic necessities to the victims of the country's worst-ever natural disasters. Similarly, PIAC helped displaced people in the post-9/11 war on terror in the northern part of Pakistan. Evidence of corporate CSR initiatives presented in earlier sections reveal that most of the companies support NGOs for community development projects addressing socio-economic and human rights issues, including women's and children's rights.

Local values and CSR

> I also support charities that provide food, clothing and shelter to the poor or orphans. The organization has also sponsored so many people who are not able to go for Umrah or Hajj. This dedication satisfies my faith and service to religion. We also establish medical camps in poor and rural areas as well as in the slums of big cities like Karachi, Lahore, Faisalabad etc. This balance of the corporate and adherence to our faith: this is how to do good CSR.
>
> (Senior Manager, Shafi Gluco Chem)

Although all organizations appear to engage in CSR that is familiar to Westerners, there is also a view that there is a need to ensure that long-established local socially responsible activities of firms are recognized. Importantly, these practices are grounded in Islamic traditions of obligations to the poor. Some organizations engage in socio-economic and community development in the names of elders or forefathers to secure prayers for their time in the afterlife and also in order to 'do God's work'. A senior manager from a private firm noted that the 'Seth' (a local term for owner) had established two foundations: one in his father's and one in his mother's name. These two company foundations supported community development programmes in education and health, and provided vocational training to women in poor households and national emergency relief. He stated that they had 'done remarkable community work and spend lots of money'. The work, the manager suggested, was underpinned by religious conviction, and good acts earn *dua* (a prayer or blessing) from the poor and, therefore, 'God's pleasure'.

This view is further explored in research by Khan and Lund-Thomsen (2011). Their study of soccer ball manufacturers in Sialkot, Pakistan, a privately owned firm, has challenged conventional thinking about CSR. They identified a counter-discourse, challenging the motivation behind CSR, with local manufacturers sharing the view that CSR was 'part of the wider historic project of Western imperialism in the developing world through which economic resources are extracted from local manufacturers' (p. 73). In other words, they were concerned that 'foreign' views of CSR would be seen as 'right' and that long-established socially responsible practices, often grounded in religious (Islamic) values, were made less visible; thus CSR is considered by some as a neo-colonial agenda in postcolonial times.

This position was expressed openly by one manager of a regional private firm. He argued strongly that CSR was a foreign influence on local business, a vehicle to create Western approaches to local issues and dilute local values. In the view of one senior manager, CSR and other practices were deliberately exported from the West to influence poor countries. Specifically:

> The West does not know that we as Muslims have the concept of Zakat [where] we provide monetary help to deserving poor people. Zakat is hundreds of years old and CSR is only decades old: new name only. We comply with the country's laws, take due care of our employees and also do good work on community welfare.

Of course, it is possible that some national firms may have felt the 'big' initiatives of larger firms to be regarded as more worthy than more traditional, local charity, and, further, may weaken the influence of the latter. However, there was also a genuine concern that the traditional Eastern value obligations of those of substantial means towards the poor may be weakened.

Conclusions

What is striking about the involvement of firms in CSR in Pakistan is the range and scope of their interventions. Indeed, it could be argued that through their commissioning of third sector organizations, the impact of community organizations and NGOs can be scaled up effectively. In the absence of government resources and reach, many local communities have secured access to not only disaster relief or community empowerment support, but also the provision of public services, such as education and health, provided by the CSR activities of firms directly or through the support of intermediary organizations. By virtue of its objectives, CSR requires businesses to address socio-economic inequalities and environmental concerns facing society. CSR in Pakistan appears to be mixture of legal and voluntary duties.

The efforts of the federal government to create more formal duties regarding the enactment of social responsibility in organizations is also an important factor that shapes CSR's character in Pakistan. Further work is required to assess, in particular, whether Pakistan's legal intervention in social accountability intensifies the focus to be seen to be engaging in CSR activities. Certainly, firms emphasize high-profile, philanthropic-type activities on their websites, perhaps in order to enhance their corporate reputation and image, and some may do little more than this. However, we have identified examples of firms that support social provision that could arguably extend well beyond reputation management. Our brief assessment reveals a mixed picture. As in many countries, some organizations are simply playing lip service to CSR practice, albeit that their promotional accounts of CSR are promising. Others have been independently assessed as exemplars, whose CSR practice has made a difference to poverty, community well-being and the positive development of traditionally disadvantaged groups at the grass roots level.

Further, in the for-profit sector, there is a distinction between the views held on CSR depending on whether organizations are local or multinational. MNCs in Pakistan operate in a manner that closely mirrors their Western counterparts, perhaps unsurprisingly, as many MNCs in Pakistan are foreign owned. Some Pakistani-owned firms may view CSR as a foreign concept, underpinned by a lack of respect for traditional forms of social responsibility, grounded in religious and community duty. Future research is needed to establish if religious traditions informing beneficence for the 'deserving poor' include or exclude some traditionally disadvantaged communities (that may be regarded, traditionally, as less deserving) from the benefits of CSR. From an empirical and thus an emerging theoretical perspective, one size does not fit all. Further, although there was good evidence of gift giving, on reflection, this was not always with a focus on the sustainability and empowerment potential of the CSR actions taken.

However, although the focus of this chapter is firms, there are also risks to the sustainability of vital areas such as health and educational provision, or in any area that is essential for the long-term growth and development of societies. In developed economies, health and education are regarded as public goods, provided by government. The enhancement of well-being and quality of life depends on building individual and community capabilities: what is provided through CSR needs to enable communities to develop and grow (Sen, 1995, 2001). The beneficence of firms should not be confused with clarity regarding the obligations and duties of the state. In Transparency International's Annual Corruption Perception Index, developing countries usually make up the bulk of the most poorly ranked countries; moreover public sector organizations of Pakistan come top on corruption, malpractices and poor governance. The transfer of wealth from the rich to the poor does not invariably build the resilience and sustainability of communities or sharpen a sense of social duty in governments. In the context of developing and emerging economies, an important agenda for CSR research in the future will be the relationship between the level of the CSR activity of firms as a potential disincentive for government modernization, transparency and renewal with regard to public services provision.

References

Ali, I., Ur Rehman, K., Ali, S.I., Yousaf, J. and Zia, M. (2010) 'Corporate social responsibility influences, employee commitment and organizational performance', *African Journal of Business Management*, 4(12): 2796–801.

Ahmad, S.J. (2006) 'From principles to practice: exploring corporate social responsibility in Pakistan', *Journal of Corporate Citizenship*, 24: 115–29.

Amaeshi, K.M., Adi, B.C., Ogbechie, C. and Olufemi, O.A. (2006) 'Corporate social responsibility in Nigeria: Western mimicry or indigenous influences?', *Journal of Corporate Citizenship*, 24: 83–99.

Arora, B. and Puranik, R. (2004) 'A review of corporate social responsibility in India', *Development*, 47(3): 93–100.

Bowen, H.R. (1953) *Social Responsibilities of the Businessman*, New York: Harper.

Carroll, A.B. (1979) 'A three-dimensional conceptual model of corporate performance', *Academy of Management Review*, 4: 497–505.

Carroll, A.B. (1994) 'Social issues in management research: experts' views, analysis and commentary', *Business and Society*, 33(1): 5–29.

Charmaz, K. (2006) *Constructivist Grounded Theory*, London: Sage.

Christensen, J. and Murphy, R. (2004) 'The social irresponsibility of corporate tax avoidance: taking CSR to the bottom line', *Development*, 47(3): 37–44.

Crane, A. and Matten, D. (2007) *Business Ethics*, 2nd edn, Oxford: Oxford University Press.

Engro Corporation (EngroCorp) (2011) *Annual Report 2011*. Available online at http://engro.com/wp-content/uploads/2012/03/F-E-Corp%20AR%202011.pdf (accessed 4 June 2012).

Fig, D. (2005) 'Manufacturing amnesia: corporate social responsibility in South Africa', *International Affairs*, 81(3): 599–617.

Freeman, R.E. (1984) *Strategic Management: A stakeholder approach*, Boston, MA: Pitman.

Friedman, M. (1970) 'The social responsibility of business is to increase its profits', *New York Times Magazine*, 13 September.

Garriga, E. and Mele, D. (2004) 'Corporate social responsibility theories: mapping the territory', *Journal of Business Ethics*, 53: 51–71.

Government of Pakistan (2009) *Companies (Corporate Social Responsibility) General Order, 2009*. Available online at www.secp.gov.pk/corporatelaws/pdf/CSR.pdf (accessed 21 March 2012).

Haigh, M. and Jones, M.T. (2006) 'The drivers of corporate social responsibility: a critical review', *Business Review*, 5: 51–71.

Hameed, S.K. (2010) 'Corporate social responsibility (CSR) theory and practice in Pakistan', unpublished Master's thesis, Swedish University of Agricultural Sciences. Available online at http://stud.epsilon.slu.se/2096/1/hameed_s_k_101222.pdf (accessed 19 January 2013).

International Monetary Fund (IMF) (2006) *World Economic Outlook: Financial systems and economic cycles*, Brussels: International Monetary Fund.

Jamali, D. and Mirshak, R. (2007) 'Corporate social responsibility (CSR): theory and practice in a developing country context', *Journal of Business Ethics*, 72: 243–62.

Jamali, D. and Sidani, R. (2011) 'Is CSR counterproductive in developing countries: the unheard voices of change', *Journal of Change Management*, 11(1): 69–71.

Jaseem, A.S. (2006) 'From principles to practice: exploring corporate social responsibility in Pakistan', *Journal of Corporate Citizenship*, 24: 115–29.

Khan, F.R. and Lund-Thomsen, P. (2011) 'CSR as imperialism: towards a phenomenological approach to CSR in the developing world', *Journal of Change Management*, 11(1): 73–90.

Lantos, G.P. (2001) 'The boundaries of strategic corporate social responsibility', *Journal of Consumer Marketing*, 18(7): 595–632.

Mwaura, K. (2004) 'Corporate citizenship: the changing legal perspective in Kenya', paper presented at the Interdisciplinary CSR Research Conference, International Centre for Corporate Social Responsibility (ICCSR), Nottingham University Business School, 22–23 October.

Naeem, M.A. and Welford, R. (2009) 'A comparative study of corporate social responsibility in Bangladesh and Pakistan', *Corporate Social Responsibility and Environmental Management*, 16(2): 108–22.

Procter and Gamble (P&G) (2011) *Sustainability Report.* Available online at www.pg.com/en_PK/products/PG_2011_Sustainability_Report.pdf (accessed 4 November 2012).

Sen, A.K. (1995) *Inequality Re-examined*, London: Clarendon Press.

Sen, A.K. (2001) *Development as Freedom*, Oxford: Oxford University Press.

Silverman, D. (2000) *Doing Qualitative Research: A practical handbook*, London: Sage.

Trueman, M., Cornelius, N. and Wallace, J. (2012) 'Building brand value online: exploring relationships between company and city brands', *European Journal of Marketing*, 46(7/8): 1013–31.

UNESCO (2012) *Adult and Youth Literacy, 1990–2015 Analysis of Data for 41 Selected Countries*. Available online at www.uis.unesco.org/Education/Documents/UIS-literacy-statistics-1990-2015-en.pdf (accessed 10 March 2013).

United Nations Development Program (UNDP) (2006) *Beyond Scarcity: Power, poverty and the global water crisis*, Brussels: UNDP.

Visser, W. and Macintosh, A. (1998) 'A short review of the historical critique of usury', *Accounting, Business & Financial History*, 8(2): 175–89.

Wallace, J. and Cornelius, N. (2010) 'Community development and social regeneration: how the third sector addresses the needs of BME communities in post-industrial cities', *Journal of Business Ethics*, 97(1): 43–54.

Weyzig, F. (2006) 'Local and global dimensions of corporate social responsibility in Mexico', *Journal of Corporate Citizenship*, 24(winter): 69–81.

World Bank (2006) *World Development Report 2007: Development and the next generation*, Washington, DC: World Bank.

World Bank (WB) (2010) *World Bank Country Data*. Available online at http://data.worldbank.org/indicator/SE.XPD.TOTL.GD.ZS/countries (accessed 19 March 2012).

7 Corporate social responsibility practices in Indonesia

Intermediary matters – case studies from Indonesia

*Janti Gunawan, Agnes Tuti Rumiati,
Lantip Trisunarno and Eddy Soedjono*

Corporate social responsibility (CSR) is increasingly attracting the attention of companies operating in Indonesia (Koestoer, 2007; Indonesia Business Link, 2011), including the Government of Indonesia. Simon (2009) finds that CSR has been used as a strategic tool to obtain legitimacy and operate successfully in Indonesia. Although there are regulations in place, problems exist regarding the interpretation of the regulations, and how they should be implemented remains unclear.

Recent studies have found a trend of CSR moving from philanthropy and non-integrated activities to such activities being included within a firm's value chain, and, therefore, enhancing the strategic position of the company in the market (Indonesia Business Link, 2011; Bappenas, 2012). However, other studies have tended not to support the above position. These studies have found that the implementation of CSR programmes in Indonesia is varied and mixed across companies (Koestoer, 2007; Simon, 2009). These current findings are consistent with the results from Chappel and Moon (2005), which suggest that CSR practices in Asia are not homogeneous, and that there is no single explanatory factor to explain this heterogeneity. The authors indicate that national factors may explain why CSR practices differ between firms. This chapter will attempt to expand on the Chappel and Moon research and aims to answer why variances exist between companies implementing CSR in Indonesia. It examines the definition of CSR as stated in law and regulations, maps CSR programmes practised in Indonesia, examines the role of CSR, and identifies key stakeholders enhancing the successful implementation of CSR.

Institutional theory and stakeholder theory is used to frame the exploration of CSR practice in Indonesia. Institutional theory offers a framework to examine the interface between business and social interaction (Brammer *et al.*, 2012). The opening section introduces the country profile of Indonesia, which is followed by a review of institutional and stakeholder theories, in which the hypotheses are developed. The chapter then presents three case studies, followed by a discussion on the critical issues associated with the implementation of CSR in Indonesia.

Indonesia: country profile

Indonesia is located in Southeast Asia and has a population of 237 million (Biro Pusat Statistik, 2011). It is the fourth largest country in the world (by population) after China, India and the United States. The country consists of over 17,000 islands and over 300 different ethnic groups. The majority of the population is confined to five main islands: Java, Sumatera (Sumatra), Kalimantan (Borneo), Sulawesi (Celebes) and Papua, and more than half of the population live on the island of Java, the smallest of the five main islands. The economy is driven by the service and industry sectors, which are mainly located in Java, but in terms of employment most of the population works in the agricultural sector. The industrialization process started in the 1970s, and focused on foreign direct investment in labour-intensive industries. Industries considered strategic to Indonesia, for example cement, oil and gas, are generally government owned and heavily regulated. Recent economic development has pushed some strategic industry to relax monopoly conditions, for example in the cement and telecommunications industries, although they remain regulated. As a consequence, some of the state-owned enterprises (SOEs) in strategic industries became publicly listed enterprises (e.g., PT Semen Gresik (Persero) Tbk, a cement company).

While Indonesia is rich in natural resources, a large population spread over a large number of islands creates many challenges, and not the least is the unequal economic development that exists within the country. Java is the most advanced economy among all the islands. In 2011, following a strategic review of Indonesia, the Indonesian Government decided to move away from the generic 'one strategy fits all' development policy. The country was divided into six economic corridors, namely: Sumatra, Java, Kalimantan (Borneo), Sulawesi (Celebes), Bali–Nusa Tenggara and Papua–Maluku (Molluca) (MP3EI, 2011). Depending on the characteristics of the region, each corridor will focus on the main areas of development: agriculture, mining, energy, industry, marine, tourism and information technology. This policy is a result of the changing system of governance, whereby Indonesia started the move from a centralized government to a decentralized government system in 1998.

Current strategic development stresses the need to overcome high levels of unemployment and poverty, including addressing environmental issues. CSR has come to be viewed as an alternative to help the government to overcome these problems (Koestoer, 2007). To give a scale of the problems, Indonesia has a high unemployment rate (6.8 per cent in 2011 or about 7.7 million people), in which 70 per cent of those unemployed (5.3 million) are youth (aged between 15 and 29 years), and a high poverty rate of 12.3 per cent (Biro Pusat Statistik, 2011). In addition, the majority of the labour force is poorly educated (lower than junior high school), and the economic development of the country seems to be, in some part, at the expense of the environment, with Indonesia being one of the largest CO_2 producers in the world (UNSTATS, 2011). Thus, given that CSR stresses the need to address economic, social and environmental issues, Indonesia seems to be following the findings of Visser (2008), which show that CSR in developing countries shifts towards multidimensional issues, including social and environmental concerns.

Institutional theory and the role of CSR intermediaries

The basic premise of institutional theory is that companies need legitimacy to exist (Zucker, 1987). Companies receive normative pressures and social requirements from various social groups in which they are embedded. These include national, regional and local governments, communities, authorities and professional associations (Scott and Meyer, 1991). When companies are able to meet and maintain these requirements they gain legitimacy (Zucker, 1987). The ability to meet social requirements is achieved by mimicking others. Another mechanism to gain legitimacy is through complying with laws (DiMaggio and Powell, 1983; Doh *et al.*, 2010).

In the context of Indonesia, Law Number 25/2007 regulates investing companies. The regulation implies that companies need to conduct themselves in a socially responsible manner, stating that it is the 'inherent responsibility of the existing company, to comply with environment, values, norms and local cultures' (Law Number 25/2007, Chapter 15). Operationally, this law is translated differently by institutions depending on private or public ownership; the latter referring to the Ministry of State Owned Enterprises (SOEs) and other ministries (e.g., Ministry of Finance, Ministry of Laws, Ministry of Cooperatives and SMEs).

The Ministry of SOEs Regulation Number 05/2007 established a CSR regulation for SOEs, to determine the role of an SOE as stated in the Law Number 19/2003, which is to improve the wealth of Indonesian citizens, provide jobs opportunities and reduce poverty. This regulation recognizes two types of CSR programmes: partnerships between SOEs and small enterprises, and environmental programmes. CSR activities are financed by a maximum of 2 per cent of the SOE net profit for each programme. The small enterprise partner should comply with the following criteria: (1) be located in Indonesia; (2) have assets less than IDR 200 million; and (3) have been established for a minimum of one year. The partnership programme focuses on providing access to finance for the partner, for example through soft loans, with a complementary supporting grant in the form of education, training and access to markets. The maximum grant is 20 per cent of the soft loan. On the other hand, environmental programmes refer to philanthropy, for example supporting disaster victims, improving health services, providing religious facilities, and environmental recovery programmes. The SOE has to set up a work unit to run the CSR programme, which is responsible for developing a procedure, programme and budget, as well as running the planned activities, monitoring and reporting outcomes.

For private enterprises (i.e., non-SOEs), the type of business defines the institutional obligation of the company. By law there are several forms of business recognized in Indonesia: individual, limited liabilities and cooperatives. The individual company is ruled by Law Number 20/2008 on SMEs; limited liabilities are regulated by Law Number 40/2007; and cooperatives are governed by Law Number 25/1992. Neither SMEs nor cooperative laws mention CSR. This means that neither individual firms nor cooperatives have an obligation to undertake CSR. However, limited liability law explicitly states that CSR is an obligation of companies if their business is involved or related to the extraction of natural resources. As such, CSR is defined as 'activity that can sustain economic development that can improve the quality and environment of the company and local community' (Law Number 40/2007, chapter 74). CSR activities are financed by company operational income, in which case CSR can be classified as an operational expense. Simon (2009) argues that the obligation of CSR as attached only to those companies extracting natural resources neglects the true value of CSR. Companies may conduct CSR to improve their stock value and neglect socio- and environmental sustainability aspects. Nonetheless, Simon finds that some non-extraction companies conduct CSR because the companies hold genuine concerns for environmental and community/social values, rather than simply a commitment to the law. This account, then, offers the following propositions:

P1:   *The motivation to conduct CSR differs between SOEs and private enterprises.*

P1a: *CSR in SOEs is conducted because of government obligation and therefore is more reactive.*

P1b: *CSR in the private natural extraction enterprises is conducted because of the law enforcement as well as company concerns for its sustainable business. It is more proactive.*

As mentioned earlier, in terms of ownership, companies in Indonesia may be government owned or privately owned, and in terms of business forms, these companies may be limited liability. Some of the limited liability SOEs are semi-privatized. This means that semi-privatized companies need to comply with both the Ministry of SOEs' regulation as well as the limited liabilities law on CSR. Thus, it is possible to offer the further proposition:

P2:   *Dual roles of semi-privatized SOEs lead to dual roles of CSR. This creates operational gaps in the CSR accountability.*

Previous CSR studies adopt stakeholder theory to explain how various actors are defined in the CSR implementation process (Garriga and Mele, 2008). CSR, understood from this perspective of implementation, stresses that corporate activities should be taken beyond the concern of the company's shareholders. A corporation should not be considered purely a profit-oriented entity, but should also comply with social concerns. While it can be argued that investors monitor company governance and are likely to avoid investing in low social performance organizations, stakeholder theory provides a broader understanding of the social network in which companies are placed (Doshi and Khokle, 2012). It identifies a company's internal actors (e.g., employees, labour union) and external actors, both directly (e.g., industry association, consumers) and indirectly associated with the company, such as competitors and the media.

Among the important stakeholders in CSR implementation is the intermediary. An intermediary, or 'middle man', mediates between stakeholders and plays an important role in helping the company to understand its social environment (Stapleton and Woodward, 2009). Intermediaries may take various forms, such as statutory bodies, charitable and voluntary organizations, environmental groups, trade unions, financial organizations, research centres and networking facilitators. Intermediaries exist because social and economic goals need to be integrally connected. Nonetheless, understanding the social needs and various characteristics is not easy (Porter and Kramer, 2009).

Howells (2006) argues that intermediary services cover the understanding of the client, diagnose a need and conduct scanning and information processing. The intermediary will further broker the linkage between clients and other institutions, which may involve knowledge processing and integration between the client as well as the intermediary institution. The delivery of services may also cover training, certification and reporting. Importantly, it is not a one-off service, but a long-term and one-to-one service. On the other hand, companies may not have adequate human resources to respond to varying social needs. From an economic point of view, companies focus on efficiency, and outsourcing CSR responsibility offers economic benefits. Furthermore, social demands from communities can require local knowledge and skills, which companies may not be able to provide. In SOEs, charity is part of their CSR programmes and is regulated by law. Considering that institutional frameworks differ between SOEs and private enterprises, the following propositions are made:

> *P3: Intermediaries play an important role in the CSR execution programme.*
> *P3a: Intermediaries are positively associated with CSR execution in the SOEs because of the ability to meet social values.*
> *P3b: Intermediaries are positively associated with CSR execution in the private enterprise because of its ability to meet both economic and social values.*

Case studies

Bonoma (1985) advocates conducting case research for the initial investigation of phenomena about which little is known, which relatively speaking is the case with CSR in Indonesia. Case study research can be used as a basis for theory development (Eisenhardt and Graebner, 2007), and allows answers to be found for 'how' and 'why' questions (Yin, 2002; Ghauri, 2004). The following three case studies each offer an analysis at company level, with the respondents being directors or managers of the CSR unit. The selected companies are located in Java, which was targeted as it is the most economically dominant island, and accounts for 61 per cent of the country's GDP. In the first case, the company is privately owned, while the other (providing two case studies) is an SOE.

Case 1: PT Holcim Indonesia

PT Holcim Indonesia (www.holcim.co.id) is a cement and concrete producer. It is a publicly listed company in Indonesia and is a subsidiary of the Swiss Group Company, which operates in around 70 countries. As a cement producer, the company exploits natural resources and therefore should comply with chapter 74 of Law Number 40/2007 in regard to CSR requirements. Sustainable development activity has been reported each year since 2006 (so beginning before the launch of the Indonesian government policy on CSR). CSR activities at the company cover social, economic and environmental aspects. The social programme focuses on health and safety, the economic programmes develop entrepreneurship, including skills training and microfinance assistance, while the environmental programme deals with water supply, sanitation and waste management. It is clear the company goes beyond the CSR requirements set by the Indonesian government. As a multinational enterprise Holcim CSR refers to the achievement of the United Nations' Millennium Development Goals, and as a resource extraction company Holcim implements the Ministry of Environment guidelines. The company has achieved national awards in the environmental programme.

In running the CSR programme the company facilitates the establishment of a Community Advisory Panel (CAP), which consists of various stakeholders who contribute to the selection, planning, management and evaluation of CSR activities. The CAP acts as an intermediary that links the company's strategic initiative to society through social mapping and regular meetings that discuss the requirements of the society and concerns about the company. The follow-up actions of the mapping and meetings were CSR activities such as skills training for local communities. This training may be related or unrelated to the company's value chain activities, and include scholarship, and social and environmental activities such as biodiversity and health and safety programmes. The business-related training for the community mainly involves training for masons, for example to improve the quality of work and to update their knowledge as the building industry moves towards greener industry. Such CSR activities become possible because of the collaborative knowledge and actions of the various stakeholders. For example, the community provides inputs of its needs and local enterprises offer to be trained as trainers for the community, which in turn are aligned with the company goals, as discussed by Howells (2006).

Case 2: PTP N X

PTP N X is an SOE operating in the agricultural sector, located in East Java (www.ptpn10.com). The stakeholders of the company include national and local government. One of the national government programmes is piloting a teaching industry at the local level in East Java province. Teaching industry refers to the establishment of a small factory at a vocational school, to facilitate skills learning so that graduates can support the development of private enterprises. Intermediary actors from the local university, Institut Teknologi Sepuluh Nopember (ITS), were selected by national government to examine the needs of vocational schools' stakeholders. Vocational teachers considered the national government's intention to develop a teaching industry as too ambitious, as teachers are still struggling to deal with the lack of infrastructure, capacity issues and curriculum development. Establishing a teaching factory requires business knowledge and skills, which most of the teachers don't have. At this point, the role of the industry partner has only involved receiving intern students. In the future, it is hoped that the industry partner will help in guiding curriculum development and the transfer of business knowledge and networks. The school enterprise client requested that the teaching factory should work closely with the enterprise partner, and improve its delivery. Considering the gap between the needs and demand, the intermediary approached PTP N X and PT Agrindo, a large agricultural machinery company, to support a teaching industry pilot project. PTP N X agreed to support local schools' development by providing transportation and accommodation allowances for teachers. This in turn allowed teachers to attend skills training, which led to improving the curriculum, facilitating a network with enterprise clients and promoting the schools' products through the facilitation of intermediaries. From the side of private enterprise, PT Agrindo were also willing to support teachers' upgrading programmes by accepting them as apprentices in the company. The CSR activities of both PTP N X and PT Agrindo became possible because of intermediary networks and facilitation. Universities can act as intermediaries to facilitate the linkage between stakeholders, and ensure the legitimacy of SOEs. Howell (2006) argues that the role of universities as intermediaries includes the process of knowledge transfer. In this case, the team at ITS was able to identify the partner for stakeholders, providing support in the implementation and reporting, which is necessary for companies.

Case 3: PTP N X and rural development

One mandate for PTP N X's CSR programme is also rural development. The following case describes how part of its programme benefited local farmers. Brenjonk is a farmers' group, established in 1991 in Trawas Village, Mojokerto District, East Java Province. The village is located within a resort area, near Surabaya, the capital of the province. When tourism in the area was growing, farmers sold their land, but after a few years realized there was not enough income to support themselves and their families. In an effort to generate more sustainable incomes, the farmers, through government support, were encouraged to shift to organic farming. However, access to markets is difficult for farmers with no marketing skills, limited logistic networks and poor infrastructure.

CV. Media Inovasi Kita is a small company based in Surabaya that specializes in providing small to medium-sized enterprises (SMEs) producing food products with better access to markets. Major issues facing SME food producers is the fact that they have no links with the suppliers of retail food chains, and problems surround maintaining quality standards for their products. What is needed is the establishment of secure networks for the organic farmers to sell their produce and grow their businesses. In an effort to build a reliable cooperative, Media Inovasi Kita met with farmers to discuss a business partnership opportunity. From 2009, Media Inovasi Kita became a marketing partner of Brenjonk, to facilitate the selling of their organic vegetables and rice to markets in Surabaya.

Another problem facing farmers is the difficulty of expanding production as the business grows. Farmers are very restricted in terms of land ownership and access to land is limited. One possible solution is to build small screen farming (greenhouses). As the marketing partner, Media Inovasi Kita investigated various schemes that would allow farmers access to finance. The company approached PTP N X with a CSR proposal to obtain finance for farmers to build their own greenhouses. The CSR proposal was accepted because the marketing partner became the guarantor for farmers, who were provided with soft loans. Under normal circumstances PTP N X would not be able to provide direct loans to farmers due to regulation requiring CSR clients to have been established for the minimum of a year, and to be monitored. Through the intermediary's guarantee, the Brenjonk farmers were able to obtain soft loans to develop their cooperative business. Another positive benefit arising from this case was PTP N X being able to provide training assistance for farmers. In this case, Media Inovasi Kita was the intermediary that allowed PTP N X to be able to securely disburse a soft loan from its CSR fund, for the benefit of the community. In fact, from this CSR activity the company found that community requests grew higher than the company capacities in terms of finance and human resource capital.

Discussion and conclusion

Based on the preceding accounts, the motivation to conduct CSR can be seen to differ between SOEs and private enterprises. CSR in SOEs is conducted because of government obligation and is more reactive, while CSR in the private natural extraction enterprises is conducted because of law enforcement requiring a company to be concerned for its sustainable business, therefore more proactive. Institutional theory shows that companies conduct CSR to obtain legitimacy (Doh *et al.*, 2010; Brammer *et al.*, 2012), and the three cases discussed above showed that perspectives on legitimacy differ from one company to another. The multinational company, Holcim, considers compliance with global standards will maintain its legitimacy, while the SOE stresses that complying with domestic regulations ensures the company's legitimacy within the local and national context. Taking an international perspective, Holcim pushes the company to be more proactive than the domestic business of PTP N X in implementing CSR. These findings parallel those of Garriga and Mele (2008), who claim that territory defines the responsibility of the company. It can also be argued that dual roles of semi-privatized SOEs lead to dual forms of CSR. This creates operational gaps in CSR accountability. Nonetheless, such a proposition cannot be drawn out fully from the account given here as PTP N X is a fully state-owned enterprise. This leads to the suggestion that future research may usefully investigate the implementation of CSR in semi-privatized companies in Indonesia.

This chapter also argues that intermediaries play an important role in the execution of a CSR programme. Intermediaries are positively associated with CSR execution in SOEs because of their ability to meet social values, while they are positively associated with CSR execution in the private enterprise because of their ability to meet both economic and social values. The case of PTP N X shows that the execution of CSR in this SOE was driven by external pressure and adoption of a bottom-up approach. Intermediaries – for example university and marketing partners for the farmers – shape the form of CSR activities for SOEs. Parallel to findings by Howells (2006), intermediaries may take many forms, such as a university, or a private or community-based partnership. The role of intermediaries in the CSR process is very important, but CSR regulation has not addressed their role.

On the other hand, the Holcim case demonstrates how a multinational company can have a clear strategy for CSR, which goes beyond the requirements set by government regulation. This intent is driven more by international pressures due to its global presence. At the execution level, an intermediary body, such as the Community Advisory Panel, acts as an important institution to provide inputs for the CSR programme on how and why the company should respond to societal demands. As the CAP consists of multi-stakeholders, the intermediary negotiates both the social and economic concerns of the company.

Intermediaries can be seen to work at different operational levels. For example, the Holcim case presents an intermediary at the local level, while the PTP N X cases provide examples of intermediaries at the provincial level. Future study may investigate how intermediaries can work at different levels to support CSR practice, and how knowledge is shared, and whether CSR practices can be learned and disseminated systematically. In the context of Indonesia, the definition of CSR and the scope of CSR activities have largely been limited to SOEs and private natural extraction companies. In addition, triple bottom line issues – social, economical and environmental aspects of CSR – have not been fully integrated, but managed separately. This gap calls for further research on policy advice and operational management on CSR in developing countries. Visser (2008) argues that CSR in developing countries is often driven by international standards, and aims to achieve global consistency of operating units. The case of Holcim can help remind us of how policy can be developed to manage CSR in the context of a developing country, such as Indonesia, and how the example of a CAP can be used to formulate a tool to bridge the gap between stakeholders' interests.

The account provided here can be said to capture the activities of Indonesian companies operating in the transition economy. Indonesia has shifted from a centralized to a decentralized government system. Interestingly, the decision-making process in SOEs is still centralized. Considering the challenge of CSR implementation to respond to local demand, further consideration of how CSR is managed in an SOE would be beneficial. As discussed here, institutional and stakeholder theories are helpful in examining cases. However, to date, the role of intermediaries and how they relate to sustainable aspects of CSR has only just begun to be explored. In addition, given that a transition economy has led to the semi-privatization of SOEs, the further development of CSR practices in Indonesia remains open to investigation.

References

Bappenas (2012) *CSR Implementation in East Java*, workshop report, Jakarta: Bappenas.

Biro Pusat Statistik (2011) 'Penduduk Indonesia menurut provinsi'. Available online at www.bps.go.id/tab_sub/view.php?tabel=1&daftar=1&id_subyek=12&notab=1 (accessed 29 April 2012).

Bonoma, T.V. (1985) 'Case research in marketing: opportunities, problems, and a process', *Journal of Marketing Research (JMR)*, 22(2): 199–208.

Brammer, S., Jackson, G. and Matten, D. (2012) 'Corporate social responsibility and institutional theory: new perspectives on private governance', *Socio-Economic Review*, 10: 3–28.

Chappel, W. and Moon, J. (2005) 'Corporate social responsibility (CSR) in Asia: a seven-country study of CSR web site reporting', *Business & Society*, 44: 415–41.

DiMaggio, P.J. and Powell, W.W. (1983) 'The iron cage revisited: institutional isomorphism and collective rationality in organizational fields', *American Sociological Review*, 48: 147–60.

Doh, P.J., Howton, S.D., Howton, S.W. and Siegel, D.S. (2010) 'Does the market respond to an endorsement of social responsibility? The role of institutions, information and legitimacy', *Journal of Management*, 33(6): 1461–85.

Doshi, V. and Khokle, P. (2012) 'An institutional perspective on corporate social responsibility', *Vikalpa*, 37(2): 98–108.

Eisenhardt, K.M. and Graebner, M.E. (2007) 'Theory building from cases: opportunities and challenges', *Academy of Management Journal*, 50(1): 25–32.

Garriga, E. and Mele, D. (2008) 'Corporate social responsibility theories: mapping the territory', in Crane, A. Matten, D. and Spence L.J. (eds) *Corporate Social Responsibility: Readings and cases in a global context*, Abingdon: Routledge.

Ghauri, P. (2004) 'Designing and conducting case studies in international business research', in Marschan-Piekkari, R. and Welch, C. (eds) *Handbook of Qualitative Research Methods for International Business*, Cheltenham: Edward Elgar.

Howells, J. (2006) 'Intermediation and the role of intermediaries in innovation', *Research Policy*, 35: 715–38.

Indonesia Business Link (2011) 'Responsible and sustainable business practices across value chains: an ILO-OECD dialogue with the business community in Indonesia'. unpublished seminar report, Jakarta, 30 November.

Koestoer, Y.T. (2007) 'Corporate Social Responsibility in Indonesia: Building internal corporate values to address challenges in CSR implementation', paper presented at the seminar on Good Corporate and Social Governance in Promoting ASEAN's Regional Integration, Asean Secretariat, Jakarta, 17 January.

Law number 25/2007 on Investment. Available online at www.embassyofindonesia. org/ina-usa/economy/pdf/laws/Investment_Law_Number_25-2007.pdf (accessed 19 February 2013).

Law number 40/2007 on Limited Liabilities. Available online at www.bapepam.go.id (accessed 19 February 2013).

Law number 25/1992 on Cooperatives. Available online at www.depkop.go.id (accessed 19 February 2013).

Law number 20/2008 on SMEs. Available online at http://bi.go.id (accessed 19 February 2013).

Ministry of SOEs regulation number 05/1997 on CSR for SOEs. Available online at www.bumn.go.id (accessed 19 February 2013).

MP3EI (2011) *Masterplan Percepatan dan Perluasan Pembangunan Ekonomi Indonesia 2011–2015*, Jakarta: Ministry of Economic Coordination.

Porter, M. and Kramer, R. (2009) 'The competitive advantage of corporate philanthrophy', in Crane, A., Dirk, M. and Spence, L.J. (eds) *Corporate Social Responsibiltiy: Readings and cases in a global context*, Abingdon: Routledge.

Scott, W.R. and J.W. Meyer (1991) 'The organization of societal sectors: propositions and early evidence', in Powell, W.W and DiMaggio, P.J (eds) *The New Institutionalism in Organizational Analysis*, Chicago, IL: University of Chicago Press.

Simon, H. (2009) 'CSR in Indonesia: a qualitative study from a managerial perspective regarding views and other important aspects of CSR in Indonesia', Bachelor's thesis, Hogskolan Gotland University, Visby, Sweden.

Stapleton, P. and Woodward, D. (2009) 'Stakeholder reporting: the role of inter-mediaries', *Business and Society Review*, 11(2): 183–216.

UNSTATS (2011) 'Environment statistics country snapshot: Indonesia'. Available online at http://unstats.un.org/unsd/environment/envpdf/Country_Snapshots_Aug% 202011/Indonesia.pdf (accessed 29 April 2012).

Visser, W. (2008) 'Corporate social responsibility in developing countries', in Crane, A., McWilliams, A., Matten, D., Moon, J. and Siegel, D. (eds) *The Oxford Handbook of Corporate Social Responsibility*, Oxford: Oxford University Press, pp. 473–9.

Yin, R.K. (2002) *Applications of Case Study Research*, 2nd edn, Thousand Oaks, CA: Sage.

Zucker, L.G. (1987) 'Institutional theories of organization', *Annual Review of Sociology*, 13: 443–64.

8 CSR sponsor as change maker

Community development programs in Thailand

Patnaree Srisuphaolarn

Although the role of business in society has been debated broadly since the 1970s, contemporary views suggest the business of a company is not restricted to making profit and maximizing shareholder value (UNCTAD 2011; UN 2012; WBCSD 2012); more emphasis is placed on stakeholders. The term *stakeholder* is defined broadly to include both business-related people and entities such as employees and suppliers, and non-related people and entities such as communities, situated near a company site and communities in general (Freeman 1984; Yodprudtikan *et al.* 2006). Companies—from multinationals to small and medium-sized businesses—increasingly appreciate the rationale of extending resources to upgrade standards of living in communities (Dixon and Clifford 2007; Thorne *et al.* 2008; Fisher *et al.* 2009); they aim for sustainability, and care for people occupying the bottom of society. In line with this movement, community engagement draws the attention of readers in the CSR literature. Most cases illustrate how a company contributes to a community altruistically, but community engagement is often portrayed as one-sided, with a community as participant in a project initiated by a person or entity from outside the community. This chapter illustrates cases from the context of Thailand in which community members make changes from the inside out, demonstrating how a company acts as a catalyst for change. In these cases, companies do not go to a community and solve problems directly; they convince and support a community to get involved in a learning process so community members discover problems and resolutions on their own. Companies commit to creating social capital and upgrading human resources for greater sustainability, one of self-reliance. These acts demonstrate that economic, environmental, and social developments are achievable without sacrificing or destroying the others.

CSR, community engagement, and sustainability

Rationales for including community engagement in a company's CSR project are numerous. Generally found in CSR literature are rationales based on stakeholder theory, resource-based views, corporate citizenship, corporate shared values (strategic CSR), and sustainable development. These theories can be grouped into three subgroups according to perspectives concerning CSR: altruism, strategic management, and a hybrid of the two. The altruism perspective encompasses stakeholder theory and corporate citizenship, and strategic management includes corporate shared values and bottom of the pyramid. The hybrid group includes sustainable development and resource-based views.

When a company views community engagement altruistically, it employs either stakeholder theory or corporate citizenship. Stakeholder theory suggests responsibility is not limited to maximizing shareholder wealth, but extends to other stakeholders such as employees and suppliers (Freeman 1984). Contemporarily, stakeholders extend to under-represented groups such as people living below the poverty level. Corporate citizenship suggests CSR is a means to express harmony with a community, which can be defined broadly as an entire country. Disputes between companies and communities are ongoing issues in business ethics (Eweje 2006; Brueckner and Mamun 2010), and community development is a means to preempt disputes.

Companies can perceive community engagement as a means to achieve strategic goals. Corporate shared value contends that a company achieves sustainability by creating shared value (CSV) among related communities (Porter and Kramer 2011). This view focuses on strategic management, integrating a community as part of a value chain. The concept of bottom of the pyramid (BOP) belongs to this school of thought (Prahalad and Hammond 2002). Through goods and services innovations, corporations help people below the poverty level by offering products at affordable prices (Hart and Christensen 2002). A supporting assumption of BOP is that consumption ability is a sign of better living standards, which appears positive superficially. However, such people become dependent on company products in the long term. In the short term, people occupying the BOP are placed at the end of a company value chain as consumers, still having to struggle to find the income to consume product innovations. Focus is on the well-being of the company, not the community.

The hybrid view of community development encompasses sustainable development and triple bottom lines. Sustainable development is concerned with the macro-environment; companies should ensure corporate activities do not reap only economic benefits without considering social and environmental impacts (United Nations 2012). A concept that represents sustainable economies is the triple bottom line, balancing economic, social, and environmental impacts of corporate activities. Some research examines how companies balance financial and social/environmental performance (Hacking and Guthrie 2008; Hubbard 2009), but no research extends this balance to find an optimum position where both company and community enjoy benefits (Savitz 2006). Extension of the triple bottom line in this direction places a company in the same position suggested by BOP, where community is merely a source of company prosperity.

Resource-based views focus on how a company develops core competencies that are imitated with great difficulty (Barney 1991). Extension of this theory to community development indicates that companies use competencies in such projects. For example, a core competency of Intel is computer literacy; thus, its projects involve building computer centers and educating community members on computer technologies (Campbell 2012). Although companies conduct community-need assessments, the role of communities is limited to informants and beneficiary recipients. Since a latent need exists for marketing, communities could inform companies about immediate problems and needs, but they might not know the causes of current problems, and no guarantee exists that a community would not become dependent on the company.

A common theme emerges when reviewing these areas of the literature. While emphasizing sustainability, businesses often interpret sustainability in a way that serves company goals rather than enhances community sustainability itself, reflecting both neoclassic economic thought concerning how a company conducts business and the hierarchy of societal groups in which the company is on top and the community lies somewhere below. Though the community enjoys better facilities, it remains dependent on the business. Some scholars argue worldwide sustainability is too abstract; community is the more appropriate unit of analysis for sustainable economies (Bridger and Luloff 1999). Sustainability should equate to a community's autonomy, identifying its own problems and solving them in its own ways.

Community sustainability

Community sustainability focuses on self-reliance. It does not deny market mechanisms, but emphasizes the strengths of social and human capital in a community (Bridger and Luloff 1999). Asset-based community development theory suggests social and human capitals are achievable in a community by mobilizing assets both in individuals and in networks already present in the community (Fisher *et al.* 2009). A supporting theory of social- and human-capital creation is the knowledge-creation spiral model proposed by Nonaka and Takeuchi (1995). It contends knowledge creating is a process of socialization, externalization, combination, and internalization. A person expresses knowledge explicitly by socializing. Capturing explicit knowledge from others, a receiver combines the new knowledge into his or her own internal knowledge stock. By internalizing new knowledge, he or she possesses more stock with which to socialize in a subsequent round of knowledge creation. However, some communities are unaware of their own problems, requiring someone from the outside to act as trigger. Carrigan *et al.* (2011) use innovation diffusion theory to explain how a campaign to engage a community in environmentally friendly packaging consumption for retailers was conducted and diffused from the United Kingdom.

Combining innovation diffusion and knowledge management is crucial if community development sustainability is to be achieved. Based on an assumption of low community mobility, sources of knowledge arrive from outside. Thus, the theory of innovation diffusion explains the process of new knowledge dissemination. Knowing how to absorb knowledge and create a new body of knowledge is inevitable to upgrade social and human capitals to achieve the ultimate goal of sustainability.

The next question concerns what new knowledge should be diffused to a community. Experiences with community development in many developing countries suggest management knowledge—not knowledge of professions— is lacking in most communities (Das 2009). Management knowledge is the greatest contribution a company can make to foster community sustainability. Succinctly, a company contributes the most when it teaches a community how to manage. Educating is the goal of educational institutions, but in developing economies where institutions are few, companies can help fill the void. Similar to the innovation diffusion process, companies can disseminate knowledge on how to manage a community through the theory of knowledge creation and management, but one question remains: how?

Nonaka and Takeuchi (1995) argue there are two kinds of knowledge: implicit and explicit. Implicit knowledge is crucial for knowledge creation in Asian cultures. Coaxing implicit knowledge from a person requires a place for two parties to share and absorb knowledge. The theory is built on Japanese examples where trust already exists among members of a company. If this theory is applied to community development, it is crucial to build trust as an initial step. The knowledge-creation model proposed by Nonaka is intended for organizations in which hierarchy is a means to force participation in the entire process. Adaption is required if outsiders use this model in a community. Cases described in this chapter illustrate a dialogue method to create a spiral of knowledge that in turn creates cycles, and an intermediary that links a community and company as a supporting mechanism to diffuse and create knowledge.

Uneven development in Thailand

Since the first Economic and Social Development Plan launched in 1951, Thailand has been criticized as a country that developed unevenly, resulting in inequality between urban and rural areas (Dixon 1999). Although it tried to industrialize, the country struggled in the middle where there exist neither cost nor differentiation advantages to compete in worldwide markets. Aiming to raise the standard of living for citizens, it ended up highly unequal (according to the National Economic and Social Development Board, Thailand, the Gini Index of Thailand was 0.485 in 2009, slightly better than 0.507 in 1998 (NESDB website, 2012)).

One of the greatest inequalities is apparent in access to quality education, especially in rural Thailand (Doner 2009). Continuous and lifelong learning are not known well. Much of the population is financially illiterate, especially in the case of farmers who largely occupy the BOP in the Thai economy. When farmers lack sufficient knowledge, it results in at least two problems. First, they know how to farm, but do not know how to manage farming profitably. Second, they are miserable not knowing how to alleviate the problem. The green revolution led to increased dependency on extra-community economies (e.g., middlemen, fertilizer and seed sellers), requiring new technology and inputs to farming (e.g., chemical fertilizers, insecticides, pesticides, machines) that increase costs. Since farms largely produce commodities, farmers have no control over price, and farmers become part of a large value chain in agribusiness. Lacking knowledge and a means to acquire information, farmers do not enjoy negotiation powers (as a result, some parents, for example, only continue growing rice by using money sent from their children who work as factory laborers in big cities).

Industrialization leads to labor mobility from rural agricultural areas to urbanized trade and manufacturing sectors. Some mobilization is seasonal, and the process weakens connections among members of rural communities during the period between harvesting and planting. Exacerbating the problem is a cultural gap between those who urbanize and those who remain rural. Trust—a valuable social capital—dilutes.

Until recently, there were no labor or political parties that represented disparate groups of people. The Pauthai Party, the primary party of the current administration, launched campaigns such as the Village Fund to empower poor people, a fund intended as capital for village enterprises to ease inequality of access to capital. With little to no knowledge of management, the fund was used for consumption of luxury items (e.g., trucks, motorcycles, electrical appliances, mobile phones, etc.) instead of investment, resulting in higher debt rather than higher income (Doner 2009). The debts turned into non-performing loans since they were used for hedonic consumption rather than to generate income. Consumerism diffused to rural areas, but good education had not.

A preliminary survey of four of the 77 provinces in Thailand (as of 2012) shows that social capital is below satisfactory (ABAC Poll 2011)—evidence that Thai communities are stratified and weakening. There is no buffer or safety net when community members fall into trouble. Poverty in Thailand relates to debt problems rather than inadequate food and housing, and eroding social capital is a current issue. Community development in Thailand does not deal with building infrastructure but with qualitative aspects of development such as community self-sufficiency and autonomy to manage well-being.

Community development as CSR in Thailand

Outsourcing community development operations: Community relationship has long been a tradition in Thai culture. Until recently, most CSRs were passive, responding to community requests for donations for religious or cultural causes (Srisuphaolarn 2013). A company engages in community development—both area- and issue-based—because such projects are unrelated to the company's core business. While Western literature on the triple bottom line suggests a company should find an optimum position where both company and community enjoy benefits, the idea is not received well in Asian cultures; the public perceives such practice as deceptive CSR (Srisuphaolarn 2012).

Since community development is not a company's core business, many companies collaborate with experts such as non-profit organizations (NPOs) and government agencies (Srisuphaolarn 2010). Some companies tried to be active by conducting surveys of community needs, but received cold receptions. Communities do not trust that a company is willing to work with them in the long run toward community sustainability; they are skeptical that a project is for the company's benefit alone (Rodrungruang and Kojabhumi, interview 2012). Consequently, most community development CSR projects are conducted by third-party organizations or NPOs such as Kenan Asia, the Population Development Association, and Habitat, which are keen on community development (Srisuphaolarn 2010). Companies remain the sponsors while third-party organizations are the operators. Companies occasionally send employees to join a project, but only as visitors. Hence, there is little relatedness between companies and communities. To a community, CSR appears as mere societal marketing for public relations purposes.

Community development focusing on social capital creation: Companies are primary project carriers in two cases of community development CSR: SCG (Siam Cement Group) and PTT (Petroleum Authority of Thailand). After much experience with CSR, these two companies discovered clear goals associated with CSR for community development. To achieve sustainability, social capital must be created or strengthened. The cases discussed here illustrate how trust is built and how a community is empowered to manage a project on its own. At the completion of the projects, the communities—in a sense—became social enterprises. One became a famous homestay spot in addition to an informal learning center for neighboring villages. The other became a learning center for other communities for developing sustainable communities. Local production linked with local market development and financial cooperation in which members received dividends from community ventures. The following section describes the two projects in detail.

Case studies

Two CSR projects from SCG (Siam Cement Group) and PTT (Petroleum Authority of Thailand) were selected from 14 cases identified as highly socially responsible companies in a prior survey (Srisuphaolarn 2010). These cases illustrated the highest level of community engagement and proved highly sustainable over 20 years (studies of development of CSR patterns in Thailand demonstrate that the public evaluate CSR projects only when conducted continuously and resulting in concrete outcomes (Srisuphaolarn 2013)). According to the survey, criteria for identifying socially responsible companies included project continuity and outcome tangibility. The cases also demonstrate a two-way, dynamic process of engagement between company and community. The relationships are horizontal rather than the typical hier-archical structures observed in most community engagement cases appearing in extant literature. Companies and communities were co-creators of projects that improved standards of living.

The author used an ethnographic method to examine the entire process of how the projects were conducted and how communities evaluated both the project and the sponsoring companies (Westney and Maanen 2011). In addition to reviews of secondary data, four field studies and 21 interviews—both individual and group—were conducted during February and March of 2012.

SCG check dam project and community development at Sa-sob-hok village

Background: King Rama XI founded SCG in 1913 as a cement factory to support modern businesses (company credos illustrate strong responsibility to Thai society, so the company is regarded as a first-mover in modern CSR). SCG Lampang is a subsidiary of SCG, located in the north of Thailand approximately 100 kilometers south of Chiang Mai. Primary businesses are mining and producing cement powder. Commensurate with the company's credo of social responsibility, company policy mandates minimizing impact on surrounding communities (e.g., noise, airborne particles, etc.). The company operated under a mining concession covering 13.6 km^2 of degraded forest in the Mae-Sa sub-district. The area is partially mountainous with unfertile soils due to wildfires and insufficient irrigation. The people of Mae-Sa subsist primarily on vegetable farming with minor activities in foresting.

Community development: The company initiated the check dam project as a trial against wildfires that occurred annually during the dry season (wildfire is a chronic area problem, with fire mostly manmade. The activity is rooted in traditional values, when the forest was thick and dangerous and setting fire was considered a good deed—a viewpoint that today remains only among older villager generations). The check dam was built easily using leftover wood from the forest, and the mechanism was simple. To preserve water, a flowing stream was slowed by erecting a wooden barrier (an action representing local wisdom used by the Miao as a means of irrigation, and reintroduced by King Bhumibol following his work in community development over decades). Proven success-ful, the company wished to extend the knowledge to the larger community. However, villager response was cold. Only after successes from Sa-sob-hok village, one of six villages surrounding SCG Lampang, did more villages sign up for the project. The outcome of the project was not limited to numerous check dams, but included better irrigation, more wild plants for foraging, and closer relationships among villagers. More communication was established, more collaboration was achieved, and more projects were initiated by villagers.

Success of Sa-sob-hok village: According to the theory of innovation diffusion, an opinion leader is the channel that triggers change. Announcing the projects to six nearby villages, SCG Lampang received only one reluctant response from a village head. The company changed its strategy by inviting villagers to a study trip to Chiang Mai Learning Center to learn from a real site the benefits of a check dam. Of 40 participants, only one was fascinated and determined to materialize the idea. This man, Somchai, became an opinion leader who changed the course of the whole village.

Obtaining villager consensus was challenging for both SCG and Somchai. They repeatedly insisted that a check dam would make a difference. Eventually, Somchai convinced the village head to use dam building as the village's annual development activity. Building the dam turned out to be a village gathering that reconnected neighbors who never communicated seriously prior to the project. Satisfied by the results, villagers agreed to build more dams. The project was endorsed formally by consensus, and community partnerships were strengthened.

Villagers learned that building a check dam requires effort, but maintaining a dam is even more difficult. Check dams cannot withstand wildfires, and realizing this, the village initiated forest patrols on a volunteer basis. This turned a wild object collector into a wildfire patrol volunteer. Neighboring villages observed environmental regeneration—more wild mushrooms, better irrigation in the summer, improved water utility, and better prevention of floods during the monsoon season. This resulted in higher productivity in farming, lower expenses to cover damage from flooding, and better livelihood in the community. With profound knowledge of how to manage its ecology system, Sa-sob-hok village recently offered an eco-tour homestay to anyone interested. Most visitors are those who were impressed by a TV commercial, broadcast nationwide, on how Somchai and Sa-sob-hok village turned a nearly degraded mountainous area into a greener watershed.

Mechanisms that drive success: The primary mechanism that drives success is creating space for everyone's voice. SCG Lampang used a dialogue approach to complete its mission. (Note that "dialogue" is a term anthropologists use in relation to field studies, though stakeholder dialogue is also common in CSR literature to convey sustainability (see Kaptein and Tulder 2003).) Dialogue prepares space for all concerned parties to meet and engage in constructive conversations. The problem and its cause could be consensually identified through dialogue. Good dialogue makes people question the status quo and raise awareness to create change. It requires skills, especially when differences in knowledge and social values are involved. SCG Lampang collaborated with Thailand Research Fund experts in a study to learn how to guide constructive dialogues.

In addition to dialogue, the quality circle of PDCA—plan, do, check, and act—was introduced to villagers as a principle of project management. Dialogue was a preparatory process for villagers to establish objectives. PDCA is an effective management tool to control quality and ensure continuous improvement. Once objectives are set, participants must learn to plan, implement, and check whether there are gaps between targets and realized outcomes. If corrective actions are needed, participants must act accordingly. This process was conducted naturally through periodic community meetings. It is a learn-by-doing process, with experienced coaches attending every meeting, ready to add support when problems arise. Resolutions to address unintended consequences and plans for the new project were constructed at village meetings. Reinforcement mechanisms were added to ensure completion of the project within the timeframe. A governance system was designated clearly from the beginning; the project must be run by consensus and by villagers, and SCG Lampang announced it would support the village with anything except money. This measure prevented corruption, often the case when only money pours into a village absent true community partnership.

PTT and its project at Bangnamphueng

Background: PTT was founded in 1978 as a state-run enterprise, the Petroleum Authority of Thailand. It was committed to economic and social development when founded to ensure sufficient energy for the country. PTT's early CSR projects dealt with renewing degraded forests responsively at the request of cooperation from the Forestry Department. Experience with conducting CSR ensured community engagement and commitment were essential to community development success. Its new CSR project objective was to foster a self-sufficient economy as a tool that leads to long-term social enterprises.

Bangnamphueng is a small sub-district, located near a prominent industrial area in southeast Bangkok, with a population of 4,800 in 2011. It was originally an agricultural area, but it urbanized gradually. Under expanding industrialization in the late 1980s, inhabitants moved to other areas for work and education. The turning point was the 1997 financial crisis, and an inflow of laid-off factory workers meant an increasing population. However, there were fewer arable lands for farming due to speculative land purchases during the economic bubble. A small community development plan was implemented and was briefly successful; however, the community remained fragmented and economically vulnerable.

Self-sufficient economy: Just as the check dam was the means by which SCG developed Sa-sob-hok's standard of living, a self-sufficient economy was the means PTT used to develop Bangnamphueng. King Bhumipol proposed the self-sufficient economy, focusing on sensible investments and consumption. The theory was reintroduced in response to the 1997 economic crisis, when people were especially aware of speculative investments and hedonic consumption. Although the term was translated into English as self-sufficient, it means self-reliance in which community members:

> would still be linked to larger economic structures, but they would have vibrant local economies which would better protect them from the whims of capital than is currently the case . . . Self-reliance entails the development of local markets, local production, local processing of previously imported goods, greater cooperation among local economic entities and the like.

> (Bridger and Luloff 1999: 381)

The concept focuses on interdependency among people in a community rather than one-way dependency on markets that limit bargaining power. Rather than focusing on scaled economies, it focuses on economies of scope; rather than focusing on speed of growth, it focuses on steadiness of growth. The theory suggests that only when a person has a strong foundation can he or she step toward the next investment or consumption. A foundation of doing business is having enough capital to invest. Applied to household financial management, a person needs to increase income and decrease expenses to maintain wealth for further investment and consumption. There are many similarities in the core values underpinning the theory and movement, including minimization of one's own needs as suggested by classical economists.

Observing rising consumerism and household debt, PTT decided to institute the self-sufficient economy in communities nationwide. It selected 84 sub-districts as project participants, Bangnamphueng being one of them. The selection criterion was a community's potential to implement the project. Bangnamphueng had previously implemented self-sufficiency in farming ten years earlier, but it was limited to a small group. It had its own Sunday market to distribute farm produce, but transactions were small in both volume and value. Furthermore, Bangnamphueng was a good representative of urbanized farming areas in which household debt was a growing problem. Household income was not low, but most households struggled to make ends meet.

Bangnamphueng was equipped with some resources, but they were not utilized or managed well. As an outsider, PTT faced the challenge of building trust within the entire community. Unlike SCG, PTT used intermediaries to convey its ideas to community members, and convinced them to join. The intermediaries were members of the community who worked as PTT's local staff. Their jobs were to identify opinion leaders, trigger lively meetings at which everyone could voice their opinions freely, and monitor project implementation. The PTT local staff met Manus, head of a self-sufficient experimental farming group, to act as opinion leader. Similar to SCG was the guiding principle that the project must be run by consensus. While SCG used PDCA circles as a guiding principle, PTT prepared a project management guide for each local staff member to follow. The guide covered all significant management aspects (i.e., planning, organizing, staffing, coordinating, report-ing, and budgeting). PTT project managers revealed that it was the same guide used at PTT headquarters, simplified to match a community context.

The project was conducted incrementally, starting with a household social and economic status survey. Participating households completed household bookkeeping for self-assessment of financial standing. Surprised by the imbalance between income and expenses, community members realized they needed to save more money. The first project implemented was energy saving, followed by expenditure minimization. They substituted purchases of small items with producing similar items at home once they learned production techniques at the self-sufficiency learning center, sponsored by PTT. The program was scaled up to community enterprises for various product lines (e.g., farming produce, personal care, home-use utensils, and fertilizer), and farm-related items through the Sunday market. Financial cooperation was established to manage investments from community members.

Mechanisms that drive success: A key success factor is building vitality in learning. PTT promoted knowledge-sharing through a visit-your-neighbor program and dynamism of dialogues at monthly meeting. The visit-your-neighbor program enabled members to learn about problems and solutions from nearby sub-districts. It promoted idea exchange and continuous improvement. The idea that copying is malignant was a community social value, but copying and development was acceptable. Hence, product improvement was the only way for participants to demonstrate ideas to others during subsequent neighbor visits. A spiral of knowledge-sharing began naturally. Interview respondents emphasized they were fond of this activity since they could socialize with people in other sub-districts who were so near yet so far prior to joining the project.

Another mechanism that institutionalized knowledge-sharing and increased social capital in the community was the monthly meeting. Members gathered to decide on issues such as the next activity to support the project, where to take a study visit, and how to organize sales units. Observing members at a gathering, the author noticed each member could offer his or her opinion freely and logically. At the assembly, there was no hierarchy—each person had one vote, and each person had an equal voice, rare in hierarchical and collectivist societies such as Thailand. It took PTT local staff members substantial time to convince community members that getting involved in a meeting could change quality of life.

Regarding the governing system, members were divided into groups according to interests or business unit. Organic fertilizer-making, garbage management, water management, charcoal, soap, dish-washing detergents, mouthwash, and farming were examples of subgroups. Each group had a head, and consensus was the guiding principle in every activity, even down to the packaging used for soap.

The guiding principle in production and marketing was to use local materials to their greatest extent. Consequently, a forgotten local vegetable, the spring bitter cucumber, was reinstated as a major ingredient in beauty soap. Naturally grown cucumbers were farmed systematically with a new technology from a community member with an agricultural college degree. Local wisdom and modern technology became complements.

With more products to offer, the Sunday market became more popular with tourists. It appeared on many TV shows, attracting tourists nationwide. With its excellent achievements, Bangnamphueng was selected to be one of six sub-districts in Thailand to become a learning center for other sub-districts during a new PTT project starting in 2012. With knowledge gained from joining the project, four community members became researchers under the Thailand Research Fund area-based research project.

Analysis

From the cases discussed in this chapter, one conclusion is obvious. Empowerment is possible only when trust is built, such as trust that an outsider (the company) is truly altruistic, trust that a project is truly deliverable, and trust that community members can create change. To create trust between community and company, relationship-building is the first ingredient. Identifying an opinion or natural leader is useful. To create proof of deliverables, small-scale pilot projects are necessary. The project should be conducted incrementally so tangible results are observable and trust develops. Once trust is built, a project can be scaled up naturally through the initiative of community members. Trust in one's own abilities to create change is assured when community members work collectively. At that point, peer support or even peer pressure is essential. To support collective works, a management tool that monitors whether members are working toward the same goal is helpful.

Both SCG and PTT spent time and energy identifying the best opinion leader. Somchai and Manus were good opinion leaders not because of their formal status in the community, but because they were knowledgeable, determined, and committed to completing the project. Both the check dam project and the self-sufficient economy project started with small-scale pilots to prove the ideas were deliverable. Eighty check dams on the first day led to thousands more. Household bookkeeping made people realize their hedonistic consumption habits, and led to expenditure-reducing measures. Success of the pilot assured community members of the project's scalability. Simultaneously and spontaneously, members initiated innovations—both product and process—through dynamic dialogues among community members. New social values and cultures (e.g., continuous improvement) became embedded as a natural process. Knowledge hoarding, observed often in Asian societies, was removed as trust in community members increased (Loveridge 2006). Both SCG and PTT emphasized self-sustainability, and thus made clear that the companies would assist the communities for a limited time. The ultimate goal was for the community to run projects autonomously, accelerating community members to learn and develop to reach independence after the company left.

While trust-building is a necessary component of community empowerment, it is important to emphasize that diffusion of knowledge concerning how to manage a project and how to create and share lessons learned in the process assists greatly. With a background in plant management, SCG focused on continuous improvement using PCDA circles as a basic tool. With experience in large-scale projects that run nationwide, PTT used a formal operating manual—a project management guide—as a basic tool to educate community members on how to manage. In the case of SCG, continuous improvement tools were transferred gradually to the community at village meetings. In the case of PTT, intermediaries or PTT local staff members explained how to follow the project management guide at monthly meetings. The manual showed step-by-step how to plan, organize, set up a budget, monitor a project, and report comments and suggestions from the PTT project manager committee. Similarly, community members learned about the importance of management. Without proper management, the project would not be monitored, evaluated, or improved, explaining why prior community development projects initiated by the central government were unsuccessful. They learned that the entire process of plan, do, check, and act is the core of project management.

In addition to transferring management knowledge, both cases illustrate how knowledge is managed so interactions between implicit and explicit knowledge from company to community and interactions between community members are conducted properly. Both SCG and PTT constructed a condition that created knowledge-sharing space. *Ba*, as termed by Nonaka and Takeuchi (1995), was absorbed naturally by community members. In the case of SCG, the company used village meetings to conduct dialogues with community members. After these formal meetings, representatives would go out for drinks to exchange ideas with small groups of friends—an activity that might be labeled with the term "nomi-nication," as coined by Nonaka and Takeuchi (1995) from the Japanese "nomi" meaning "drinking" and the English "communication." The term refers to social drinking, whereby people communicate freely as friends rather than based on social status, such as buyers and sellers, bosses and subordinates, etc. In the case of PTT, the company used monthly meetings and a visit-your-neighbor program. Community members residing in different villages had the opportunity to mingle and learn from each other. Results from interviews confirmed that this friendly atmosphere had not been created prior to the company's intervention; it used to be a formal meeting that community members gathered at to listen to new policies top-down from central government, most of which were irrelevant to community members. The monthly and village meetings PTT and SCG introduced were different. They were places where members set their own goals and the means to achieve them, and the atmosphere was more relevant and approachable. They could use these meetings to ask for guidance when confronted with problems that arose during project implementation. This way, the project ran smoothly until a goal was achieved. Once successful, community members had more confidence to get involved in other projects. The findings in this study depict sustainable communities, and lessons learned are summarized well as follows:

> In the process of aggregating human beings into a relatively small area and providing the necessary forum for civic life, the sustainable city serves as a medium for decentralizing and localizing economic production and commerce and thus preserving the social surplus of the local economy for the community's self-sufficiency and self-enhancement.
>
> (Yanarella and Levine 1992: 305, quoted in
> Bridger and Luloff 1999)

Discussion

This study demonstrates cases that apply theories to community development, innovation diffusion, and knowledge management. The role of the company as CSR sponsor is to put the pieces together. It connects villages to the outside world (e.g., learning centers) so they are knowledgeable in what they are doing. The companies empower them to manage their own problems. Hierarchical management, found often in most government-centered development projects, merely places communities near the bottom of the social pyramid. They do not possess sufficient autonomy to manage their own futures. Collaboration with companies leads to stronger community partnerships.

Corporations outperform governments regarding community development for at least two reasons. One is the limitation of bureaucracy, and the other is results-oriented foci and lesser degrees of formalization in private corporations. While centralized, it is difficult to design a context-based solution for each community. Governments issue policies and guidelines, and require cooperation from communities to implement them. However, communities lack core knowledge on how to realize an idea. No continuous support is available, the missing link in community development in the country. Furthermore, remuneration given to government officers is based primarily on project success. Opportunistic officers can use communities as a means to get promotions by forcing communities to complete a project without thorough understanding of the benefits the community earns from completion. Consequently, trust between communities and outsiders is low, if not coercive.

Community members do not perceive private companies as authorities as they do government agencies. Contact is relaxed. In addition, the company could empower the community by equipping them with management knowledge, which is necessary and most needed. Companies normally evaluate investments based on profits and losses, but communities also feel pressure to realize a good return on investments to receive further support. This suggests that the role of business in developing economies is twofold. One is as educator of management practice, and the other is as connection between community members and abundant resources outside. The former connects the missing link to community development, and the latter fulfills the government's failure to redistribute resources. Recent literature emphasizes the role of large corporations, especially multinational companies, in developing economies through CSR (e.g., poverty alleviation) (Ragodoo 2009; Bardy *et al.* 2012). However, instead of the traditional method of philanthropy, the company empowers the community to conduct the entire management process by acting as coach and supporter. Monetary support is necessary but insufficient; assisting them to learn is essential.

Conclusion

One of the deep-rooted problems with community development in Thailand, especially in rural areas, is lack of autonomy perceived by communities.

Government developmental policies that emphasize industrialization and fail to develop rural communities into autonomous social groups make rural communities economically and socially vulnerable. Lack of autonomy also means depending on centralized authorities and the outside world. With existing institutional voids in many forms, companies can conduct CSR projects in ways that support realization of sustainable communities. The distribution mechanism governed by the invisible hand can be impacted by the visible hand of these managers.

This study illustrates how companies turn communities at the lower level of society from consumers into efficient producers. Unlike strategic CSR, which places communities into upper positions in a company's value chain, the CSR of SCG and PTT places communities at the upper levels of the pyramid. The community becomes an independent producer with more bargaining power over numerous buyers. This altruistic CSR reflects different concepts from what Western academia and practitioners suggest, but as the cases discussed here demonstrate, Asia receives it well.

The rationale for conducting CSR is an ongoing debate. While mainstream literature argues CSR should result in business gains, recent literature draws attention to compassion and spiritual aspects (Bejou 2011; Kraisornsuthasinee 2011). Asian values based primarily on Confucianism and Buddhism emphasize duties among parties in society. If CSR is a means to reflect roles of business in society, interpretation of CSR in Asian contexts should be re-examined.

References

ABAC Poll (2011) *Survey on the Thai Family: Case studies of households in four pilot areas—Phanga, Samuthsakorn, Yasothorn and Nakorn Sawan.* Available online at www.abacpoll.au.edu/internetpolls.html (accessed October 1, 2012).

Bardy, R., Drew, S., and Kennedy, T.F. (2012) "Foreign investment and ethics: how to contribute to social responsibility by doing business in less-developed countries," *Journal of Business Ethics*, 106: 267–82.

Barney, J.B. (1991) "Firm resources and sustained competitive advantage," *Journal of Management*, 17: 99–120.

Bejou, D. (2011) "Compassion as the new philosophy of business," *Journal of Relationship Marketing*, 10: 1–6.

Bridger, C.B. and Luloff, A.E. (1999) "Toward an interactional approach to sustainable community development," *Journal of Rural Studies*, 15: 377–87.

Brueckner, M. and Mamun, M.A. (2010) "Living downwind from corporate social responsibility: a community perspective on corporate practice," *Business Ethics: A European Review*, 19: 326–48.

Campbell, R. (2012) "Approaches to working together with local communities," paper presented at the Asian Forum on Corporate Social Responsibility, Bangkok, October.

Carrigan, M., Moraes, C., and Leek, S. (2011) "Fostering responsible communities: a community social marketing approach to sustainable living," *Journal of Business Ethics*, 100: 515–34.

Das, S.C. (2009) "Status and direction of corporate social responsibility in Indian perspective: an exploratory study", *Social Responsibility Journal*, 5: 34–47.

Dixon, C. (1999) *The Thai Economy: Uneven development and internationalization*, London: Routledge.

Dixon, S.E.A. and Clifford, A. (2007) "Ecopreneurship: a new approach to managing the triple bottom line," *Journal of Organizational Change Management*, 20: 326–45.

Doner, R.F. (2009) *The Politics of Uneven Development: Thailand's economic growth in comparative perspective*, New York: Cambridge University Press.

Eweje, G. (2006) "The role of MNEs in community development initiatives in developing countries: corporate social responsibility at work in Nigeria and South Africa," *Business and Society*, 45(2): 93–129.

Fisher, K., Geenen, J., Jurcevic, M., McClintock, K., and Davis, G. (2009) "Applying asset-based community development as a strategy for CSR: a Canadian perspective on a win-win for stakeholders and SMEs," *Business Ethics: A European Review*, 18: 66–82.

Freeman, R.E. (1984) *Strategic Management: A stakeholder approach*, Boston, MA: Pitman.

Hacking, T. and Guthrie, P. (2008) "A framework for clarifying the meaning of triple bottom-line, integrated, and sustainability assessment," *Environment Impact Assessment Review*, 28: 73–89.

Hart, S.L. and Christensen, C.M. (2002) "The great leap: driving innovation from the base of the pyramid," *MIT Sloan Management Review*, Fall: 51–6.

Hubbard, G. (2009) "Measuring organizational performance: beyond the triple bottom line," *Business Strategy and the Environment*, 19: 177–91.

Kaptein, M. and Tulder, R.V. (2003) "Toward effective stakeholder dialogue," *Business and Society Review*, 108: 203–24.

Kraisornsuthasinee, S. (2011) "CSR through the heart of the Bodhi tree," *Social Responsibility Journal*, 8: 186–98.

Loveridge, R. (2006) "Developing institutions—'crony capitalism' and national capabilities: a European perspective," *Asian Business & Management*, 5: 113–36.

Nonaka, I. and Takeuchi, H. (1995) *The Knowledge-creating Company: How Japanese companies create the dynamics of innovation*, New York: Oxford University Press.

Porter, M. and Kramer R. (2011) "Creating shared value: how to reinvent capitalism—and unleash a wave of innovation and growth," *Harvard Business Review*, January/February: 62–77.

Prahalad, C.K. and Hammond, A. (2002) "Serving the world's poor, profitably," *Harvard Business Review*, September: 48–57.

Ragodoo, N.J.F. (2009) "CSR as a tool to fight against poverty: the case of Mauritius," *Social Responsibility Journal*, 5: 19–33.

Savitz, A.W. (2006) *The Triple Bottom Line*, San Francisco, CA: Jossey-Bass.

Srisuphaolarn, P. (2010) "The development of CSR definition and pattern in Thailand," unpublished report, Kasetsart University, Bangkok.

Srisuphaolarn, P. (2012) "The public's evaluation of socially responsible companies: evidences from Bangkok," *Chulalongkorn Business Review*, 34: 63–93.

Srisuphaolarn, P. (2013) "From altruistic to strategic CSR: how social value affected CSR development—a case study of Thailand," *Social Responsibility Journal*, 9: 56–77.

Thorne, D.M., Ferrel, O.C., and Ferrel, L. (2008) *Business and Society: A strategic approach to social responsibility*, 3rd edn, Boston, MA: Houghton Mifflin.

United Nations (UN) (2012) *Report of the United Nations Conference on Sustainable Development*. Available online at www.uncsd2012.org/content/documents/814UNC SD%20REPORT%20final%20revs.pdf (accessed November 13, 2012).

United Nations Conference on Trade and Development (UNCTAD) (2011) *World Investment Report 2011*, New York: United Nations.

Westney, D.E. and Maanen J.V. (2011) "The casual ethnography of the executive suite," *Journal of International Business Studies*, 42: 602–7.

World Business Council for Sustainable Development (WBCSD) (2012) "Vision 2050: the new agenda for business." Available online at www.wbcsd.org/vision2050. aspx (accessed November 16, 2012).

Yodprudtikan, P., Preeyapant, V., Charoenngam, S., Trivithayanurak, S., Shrestha, S., Angkularad, K., Chansa, P., Yangprayong, R., Junson, J., Sophontanased, P., and Laitae, P. (2006) *CSR Development in the Business Process: Phase 1: The study of attributes, components and tools for development*, Bangkok: Thaipat Institute.

9 Corporate and community processes of engagement

A framework to address multi-level CSR issues and situations

Maria Elena B. Herrera and
Francisco L. Roman

Over the past two years, the authors have conducted research in ten countries: Cambodia, China, India, Indonesia, Laos, Malaysia, Philippines, Singapore, Thailand, and Vietnam. These countries in general and their governments in particular increasingly expect companies to act responsibly. Corporate social responsibility (CSR) strengthens the linkages between the company and its stakeholders, especially through community engagement initiatives that enable the company to identify needs and thereby to create acceptable and sustainable CSR programs. In this chapter, we present approaches to CSR that include the management of the business footprint, resulting in the creation of value for the company as well as for its stakeholders. Michael Porter and Mark Kramer (2011) call this the creation of shared value—"creating economic value in a way that also creates value for society by addressing its needs and challenges." The framework presented in this chapter is based on a series of research projects conducted by the AIM RVR CSR Center (2011b, 2011c, 2011d).

The umbrella phrase "strategic CSR" is adopted in this chapter, and is defined as the internal alignment of the firm's CSR into its overall corporate strategy. As such, strategic CSR also includes the transition from aligning to fully embedding CSR in both the overall corporate strategy (formulation) and operations (implementation). This "triple fit" covers: (1) corporate strategy and CSR; (2) the market or industry environment needs; and (3) the interests of the corporation's direct and indirect stakeholders. Further, the chapter highlights the community engagement process in creating a sustainable partnership between a company and its stakeholders and underscores three issues related to the macro-environment, stakeholder concerns, and company impact or footprint in developing a community engagement strategy. The issues are explained primarily through an Influences Framework with supporting frameworks on footprint analysis and community engagement.

Toward strategic CSR

CSR involves the interface between a company and its environment. The purposes of CSR include mitigation of all negative impact and the maximization of the positive impact of operations. Initiatives can be classified based on both the specific intent and target beneficiaries using a Typology of Intent (AIM RVR CSR Center, 2011d; see Figure 9.1).

Corporate intentions are classified as follows: compliance, minimizing harm, creating stakeholder value, and shared value. These intentions are matched to specific beneficiaries depending on the particular activity. Beneficiaries are classified as follows:

- *Unrelated*—Those who do not have a direct connection to the company and may not be impacted by or have an impact on its operations.
- *Primary internal*—Stakeholders who are internal to the organization (i.e., employees).
- *Primary external*—Stakeholders who are part of the company's supply chain (i.e., suppliers and consumers).
- *Secondary*—Stakeholders who are not directly linked to the supply chain, but are affected by company operations (i.e., host community).
- *Mediating*—Stakeholders who may not be affected directly by company operations, but represent a particular stakeholder group or cause.

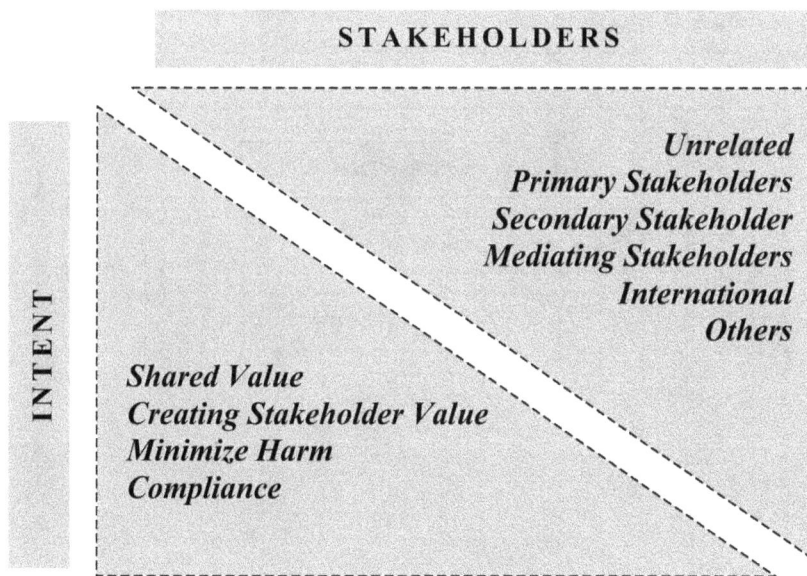

Figure 9.1 CSR Typology of Intent.
Source: AIM RVR CSR Center, Herrera *et al.* (2011d).

- *International*—Those who can influence corporate behavior, including through public opinion concerning the corporation (including foreign investors and consumers).

Strategic CSR focuses on aligning the company's social development initiatives with its business strategy and on embedding CSR into the organization (i.e., its processes, procedures, and policies). An integrated CSR strategy considers two factors—context and coherence. Context refers to the need for alignment with the external and internal realities of the corporation. Coherence refers to the internal integrity (completeness and consistency) of CSR programs and includes the level of efficiency and effectiveness in implementing them. This core framework is meant to be used by practitioners when embedding CSR into corporate strategy and operations. Its use is explained more fully in the AIM RVR CSR manual *Towards Strategic CSR* (2011d).

The Integrating CSR Framework (AIM RVR CSR Center, 2011d: 6–9; see Figure 9.2) consists of four stages:

- *Assessment* is similar to situation analysis and includes an external stakeholder mapping and macro-analysis of the political, social, cultural, and economic realities. Internal assessment includes review of the business footprint and current programs, as well as the social climate.

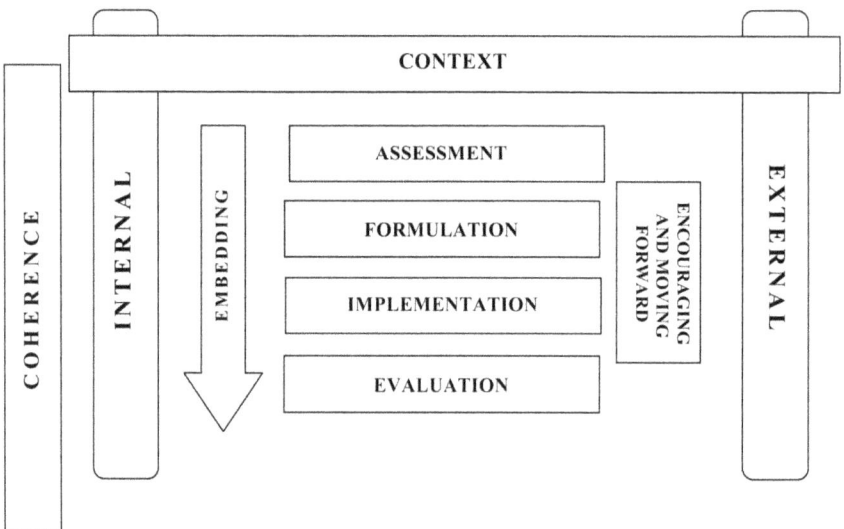

Figure 9.2 Integrating and aligning CSR.
Source: AIM RVR CSR Center, Herrera *et al.* (2011d).

- *Formulation* involves development of approaches and key components of each approach, including corporate giving, compliance, targeted value chain management, stakeholder engagement, communication methods, and forms of relationship-building such as partnerships.
- *Implementation* requires a time-based operational plan, including the clear tasks with appropriate financial and human resources.
- *Evaluation* requires mechanisms to ensure that program outputs are delivered and desired outcomes are achieved. In particular, this should include an assessment of stakeholder outcomes relative to expectations and a review of accountabilities and key success factors.

Footprint and stakeholder analysis

Companies with a better understanding of their impact on communities and the environment can formulate initiatives that create shared value. Assessment involves footprint and stakeholder analysis. Footprint broadly refers to the impact of the company's operations on the environment and on society, including economic (i.e., employment, tax, livelihood for local communities); environmental (i.e., degradation, pollution, loss of biodiversity); and social (i.e., security threats, human rights concerns, changes in social structure, effects on local tradition and culture). Footprint analysis involves evaluation of each of the activities in the value chain in terms of the economic, environmental, and social impact of company operations (see Figure 9.3).

A light footprint might refer to waste and gas emissions from product distribution, while a mining company might leave a much heavier footprint, not only from creating pits and mountains out of forestland but also by displacing communities from their ancestral lands. Footprint analysis is similar to Porter and Kramer's inside-out approach whereby the impact of each process in the value chain is evaluated. The process also facilitates the identification of stakeholders' concerns, possible partnerships' needs and opportunities in the value chain—including sourcing, manufacturing, warehousing, shipment, sales and marketing, and retail distribution.

Individuals or groups are affected in varying degrees by the company's operations. The Typology of Intent categorized a variety of stakeholders including employees, shareholders, and investors (internal), suppliers and customers (external), government, non-governmental organizations (NGOs), media, and international organizations. Stakeholder analysis would include a review of: stakeholder concerns (current versus potential and desires versus fears); knowledge (shared, "theirs" and "ours"); capacity and assets (financial and human); and mindsets and attitudes (articulated, observable, and concealed). Stakeholders' interests and concerns vary. Any stakeholder's degree of influence depends on their knowledge, capabilities, and competencies.

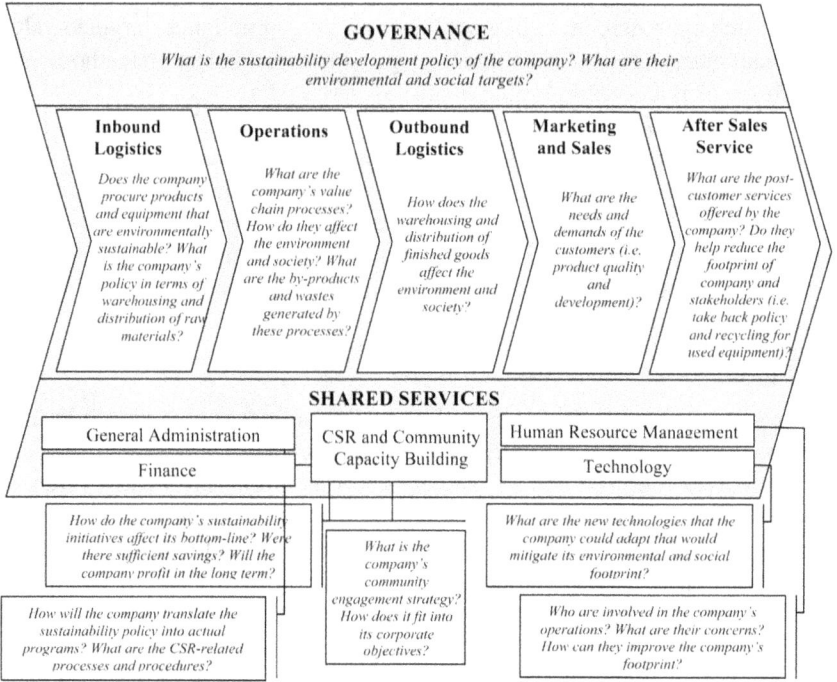

Figure 9.3 Footprint analysis.
Source: Herrera and Alarilla (2012).

Table 9.1 Stakeholder type: roles and wants

Stakeholder type	Role/impact to the company	Wants
Employees	Workers	High wages; safe and comfortable workplace
Shareholders and investors	Financiers and overseers	High profitability
Suppliers	Availability of acceptable raw materials and components	Fast payment and long tenure
Consumers	Purchase the finished goods and services	Affordable quality goods and services
Society	Public opinion makers on corporate citizenship	Employment and social development programs
Moderating/ mediating stakeholders	Influence image/ reputation and operation of the company	Socially responsible company

Influences Framework

The Influences (Hexagon) Framework (Figure 9.4) aids in understanding the factors affecting the practice of CSR in a country or locality and allows stakeholders to understand how they can influence CSR practice. It can also be used by a company to analyze its market and non-market business environment. The Framework contributes to the existing literature on institutional assessment by providing an analysis of the dynamics of formal and informal institutions and their impact on stakeholder concerns, interests, and behavior.

As can be seen from Figure 9.4, the Framework has three clusters—Fundamental Influences, Institutional Dynamics, and Business Landscape. Fundamental Influences, including geography and geology, natural resources, history, and culture, are exogenous factors largely beyond company or stakeholder control but that help each stakeholder better understand the mindset and attitude of the communities in the location. Institutional Dynamics are a snapshot of the macro-environment of the industry—social, political, market, labor, and corporate structures. They are also somewhat beyond a company's control but can provide guidance concerning what approaches are appropriate.

The Business Landscape cluster provides more industry- and business-specific factors that directly affect the company's operations and include social and environmental concerns and initiatives, the regulatory environment, stakeholder influence, and business initiatives that directly affect the CSR agenda

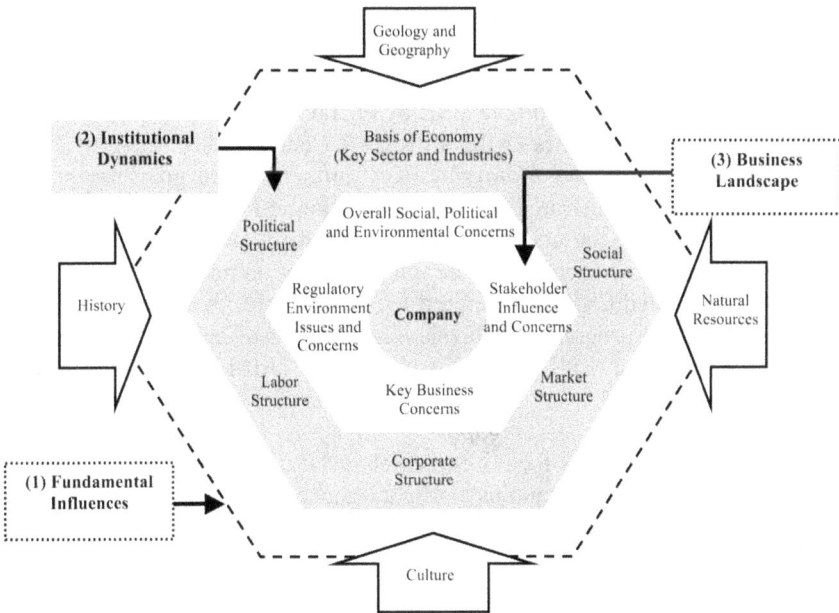

Figure 9.4 Influences (Hexagon) Framework.
Source: AIM RVR CSR Center, Herrera *et al.* (2011a).

given company-specific circumstances. For example, large companies tend to address broader social, political, and environmental concerns due to the greater scope of their operations and resources. Smaller companies have limited capability and may focus on a few modest initiatives such as employee and family health and welfare. Moreover, larger companies have the capability and the network to "changes the rules of the game or playing field"—presumably for the better. The Business Landscape cluster allows firms to understand stakeholder influence and concerns, and the overall social, political, and environmental concerns, in order to identify the critical needs and issues faced by its stakeholders in the host community and society in general. The challenge for companies is to align its interests with the interests of its stakeholders.

In transforming these stakeholders into sustainable business partners, companies assess the Institutional Dynamics cluster because of the web of relationships and characteristics of key social, political, and economic institutions (both formal and informal). This cluster helps companies to identify partners based on competency, skills, and knowledge and to assess interrelated influences and concerns.

Some general observations resulting from studies undertaken when developing the Framework are presented here by country clusters:

Mekong (Laos, Cambodia, Thailand, and Vietnam): Large foreign companies and the government are key influences. Large foreign companies spearhead CSR implementation. Philanthropy dominates among large local firms. The state actively promotes CSR in the areas of environment, employee rights, and livelihood in key industries. Thailand, through its Securities and Exchange Commission, requires listed companies to have their own CSR programs. While there is no law requiring CSR in Vietnam, Cambodia, and Laos, their governments promote CSR by encouraging partnerships between local and foreign companies (AIM RVR CSR Center, 2011b: 12–20).

Islamic (Indonesia and Malaysia): Key influences are government and companies that are motivated by an Islamic tradition of charity and philanthropy. In Indonesia, the CSR focus areas are poverty, education, and health and, in Malaysia, the focus is on the integration of its multicultural society. Indonesia mandated CSR and required local companies to begin implementing their own CSR programs. Malaysia introduced an awards mechanism that offers incentives for CSR-practicing companies (AIM RVR CSR Center, 2011b: 23–8).

State-led market focus (Singapore): Singapore is a developed country with strict enforcement of environmental laws and civic-social concerns. Sustainable development remains a primary concern due to its limited natural resources. A business-friendly environment is a priority for government, which actively promotes but does not mandate CSR. Large multinational corporations (MNCs) also exert some influence on the practice and development of CSR (AIM RVR CSR Center, 2011b: 29–34).

Civil society democracy (Philippines): Philippine NGOs actively monitor and thus encourage CSR. CSR is more developed in terms of programs and awareness, and partly fills the gap resulting from the weak implementation of laws and weak state-led programs for key social and environmental concerns. Both local companies and MNCs develop CSR initiatives to address education, health, livelihood, and environmental concerns. Philanthropy motivated by religious tradition continues to be prominent, especially among local firms, and supplements CSR that is integrated into the core function of business. Multilateral and international organizations also influence CSR in the country (AIM RVR CSR Center, 2011b: 35–41).

"Mega" (population) players (China and India): Both countries are concerned about environmental pollution and the widening gap between the rich and the poor. CSR is beginning to take root partly due to the presence of large MNCs. In India, large local companies such as Tata Group, Birla, and Reliance, with their national networks, play a key role in expanding CSR. Local companies are beginning to increase their knowledge and understanding of CSR as it is increasingly seen as a competitive advantage—for example, to improve access to European and US markets and to reduce reputation risk. In China, CSR is encouraged by the government as a tool for increasing access to international markets and creating social harmony (AIM RVR CSR Center, 2011c).

Community engagement strategy and the bottom of the pyramid

The Business Landscape cluster of the Influences Framework allows the analysis of the company's macro-environment, and helps guide companies in understanding dynamics and concerns relating to the bottom of the pyramid (BOP) (see Figure 9.5). Three parameters affect the relationship between the company and its stakeholders:

1   *Overall Social, Political, and Environmental Concerns* provides a context for the community situation and the capabilities and concerns of government.
2   *Regulatory Environment Issues and Concerns* provides an understanding of the regulations that companies and its suppliers and distributors must comply with.
3   *Stakeholder Influence and Concerns* provides an understanding of the concerns, dynamics, and interrelationships among stakeholders.

Once the situation, dynamics, and concerns of the community, and particularly the BOP, as well as the company are understood, the company has a foundation for developing a community engagement strategy. On the ground feedback as well as research literature shows that engagement strategies are most effective and sustainable when stakeholders become collaborators as opposed to simply beneficiaries. This requires a reciprocal relationship based on trust that is built through successful collaboration. Stakeholder capacity-building is critical to a successful collaborative engagement strategy.

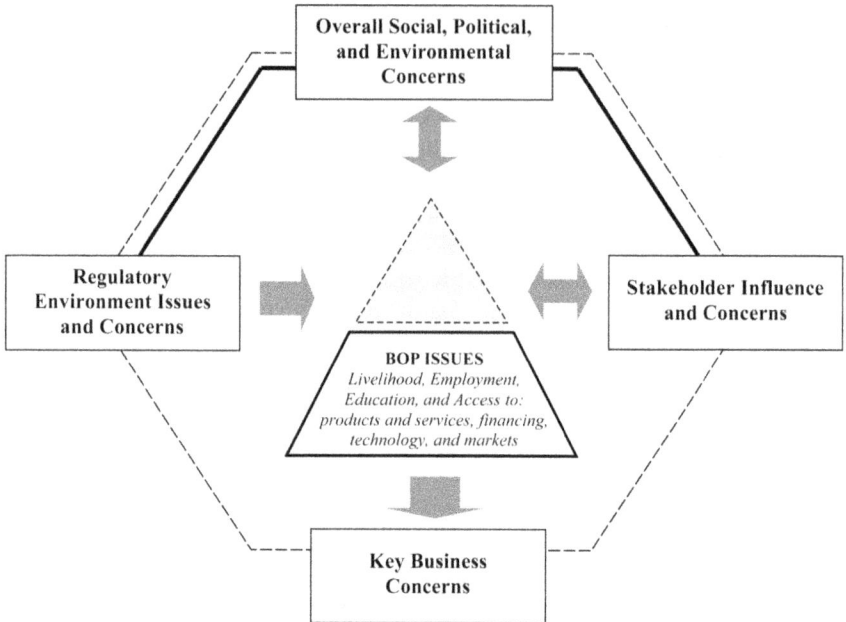

Figure 9.5 Business Landscape Framework.
Source: Herrera and Alarilla (2012).

In many developing countries, community engagement strategies focus on the two most common BOP issues of lack of access to quality products and services and lack of employment and livelihood opportunities. Additional projects address the related concerns of inadequate education, and poor access to finance, technology, and markets. A disciplined approach to creating a BOP engagement strategy (see Figure 9.6) allows the company to effectively address priority concerns in a sustainable manner. The step-by-step analysis of each part of the value chain should be aimed both at analyzing impact and evaluating possible opportunities for productive win-win engagements.

The traditional rationales for addressing BOP issues are the improvement of corporate reputation and the maintenance of its social license to operate (SLTO), which refers to community and stakeholder support. The more enlightened approach goes beyond impact mitigation and philanthropic activities toward product and service innovation (BOP marketing) and BOP partnerships, including: capacity-building in preparation for economic partnerships (e.g., as supplier or distributor) and engagement in order to improve the available talent pool. BOP engagement approaches must be aligned with the situation, concerns, and capabilities of the BOP, as well as with the situation, concerns, and competencies of the company. In order for the strategies to be sustainable, all stakeholders must be able to fulfill their roles and gain appropriate advantage.

Figure 9.7 shows the full BOP Engagement Framework; while Boxes 9.2 and 9.3 provide information, respectively, about partnerships and marketing at the bottom of the pyramid.

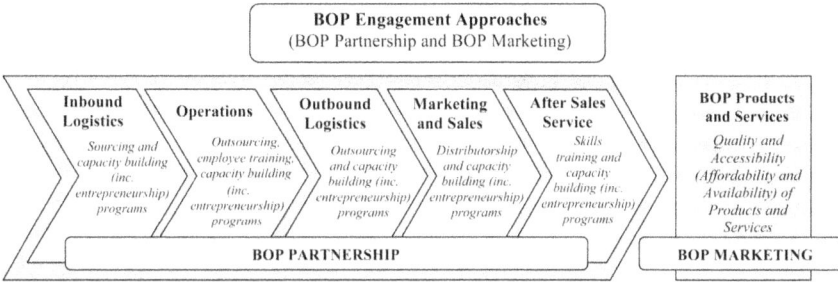

Figure 9.6 BOP engagement approaches.
Source: Herrera and Alarilla (2012).

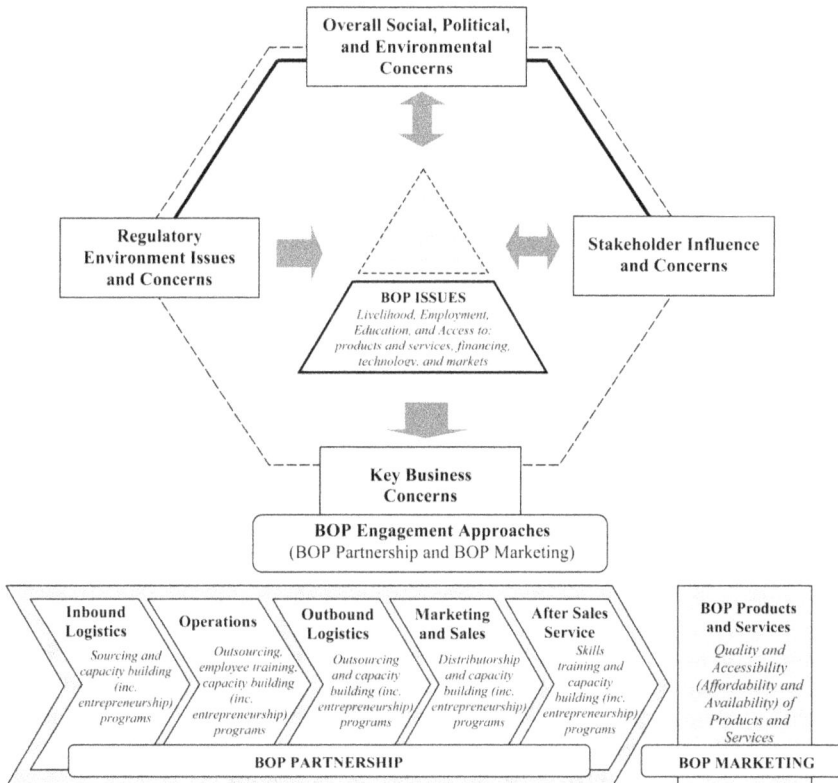

Figure 9.7 BOP Engagement Framework.

BOX 9.1 Bottom of the pyramid partnerships: vignettes

Eureka Forbes Ltd's Euroable (India)

Euroable is India's first state-of-the-art call center manned and operated entirely by persons with special needs. There are about 40 million "differently abled" persons in India. Eureka Forbes Ltd, in partnership with the National Society for Equal Opportunities for the Handicapped (NASEOH), staffed a call center entirely with individuals with special needs. In 2011, about 70 individuals with special needs were hired, while 20 are still under training. Euroable has 100 percent retention, compared to 70 percent of its other partners. The group was also able to handle an increasing number of calls, from 4,800 in April to 37,767 in July (Eureka Forbes Ltd, 2011).

Tetra Pak Pakistan's Dairy Development Program (Pakistan)

Pakistan is the world's third largest producer of milk, but wastage at source is 40 percent of total production due to poor dairy farming practices and farm-to-market roads. About ten million families depend on the milk industry, which accounts for 11 percent of the country's GDP (Tetra Pak Pakistan website, 2010). Tetra Pak implemented the Dairy Development Program to provide education and training programs as well as mechanized milking machines, farm supplies for animal welfare, feeds, and veterinary clinics. Village Milk Collection points were established and managed and operated by the local community. By 2010, Tetra Pak reported that about 27,000 farmers directly benefited, as well as the productivity of 90,000 animals. Milk collection increased from 400 liters to 8,500 liters per day (Tetra Pak Pakistan website, 2010).

Applying the BOP Engagement Framework

This section presents summaries of two case studies demonstrating the application of the BOP Engagement Framework. The first example concerns Double A, a public limited company, with headquarters in Bangkok and branch offices elsewhere in Thailand and overseas. Principally, the company operates manufacturing facilities producing many types of quality writing and printing papers, which it distributes globally. Double A's commitment to sustainability addresses environmental, social, and economic issues and engages the BOP through a partnership initiative to create sustainable sourcing of raw materials. The second example is of Smart Communications Inc., a wholly owned subsidiary of the Philippines' leading telecommunications

---

BOX 9.2 Bottom of the pyramid marketing: vignettes

Arohan Financial Services Private Ltd (India)

Businesses that are neither micro-entrepreneurs nor large enterprises suffer from limited access to credit. Arohan launched a new microfinance product called Pragati to target small business owners — "the 'missing middle' estimated at 13 million businesses that employ approximately 410 million people" (Arohan, 2011). As of August 12, 2011, Pragati loans amounting to US $380,000 were disbursed to 275 clients. Based on its five-year projections, Arohan plans to disburse US $25 million by March 2014 with a client base of 20,000 (Arohan, 2011).

Coca-Cola Philippines' NutriJuice Program

About 37.4 percent of school children are iron deficient. Coca-Cola Philippines and the Food and Nutrition Research Institute of the Department of Science and Technology formally launched NutriJuice, a fortified juice drink to address iron deficiency among children aged 6–12 years (Coca-Cola Philippines, 2009). The NutriJuice Program covers a six-month feeding period, where each student drinks one pack per school day as a vitamin supplement (Baccay, 2012). Based on the initial roll-out, the student beneficiaries demonstrated reduced rates of "anemia among iron-depleted children and increased weight and height of both anemic and underweight children" (Coca-Cola Philippines, 2009). The program has helped 200,000 rural school children (Castillo, 2012).

---

carrier, the Philippine Long Distance Telephone Company. Smart is the country's leading wireless services provider with over 52 million subscribers (Smart Communications, n.d.). As will be discussed, Smart is committed to providing innovative mobile solutions. It engages the BOP through partnership and marketing initiatives to create business opportunities and to provide quality and affordable products and services.

Case 1: Double A

Double A's CSR strategy is holistic (see Figure 9.8). As a pulp and paper company, its operations heavily impact on the environment due to the raw materials and water needs, as well as because of the waste generated in manufacturing. The successful and effective integration of Double A's sustainability strategy and initiatives is rooted in its ability to merge the external and internal issues of its operations. It was also able to fully embed

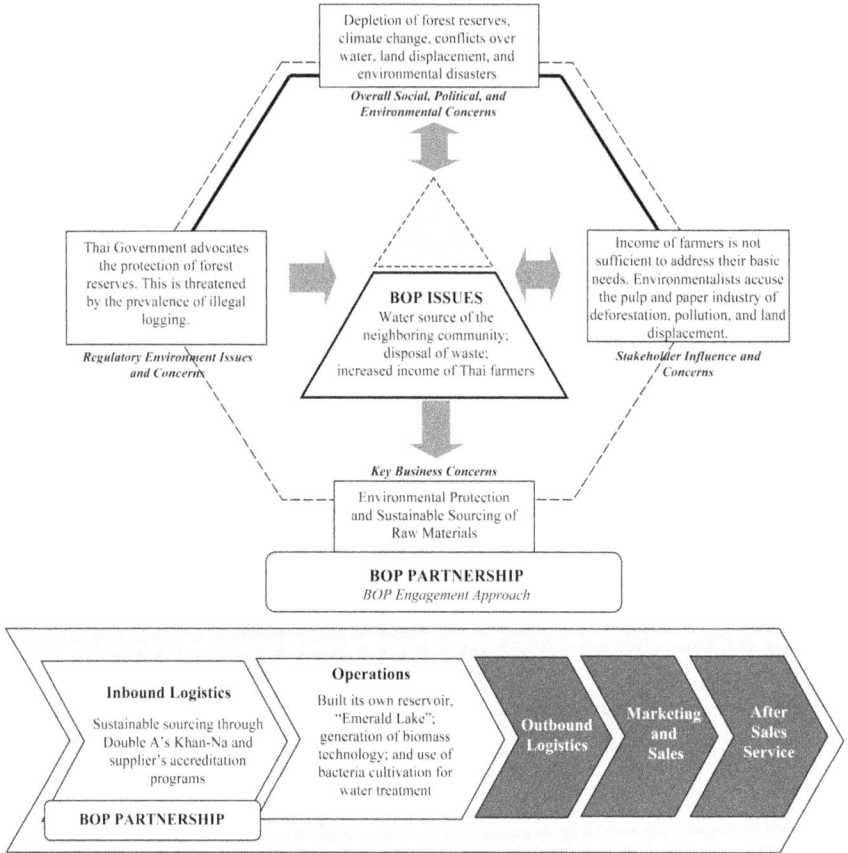

Figure 9.8 Double A's BOP Engagement Framework.
Source: Herrera and Alarilla (2012).

these programs into the company's value chain. In doing so, these initiatives are not considered as "add-ons" or "extra," but are viewed as critical to its business processes.

Situation: The Thai government strongly advocated the protection of forest reserves—about 40 percent of Thailand's total land area that illegal logging threatens. Meantime, the Thai government promoted the pulp and paper industry through "subsidies, pro-cash crop and plantation policies, tax relief and favourable import duties on machinery imports" (Lang, 2002).

The pulp and paper industry depends on the condition of Thai forests and agricultural land. The depletion of forest reserves severely reduces the supply of raw materials. Climate change, unpredictable weather patterns, and natural disasters also affect the growth of and harvest from trees. Environmentalists argue that the industry's operations create deforestation and pollution from improper disposal of waste and chemicals and accuse the industry of collusion with illegal loggers and with land displacement. Moreover, the income of Thai farmers is insufficient to address their basic needs and many live on idle land.

Engagement approaches and impact: Double A ensures that all its products are "produced with a good balance between product quality and environmental social care." Its manufacturing process focuses on the need to "cultivate," "conserve," and "generate" without interfering with nature and the ecosystem (Double A Thailand, 2012). The following are some key initiatives:

- *Conservation of water*—Double A constructed the Emerald Lake, a rainwater reservoir, with 36 million cubic meters built to conserve water during the rainy season and supply 100 percent of Double A's water during the production process. It has also adopted wash press technology to squeeze excess water from pulp for reuse and it uses recycled water for tree-irrigation.
- *Generation of biomass energy*—"Wood chips are used for pulp production, an essential raw material for paper manufacture. Residual waste like bark and lignin are mixed with rice husks to produce biomass fuel for generating electricity at Double A's own power plant" (Double A Thailand, 2012).
- *Bacteria cultivation for water treatment*—Double A uses the "bacteria digestion process" in its water treatment facility to water the factory yard, which consumes 100,000 m^3 of treated water a day (Double A Thailand, 2012).
- Double A has the lowest water consumption for the pulp bleaching process—6–7 m^3 per ton of pulp versus other companies who consume 60 m^3 per ton of pulp. Waste products (i.e., wood bark, chips, used water, and sludge) are used as fuel to produce steam/energy in the company's power plant.

Double A's sustainable sourcing imitative adopted the BOP partnership approach through the Khan-Na Program, wherein "local Thai farmers make use of the unused spaces in their farm lands by planting and cultivating the Double A Paper-Tree" (Double A Thailand, 2012). Double A's Khan-Na Program provides crop farmers with Paper-Tree seedlings. On average, farmers plant 1,200 trees on their unused land. Double A offers a buy-back guarantee for output after a 3–5 year maturity period. The Double A Consulting Team developed a communication plan that was cascaded to the different provinces followed by an Audit Team to monitor the performance of the Consulting Team. As of 2010, there were 150,000 farmers involved in the program. Other short-term results of the program include an additional income of 2.4 billion baht per year for Thai farmers to improve their livelihood. Double A operates in a carbon-negative position through the Double A Paper-Tree's carbon storage of 6.7 million tons of CO_2 equivalent per year.

Case 2: Smart Communications Inc.

As a telecommunications company, Smart Philippines tapped the underserved BOP market for mobile solutions by offering innovative products and services that are affordable and income generating (see Figure 9.9).

Situation: Starting in 1987, the Philippine government implemented policies to deregulate the telecommunications industry. Despite the liberalization of the industry, the digital divide persists, particularly between socio-economic classes. Based on the 2003 Family Income and Expenditure Survey of the National Statistics Office, "across regions in the Philippines, personal computer, telephone, and television ownership was highest in the National Capital Region and lowest in the Autonomous Region of Muslim Mindanao" (PCIJ, 2006).

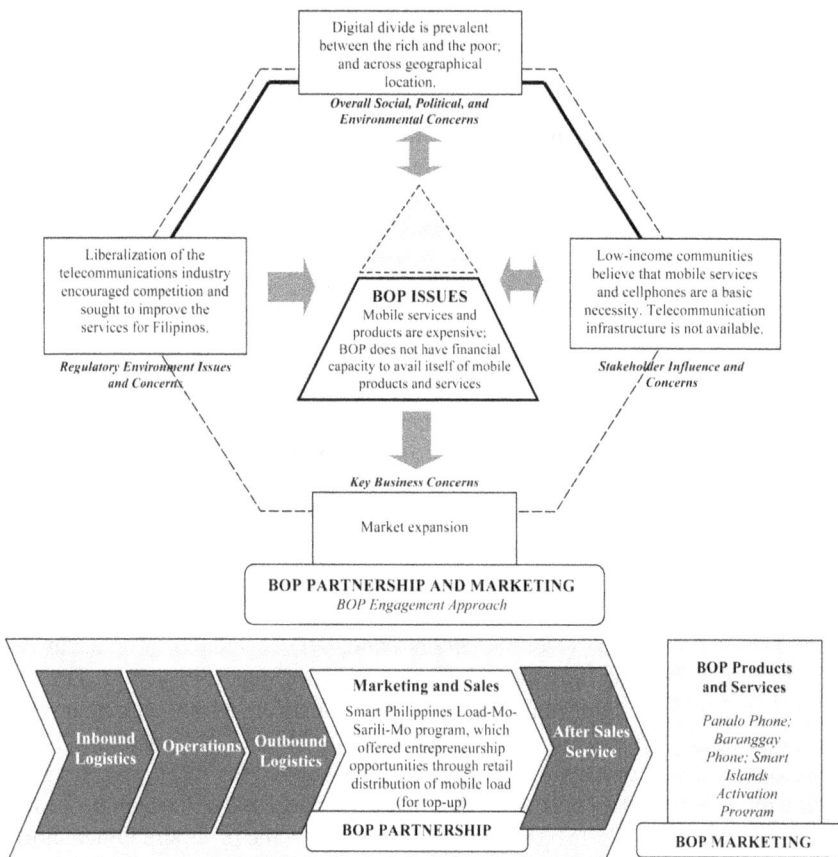

Figure 9.9 Smart Philippines' BOP Engagement Framework.

Source: Herrera and Alarilla (2012).

The country's low-income socio-economic class comprises 84 percent of the estimated population of the Philippines and 23 percent, or 11 million people, do not own a mobile phone, although they believe that it is an indispensable tool for communication (Smart Communications, 2010). Prices of mobile services must be able to fit into the daily expenditure of Filipinos at the BOP. In 2006, about 32.9 percent of Filipinos were living below the poverty line and 19.1 percent of six-person family households were earning PHP367 (US $7.50) per day. Thus, the key business concern for Smart Philippines is to expand the large-volume underserved BOP market.

Engagement approach and impact: Smart Philippines' BOP partnership initiative focused on the implementation of the Load-Mo-Sarili-Mo (LMSM) program, which seeks to augment the income of Filipinos by "using their cellphones to reload themselves or share and sell load top ups to others" (Smart Communications, 2010). The LMSM program provides business opportunities for ordinary Filipinos since the only "capital" required is their cellphone and money for load purchase. Members of the LMSM program earn from the commission that they purchase for their load and the load of their members, so their income is based on the load consumption of their network.

From 2009–10, the LMSM program generated 38,000 members, with an average of 200 activations per day. An estimated "3,000 people are already earning an average of PHP2,000 (about US $44) monthly" (Smart Communications, 2010). Smart Philippines' BOP marketing initiatives focused on providing complete mobile packages for the BOP—which includes a cellphone and load. The following products are not only for personal use, but could also provide entrepreneurship opportunities for the BOP population:

*   Smart's Talk 'N Text offered Panalo Phone (Winner Phone) as a complete phone package for US $11.60. The phone kit was sold at caravans in identified D & C low-income communities. Panalo Phone was expected to reach its target of 120,000 units by 2011 (Smart Communications, 2010).
*   The Talk 'N Text Barangay Phone is a GSM phone that functions as a payphone for shared community use by the lower socio-economic class, by providing low cash-out (US $0.069) and the lowest per minute call at US $0.023 versus US $0.186 via landline, and US $0.128 via regular mobile phones (Smart Communications, 2010). The service is ideal for emergencies in the rural and remote areas.
*   The Smart Island Activations Program (IAP) delivers "mobile money" to remote, underserved islands or municipalities. The Smart IAP rolled out to various remote Philippine communities in 2010 with the initial goal to reach at least 40 islands in the Philippines (Smart Communications, 2010).

Conclusions

Society in general increasingly expects companies to act responsibly. Companies respond to societal expectations through CSR initiatives that improve their environmental footprint and address stakeholder concerns. Strategic CSR is CSR that is aligned with external and internal business realities, is fully embedded and integrated into strategy and operations, and creates value for both the company and its stakeholders (shared value). In many countries, addressing the needs and concerns of low-income individuals and communities (i.e., the bottom of the pyramid) is a primary concern. Strategies that are beneficial for the BOP and create value for the company provide a sustainable approach. They are also increasingly driving companies to innovate, creating more shared value.

The research on company CSR activities at the BOP—while not currently generalizable—suggests that corporations are moving from treating the BOP population simply as customers toward utilizing their skills as suppliers. However, the research also reveals at least three areas for future exploration. First, corporations are contracting small-scale enterprises in their supply chain. However, the proportion in percentage of value for meeting supply requirements is less than 15 percent for many of the companies under study. This may reflect an early start or it may imply a threshold that limits CSR supply chain engagement with BOP entrepreneurs. Second, multinational corporations are still important in expanding CSR initiatives in developing economies. These corporations act as role models, especially for the large domestic conglomerates with the capacity to undertake CSR programs. At minimum, CSR supplements the "global brand" and local corporations see CSR as part of being globally competitive against MNCs in their own markets. Third, despite the impetus of CSR and CSV, interviews during the research suggested that philanthropy for the BOP population still plays an important role among Asian local corporations. One common comment in defense of philanthropy is that it is superior to CSR because there are clearly "no strings attached" to a particular initiative. This opinion appears sincere and does not represent an excuse to avoid the time and effort required to build CSR in an organization and to undertake joint initiatives with communities. Two, philanthropy as practiced in developing countries has a strong history of charity and religious gift-giving.

It is important that any strategic approach to CSR include a clear understanding of practical realities and that a community engagement strategy involving all critical and relevant stakeholders leads to collaborative, win-win programs. In conclusion, then, some final, key observations are as follows:

- *The disciplined approach is preferred to the accidental approach in identifying BOP opportunities.* Some companies end up dealing with the community and other stakeholders through the process of learning by doing. More sophisticated companies opt for a more disciplined approach by clearly understanding their situation and their stakeholders and also by learning from other companies and from key business partners. The basic principle is for the company to transcend its own vision and mission beyond the organization, and to allow the stakeholders to share ownership of CSR initiatives.

- *The identification of BOP engagement approaches must consider the Business Landscape, the concerns of the BOP, and the company's own value chain.* It is not enough for companies to develop BOP engagement programs for the poor. Companies must also garner support from their internal and external stakeholders. Finally, the BOP engagement approach must create value for all parties involved.
- *Some issues can be resolved bilaterally and others through a multilateral approach.* Some companies are aggressively creating partnerships with the community and other critical stakeholders such as international organizations, NGOs, and other socio-civic groups. When social concerns are specific to a stakeholder group, then the company could engage with the group members bilaterally. The company could also tap technical partners that specialize in the particular issue to mediate between the company and the target stakeholder. But if a social issue transcends the various stakeholders, a multilateral approach, multi-stakeholder community engagement strategy is required. The challenge for companies is to ensure a possible win-win scenario for all stakeholders involved.
- *Shareholders and stakeholders must work together to bridge resource gaps.* The profiling of current and potential stakeholders includes identifying concerns, assets, and capabilities, their mindset, and their knowledge. The challenge for companies is how to fill in the gap between the demands of the stakeholders as well as the current supply of resources—assets and human.
- *Historic "hurts" and legacy issues often constrain seemingly rational solutions.* Patience and resources are essential in dealing with the community given the difficulty of obtaining complete information. The stakeholders' projected or articulated mindset may be temporary and superficial. Therefore companies must take the time to understand the desires, fears, mindset, and attitudes of its stakeholders because these indicators and behaviors will guide the company in drafting a community engagement strategy. Companies also need to draft contingency plans while formulating the community engagement strategy because many factors are uncontrollable. Companies operate in an environment where external factors such as security threats, conflicting regulations, and deep social problems constrain initiatives. Lastly, companies must be flexible in implementing a community engagement strategy and tweak and adjust the plan—especially its implementation components—based on the progress as well as the current internal and external situations.
- *Performance monitoring must be conducted at all stages.* The assessment starts before the initiative and continues during and after it, both to adjust in-process and to incorporate lessons learned in the next initiative.

Overall, this chapter has sought to highlight the importance of community engagement in creating a sustainable partnership between the company and its stakeholders; all of which is underscored by issues related to the macro-environment, stakeholder concerns, and a company's impact or footprint in developing a community engagement strategy. We have explored these issues through the development of our Influences Framework, and through vignettes related to stakeholder engagement at the bottom of the pyramid, and the two case studies demonstrating the application of the BOP Engagement Framework. The research results suggest that progress has occurred in supply-side CSR engagement with the BOP as corporations combine internally generated initiatives with information about and inputs from affected community stakeholders.

References

AIM RVR CSR Center, Herrera, M.B. *et al.*, for the APEC Secretariat (May 2011a) *CSR in Mining for APEC Economies*, Singapore: APEC Secretariat.

AIM RVR CSR Center, Herrera, M.B. *et al.* for Deutsche Gesellschaft für Internationale Zusammenarbeit (GIZ) (2011b) *Corporate Social Responsibility in Southeast Asia: An eight country analysis*, Makati City, Philippines: Asian Institute of Management.

AIM RVR CSR Center, Roman, F.L. and Herrera, M.B. (2011c) "Exploring strategic CSR: sustaining and strengthening corporate social responsibility," unpublished report, Makati City, Philippines: Asian Institute of Management.

AIM RVR CSR Center, Herrera, M.B., Alarilla, M.C., and Uy, R. (2011d) *Towards Strategic CSR: Aligning CSR with the business and embedding CSR into the organization (a manual for practitioners)*, Makati City, Philippines: Asian Institute of Management.

Arohan Financial Services Private Ltd (2011) "Awards entry form to the 2011 Asian Forum on Corporate Social Responsibility," unpublished, Kolkata: Arohan.

Baccay, O. (2012) "DepEd to launch nutri-juice feeding program," Philippine Information Agency, July 16. Available online at www.pia.gov.ph/news/index.php?article=461342416516 (accessed September 10, 2012).

Castillo, L.V. (2012) "Lawmakers laud Coca-Cola Philippines for its corporate social responsibility," press release, July 5, Quezon City, Philippines: House of Representatives. Available online at www.congress.gov.ph/press/details.php?pressid=6269 (accessed September 10, 2012).

Coca-Cola Philippines (2009) *NutriJuice*. Available online at www.thecoca-cola company.com/ourcompany/pdf/nutrijuice.pdf (accessed September 10, 2012).

Double A Thailand (2012) "Double A to build new paper machine in Thailand," *Pulpaper News*, March 22. Available online at www.pulpapernews.com/2012/03/double-a-to-build-new-paper-machine-in-thailand (accessed September 15, 2012).

Eureka Forbes Ltd (2011) "Awards entry form to the 2010 Asian Forum on Corporate Social Responsibility," unpublished, Mumbai: Eureka Forbes Ltd.

Herrera, M.E. and Alarilla, M.C. (2012) "Developing an integrated BOP engagement strategy," occasional paper, Makati City, Philippines: Asian Institute of Management.

Lang, C. (2002) *The Pulp Invasion: The international pulp and paper industry in the Mekong Region*. Available online at www.salvaleforeste.it/documentazione/pulp_invasion.pdf (accessed September 24, 2012).

PCIJ (2006) "Navigating the digital divide," The PCIJ Blog, September 11. Available online at http://pcij.org/blog/2006/09/11/navigating-the-digital-divide (accessed September 10, 2012).

Porter, M.E. and Kramer, M.R. (2011) "The big idea: creating shared value," *Harvard Business Review*. Available online at http://hbr.org/2011/01/the-big-idea-creating-shared-value (accessed September 20, 2012).

Smart Communications (2010) "Awards entry form to the 2010 Asian Forum on Corporate Social Responsibility," unpublished.

Smart Communications (n.d.) *About Smart*. Available online at http://smart.com.ph/corporate/about/company/ (accessed April 11, 2012).

Tetra Pak Pakistan (2010) "Awards entry form to the 2010 Asian Forum on Corporate Social Responsibility," unpublished, Lahore: Tetra Pak.

Tetra Pak Pakistan (2013) *Who We Are: The company*. Available online at www.tetrapak.com/pk/about_tetra_pak/the_company/historyinpakistan/pages/default.aspx (accessed April 10, 2013).

Index

Note: page numbers in italics refer to Figures; those in bold refer to Tables.

For Product Safety Concerns and Information please contact our EU
representative GPSR@taylorandfrancis.com
Taylor & Francis Verlag GmbH, Kaufingerstraße 24, 80331 München, Germany

9 781138 377059